1988

The American Illustrated Book
in the Nineteenth Century

The American Illustrated Book in the Nineteenth Century

EDITED BY

Gerald W. R. Ward

Henry Francis du Pont Winterthur Museum

WINTERTHUR, DELAWARE

Distributed by The University Press of Virginia

CHARLOTTESVILLE

The Proceedings of the Fourteenth Annual
North American Print Conference
held at Winterthur Museum,
Winterthur, Delaware,
April 8–9, 1982

First published 1987

Library of Congress Cataloging-in-Publication Data

North American Print Conference (14th: 1982:
    Winterthur Museum)
    The American illustrated book in the nineteenth
century.

    "The proceedings of the Fourteenth Annual
North American Print Conference held at Winterthur Museum, Winterthur, Delaware, April 8–9,
1982" — T.p. verso.
    Includes bibliographies and index.
    1. Illustrated books—United States—19th cen-
tury—Congresses.   2. Illustration of books—19th
century—United States—Congresses.   3. Book
industries and trade—United States—History—
19th century—Congresses.   I. Ward, Gerald W. R.
II. Henry Francis du Pont Winterthur Museum.
III. Title.
Z479.N67   1982   096'.1'0973   87–26255

ISBN 0–912724–17–X

Contents

Foreword

PRINTMAKING IN COLONIAL AMERICA had its moments of vitality, even brilliance, but for the most part this activity remained in the hands of a few and under the shadow of English engravers and publishers. To be sure, European influence continued for several decades after American independence, but three events in the first thirty years of the nineteenth century proved to be pivotal in encouraging a major printmaking industry in the United States. American innovations and inventions gave rise to the highly specialized security-note engraving industry that attained world renown. On a broader scale two events in particular were crucial to the development of a major printmaking industry in the United States: the introduction of lithography, followed by the use of other planographic printing processes, and the rapid growth of book publishing activities.

With the expansion of public-school systems leading to a rise in literacy, more Americans began to enjoy the pleasures and benefits of reading. A developing economy supported the increasing appetite for reading materials, and an expanding market demanded newspapers, periodicals, and bound volumes that were cogent, attractive, and illustrated. These demands encouraged improvements and changes in both the art of illustration and image reproduction.

In contrast to the eighteenth century, when libraries and reading skills were the privilege of a few and work for local engravers was limited, the expanding nineteenth-century market provided employment for painters, satirists, and illustrators, as well as for engravers to reproduce their designs. So exceptional was the growth in the early years of the century that scores of foreign-trained engravers, escaping the uncertainties of Europe, came to Philadelphia, New York, and other American publishing centers to compete with native-born talent. In assessing the pronounced development of book illustration in the last century from the perspective of 1965, art historian Edgar P. Richardson observed, "the phenomenon is so familiar that we hardly noticed it; yet it has both artistic results and social implications of very great interest."

Required to deal with a topic as encompassing as book illustration in nineteenth-century America, the 1982 conference program was designed as a survey that would provide an introduction to the subject. It is our hope that both the conference and these published proceedings will encourage further study of American book illustration and stimulate interest in specific aspects of this rich subject.

The North American Print Conference as an ongoing series of conferences is a truly remarkable phenomenon. "The American Illustrated Book in the Nineteenth Century" was the title of the fourteenth conference in the series, held at Winterthur Museum in Delaware in April 1982. What is the North American Print Conference? It is hardly a formally organized entity in the manner of the National Football League. It is simply a group of curators, collectors, and others who enjoy meeting on an annual basis to exchange information and renew friendships. As professional meetings go, these are small; anywhere from 50 to 150 people may attend. There is a formal program with scheduled speakers, but an easygoing informality pervades these affairs because most of those in attendance know and respect each other and share a common interest in the history of North American graphic art. While the papers are, of course, the main focus of these events, there are many exchanges of information before, between, and after the papers, and especially over dinner.

Conferences cost money, and they are a lot of work for the host institution. How, then, does the North American Print Conference continue year after year? Who decides where the group will meet and which institution will host each meeting? The conference continues because individual members want it to continue. They care enough to cajole the administrators of their museums, libraries, or universities to provide the necessary support. They then work extremely hard planning programs, corresponding with speakers, and dealing with the seemingly endless list of details that are essential to any conference. More than one of us has gulped upon venturing to offer ourselves and our institutions to host the print conference, knowing that we will spend the next two years trying to raise money and trying to solve a multitude of problems.

There is no formal organization, but there is Sinclair Hitchings, the venerable keeper of prints at the Boston Public Library, and Jonathan Fairbanks, the genial curator of American decorative arts and sculpture at the Museum of Fine Arts, Boston, who preside (unofficially of course) over the scheduling of the North American Print Conference. Both have been known to buttonhole innocent scholars and ask the fateful question: "Would your museum (or library, or university) be interested in hosting the next meeting of the print conference?" Some volunteer; others are asked. And somehow it works.

Holding the fourteenth conference at Winterthur was fitting because it meant that the conference finally returned to the original host institution. In 1970, when Winterthur presented its sixteenth annual conference, "Prints in and of America to 1850," we had no idea that it was also the first conference in the series later to be named the North American Print Conference. Since 1970, print conferences have been held in Baltimore, Boston (three times), Fort Worth, New Bedford, New Orleans, New York, Ottawa, Philadelphia, Syracuse, Toronto, Washington (twice), Williamsburg, Winterthur, and Worcester.

Even more remarkable than the regular schedule of conferences is the number of books that have been generated by the conferences. Who would have thought when it all began back in 1970 that by 1987 there would be ten volumes of conference proceedings in print with several others in preparation? (A list of previously published proceedings appears in the Appendix.) We are proud to add *The American Illustrated Book in the Nineteenth Century* to this distinguished list of titles.

Every conference—and, indeed, every book—is the product of many hands. We are deeply grateful to the contributors who generously shared the results of their research in both oral and written form.

We also wish to thank James Morton Smith, former director of Winterthur Museum, who saw to it that we had the financial means to hold the conference. Several people saw to the smooth running of the conference, no one more so than Patricia R. Lisk, whose cool efficiency makes difficult tasks look easy. Patti also served as the copy editor and designer of this volume. Last, we salute Gerald W. R. Ward, who assumed other editorial chores and helped to bring this book into being.

E. McSherry Fowble
Ian M. G. Quimby

The American Illustrated Book
in the Nineteenth Century

Pictorial Perils

The Rise of American Illustration

NEIL HARRIS

IT MAY SEEM STRANGE, even perverse, to begin a volume on nineteenth-century book illustration by emphasizing its problems rather than its achievements. To do this, moreover, without benefit of visual material. And to concentrate, finally, on just a brief period at the century's very end. But I do so with confidence, because explications, commentaries, and celebrations are offered by other authors, most of whom draw on a wealth of visual examples.

My interest is different: to show how laymen viewed increasing illustration and fitted it into larger social changes. American illustration climaxes at a moment when pictorialism was making new claims on public attention. Its dramatic spread in book and periodical form accompanied—and was connected to—many other changes in visual expression. My subject, then, is contemporary reaction to this broad growth of picture making and the attempt to make sense of a fundamental change in message sending.

The approaching end of centuries tends to produce retrospection. It was to be expected, then, that during the 1890s many commentaries on the evolution of American art during its first hundred years appeared in print. Written mainly by critics and artists, several of these summaries concentrated on a relative newcomer exhibiting unusual vigor and promise. This newcomer, of course, was book and periodical illustration.

As they surveyed the distance that lay between the crude wood engravings of antebellum years, and the flourishing engraving industry of a later day, commentators waxed eloquent about the triumphs of national skill. A galaxy of great names had sprung up, most within the previous quarter century, many associated with specialized techniques and subjects. There were illustrators who concentrated on military camps or western scenes, or upon farm and rural settings; there were those known for their presentations of women, of blacks, or of landscapes; still others who featured eighteenth-century America, sixteenth-century England, nineteenth-century France, or the exotic Middle and Far East. However laggard the efforts of our sculptors and painters, a cohort of celebrities dominated the more intimate and domestic art of illustration—Pyle, Abbey, Pennell, Remington, Gibson, Frost, Kemble, Christy, and Smedley among them. "If we would find where in the world of art the artist is most sure of winning and keeping the heart of the people," Philip Paulding wrote in *Munsey's*, "we must turn to illustration. . . . Here the very practicality which has retarded our appreciation of ideal art is a potent factor in our enjoyment of the artist's work. We care less, as a people, for the lofty canvasses of some modern Rafael, than for the more tangible and useful excellences of beautiful books and handsome periodicals." "Perhaps in no other direction has America progressed more rapidly than in the making of attractive, illustrated books," Arthur Hoeber argued in the *Bookman* in 1899. And the progress was recent. Harold Payne, examining periodicals and children's books of the early part of the century, found them of "the crudest character, primitive in coloring as well as in expression." Hoeber himself, browsing through the first issues of *Scribner's*, fresh from the press only thirty years before, was amazed that "such performances could have passed current," their figures "wretchedly proportioned, ridiculously out of drawing and false in all the relations." Composition was even worse; "criticism fails here," Hoeber concluded, drawing a discreet veil over the more vigorous condemnation he might have employed.[1]

[1] Philip Rodney Paulding, "Illustrators and Illustrating," *Munsey's* 13, no. 2 (May 1895): 152; Arthur Hoeber, "A Century of American Illustration," *Bookman* 8, no. 5 (January 1899): 429 (this was stated in the seventh part of an eight-part article); Harold Payne, "American Women Illustrators," *Munsey's* 11, no. 1 (April 1894): 47; Arthur Hoeber, "A Century of American Illustration," *Bookman* 8, no. 4 (December 1898): 317.

The growth achieved was multiple. Some involved the evolution of technique, a mastery displayed by the younger illustrators, particularly in their capacity to adapt to new reproductive media like the halftone. Another evidence of advancement was expanded international reputation, particularly in Europe, acknowledgment by laymen and other artists that illustration deserved critical attention and respect. And finally there were the salaries, glamorous and impressive on their own, testament to the conviction of publishers and editors that pictures paid. Running through the commentaries was a sense of new status for the illustrator, as distinguished American painters began to accept illustrated commissions and an increasing number of illustrators began to produce their own written texts. As early as 1882 William A. Coffin devoted an entire paper to painter-illustrators like Robert Baum, J. W. Alexander, William Merritt Chase, and Edwin Blashfield. These commanding figures brought to the field of illustration their insistence on autonomy. And, even more important, they transmitted a special individuality. Illustration would no longer have to rely on standardized if arbitrary conventions. These artists took orders from no one and insisted upon establishing their own style of design. This was still novel in the eighties and nineties. George Wharton Edwards, describing in an 1897 article how books were illustrated, argued that it was not until the 1880s that artists could even choose their own subjects within the text. "If Sir Galahad in the lines of the manuscript grasped the heroine by the arm, then the artists must so show him in the picture." The artist "was not expected to exercise his own imagination; and so art was still in fetters."[2]

These new artist-specialists, each associated with a personal style and a category of subject material, might well have been making New York, in William Hobbs's phrase, "the world's Bohemia of illustration," and American illustrators the envy of their European counterparts.[3] Few denied the skill or originality with which so many of this

---

[2] William A. Coffin, "American Illustration of To-Day," *Scribner's Magazine* 11, no. 1 (January 1882): 106–17. Coffin would have agreed with Payne and Hoeber: "While it may be true that a good deal of the current illustration is inferior, it serves a useful purpose in the propagation of a love of art" (Coffin, "American Illustration," p. 108). George Wharton Edwards, "The Illustration of Books," *Outlook* 57, no. 14 (December 4, 1897): 817, 820.

[3] William Herbert Hobbs, "Art as the Handmaid of Literature," *Forum* 31, no. 3 (May 1901): 371.

artist generation tackled its commissions. But the achievement of this golden age was not without certain costs. Some among the celebrants grew suspicious about this new national dependence on pictures, raising questions not about artistic talent but about cultural meaning. I hasten to add that dissenters were far from a majority. Most Americans simply enjoyed their illustrations, and the literature of description is overwhelmingly favorable. But the discontents, if sometimes covert and disguised and invariably outnumbered, nonetheless exposed fundamental anxieties. And they have been largely ignored.

What were the objections to increasing illustration? They can be subdivided. First came concerns about accuracy. In this era of vigorous publication, verbal truthfulness was abused by many books and periodicals. But it was possible to check these facts; conventions and sources were clearly established. Visual inaccuracy, however, was more difficult to spot, at least without special knowledge or advance warning. And it was, apparently, common.

The *Nation*, for example, a leading critic of the excesses of illustration, grew exercised about some pictures in the *Philadelphia Public Ledger*. When it featured a story on a new French man-of-war, a ferocious, mastless boat with two towers of circular galleries for rifles and Gatling guns, the *Ledger* presented a cut of a three-masted ship under full sail. The *Nation* was furious. Absolute accuracy, it admitted, lay beyond the reach of most human beings. But newspapers had an obligation to cling to truth. The effort to feature pictures as a means of enticing readership was wrongheaded. "The reform . . . most needed in journalism today," the *Nation* concluded, "is not fresh or better means, like cuts, of spreading abroad 'things that are not so,' but improved means of making what appears in the paper more credible."[4]

The turn to pictures in documentary reporting was one thing, but many of the most prominent illustrators were tied to fiction. Here the issue of accuracy grew more complex. A series of angry letters and editorials, in bookish journals of the nineties and later, focused on a second concern: the artist's poetic license, apparently wider than the universe created by the written text. "I know that artists are privileged

[4] E. L. Godkin, "'Cuts' and Truth," *Nation* 56, no. 1453 (May 4, 1893): 326.

beings," one Edwin Carlile Litsey wrote in a letter to the *Critic*, "that they are supposed to possess attributes which would blast a common mortal. . . . And yet, beneath all their glamor and high mightiness," he continued, they ate, slept, and got sick just like everyone else. Why should they be "given the right of way above their fellow artisans who labor with letters and words?" Authors who used words incorrectly, or changed the color of a heroine's eyes, received a torrent of abuse. Artists got little, although they were themselves frequently inconsistent. When authors described ladies in straw hats, the artists dressed them in derbies; they showed the heroine in a carriage rather than on horseback as the writer intended; a wrecked auto was drawn as it bumped into a tree, not a wall. "The ineptitudes of so-called illustrations," a Dorothea Moore wrote from San Francisco, "have become so common that every one expects them."[5]

The *New York Times* Saturday Review of Books and Art was a favorite arena for critics of artistic carelessness to have their say. "It is sometimes hard to decide at the present day whether we are glad or sorry to hear that a favorite volume is to appear in an illustrated edition," the *Times* admitted. Prepared by the author's words with a vivid mental picture, it was "surely a great shock to turn a page only to be confronted by an utterly commonplace or meaningless illustration." Agreeing with the newspaper, Bret Gyle wrote in to ask the purpose of book illustration. He was confused. Pictures, he felt, appealed mainly to those unreachable by words, "unable to feel and appreciate the inward spirit of the writer." It was useless "if not absurd," he continued, "to illustrate such works as Dickens, when the author takes chapters to bring an image before us. Should our ideals, formed under the guidance of a master hand, be crushed or perverted by the conception of another?" he asked. "Surely not," was the equally emphatic answer. The spread of illustration endangered individual thought.[6]

[5] *Critic* 48, no. 6 (June 1906): 498, 499. "The Lounger," a regular feature of the *Critic*, featured three letters on illustration in this issue.

[6] "Meaningless Illustrations," *New York Times* (April 7, 1900), Saturday Review of Books and Art, p. 232. For similar sentiments, see "Illustrations That Illustrate," *New York Times* (December 2, 1899), p. 816. *New York Times* (April 21, 1900), p. 493.

Naturally enough, defenders insisted that illustration was a harmless pleasure which enhanced the impact of a great novel, but protests continued. Even great figures like Howard Pyle, Howard Chandler Christy, and Henry Hutt ("chalky nothings that are an insult to both intelligence and taste") were not immune. Why do publishers insist on illustrating everything, one letter writer asked the *Times*. "Are they trying to pauperize our imagination, or do they think the public hasn't any?"[7]

Some serious critics steered a middle course. Hobbs, a defender of illustration, did single out some poorly illustrated volumes and condemned the careless pictures of best-sellers like F. Marion Crawford's *Katherine Lauderdale* (1894) and Charles Major's *When Knighthood Was in Flower* (1898). But he enthusiastically supported literary-artist collaboration. Praising Edwin Austin Abbey's work for *She Stoops to Conquer*, Arthur Burdett Frost's illustrations for *Uncle Remus*, and the achievements of Pyle, Rufus Zogbaum, and Thure de Thulstrup, Hobbs posited the sympathy between "the man of letters and the man of art" as a great contribution of the age, so successful that illustrators occasionally inspired authors to reshape their characters. In Hobbs's view, illustration had moved from merely embellishing the text "to the dignity of a literary performance. It can no longer be regarded as a mere accessory to, but rather as a part of, the book itself."[8] Because the drift of bookmaking was toward unity of design, this meant a more creative role for the illustrator, and Hobbs was all for that. He simply opposed unconscious liberties taken with an author's conception. When harmony characterized the relationship, Hobbs saw no danger from the enhanced status of the illustrator. The pictures, in his view, were simply an element in the larger work.

But other critics became alarmed, not by the mere presence of inaccuracy, but at the challenge offered by the illustrator's imagination. The importance of the reading experience and the integrity of the author's vision were both threatened. A picture, the *Atlantic Monthly*

---

[7]Katherine Gordon Hyle to the Editor, *New York Times* (November 5, 1904). An earlier letter from John K. Hoyt had criticized Pyle. M.P., *New York Times* (November 26, 1904), p. 812.

[8]Hobbs, "Art as Handmaid," p. 380.

observed, could actually hinder understanding, for "the modern illustrator frequently leaves his author behind, and tracks off into the
human wilderness in independent quest." The *Atlantic Monthly* admitted the value of pictures for obscure things and unusual people;
essays on Tibet or China, descriptions of the making of a compass—
these were subjects demanding illustration. But novels of Indian life
were perfectly comprehensible without illustrated commentary; their
pictures simply added a burden to the reader's shoulders. Certain
illustrations could reduce "a book or a magazine to a mere picture
album."[9]

Particularly at Christmastime, the new brand of illustrated holiday
books, a genre in which the text was just about the least important
aspect of the book, showed how far prettiness might go. Elaborate
bindings, dreamy halftones, and extensive decorations all counted for
more than any words. The illustrator was charged with making the
popular book into an artifact, a commodity whose primary purpose
was less to transmit an author's intention than to adorn a library table,
or make a properly expensive present. And when the illustrator insisted
on his own artistic dignity, when he followed his own vision, he posed
a danger because of textual diversions or inacccuracies. Seriousness
of intention, then, was no absolute protection.

Some sensed the profundity of this shift toward pictorialism. As
a device to obtain public attention, the picture was unrivaled. Pictures,
as the *New York Times* pointed out in 1901, had existed before written
language; the illuminations and woodcuts of the first printed books
were "made to appeal to a wider audience." Books adopted the same
techniques as the moralities in the miracle plays; both sought objectiv-
ity, "the one by drawings, the other by action." It was no wonder then
that the contemporary writer "owed a large debt to his illustrator."[10]

But providing a traditional pedigree hardly described the expanded
treatment pictures now received. Among other places, they were invad-
ing the classroom. One educator, Estelle Hurll, found the speed of the
change breathtaking but admirable. "The curriculum of study has

[9] "The Contributors' Club," *Atlantic Monthly* 93, no. 555 (January 1904): 136–37.
[10] "Author and Illustrator," *New York Times* (January 26, 1901), p. 56.

been largely disciplinary in character, intended to train the memory and the reasoning powers," she argued, constructed to supply the mind with information. Such an approach ignored the imagination and the aesthetic sense. Only the study of pictures, she suggested, could restore this part of the human sensibility. Distinct from the earlier movement to train future artisans and designers through drawing classes, the new art education reflected a sense that pictures formed an increasing basis for judgment and ideation. They required incorporation into the program of study. Pictures had long been accepted as a fundamental part of children's literature, and they dominated textbooks for the very young. But now the picture itself was proposed as a subject for popular study. Pictorialism constituted so large a part of the adult encounter with literature and popular journalism that preparation for its appreciation seemed vital. Progressive educators were, at just this time, seeking ways to reduce the distance between the classroom and the world of daily work and leisure. Picture study formed one bridge.[11]

But the association of bright and simple illustrations with juvenile reading tastes may have helped to raise still another issue associated with the new pictorialism: its threat to cerebration, its apparent regression to a more primitive system of communication. References to stained glass and miracle plays as instruments of enlightenment did not help. Reacting to a proposal by French critic and historian John Grand-Carteret for a series of historical picture books, the *Nation* turned to this line of attack. Grand-Carteret apparently believed that those "who come to scoff at history in uninteresting type" might "remain to pray over history tricked out with all the charm of the illustrator's art." There was logic to the proposal, the *Nation* admitted, but hardly ground for satisfaction. The problem was this notion that "the growing aversion to reading, and the increasing fondness for labor-saving and the thought-saving graphic representation" signaled progress. The *Nation* saw in it only a "distinct reversion to barbarism,"

[11]Estelle M. Hurll, "Picture Study in Education," *Outlook* 61, no. 3 (January 21, 1899): 174–76. For examples, see Elizabeth McCracken, "Pictures for the Tenements," *Atlantic* 98, no. 4 (October 1906): 519–28; and Caroline A. Leech, "The Gospel of Pictures," *Chautauquan* 37, no. 5 (August 1903): 484–86.

being nothing more or less than "a recurrence to the picture-writing and sign-language of savages." The lengthy step from using images for thought conveyance to the more complex (but more accurate) method of language was, sociologically speaking, an immense advance. "Modern man can get along with the old ways," the *Nation* admitted; they might not, by themselves, destroy civilization. But it was a "civilization under difficulties, not its supreme and happy development."[12]

Several years earlier, the *Nation* had argued that dependence on pictures for news was producing a childish view of the world. Complex diplomatic disputes had been reduced to portraits of the protagonists. Youthful readers wanting to know something about the disturbances in Brussels were "satisfied with a picture of the King's palace." In fact, pictures were not, and never could be, up to the task of complex explanation. Only extended narratives could provide such interpretation. The increasing pictorialism of journalism, designed to provide a come-on for those who did not much enjoy reading, was bound to produce continuing degeneracy in mental powers and taste. Pictures, wrote John Hopkins Denison, were fine for untrained minds and children, but with "an educated audience a well-turned description is more effective."[13]

If pictures were not capable of adequately transmitting the complexity demanded by modern life, this was the more troubling because the expansion of book and magazine illustration was accompanied, at century's end, by a series of other changes emphasizing the power of the new pictorialism. And some of these trends attracted far more vigorous, aggressive criticism than did the illustrators. One such development was the rise of photographic representation. Photographs, in magazines, books, and newspapers, formed part of the new illustration; their presence appeared to relieve illustrators from certain tasks.

---

[12] [Rollo Ogden], "Knowledge on Sight," *Nation* 57, no. 1464 (July 20, 1893): 41–42. For an interesting earlier parallel, which unites this suspicion of picture making to a Protestant hostility to pictorial propaganda, see Julia Ward Howe, *From the Oak to the Olive: A Plain Record of a Pleasant Journey* (Boston: Lee and Shepard, 1868), pp. 76–77.

[13] [E. L. Godkin], "Newspaper Pictures," *Nation* 56, no. 1452 (April 27, 1893): 306–7; John Hopkins Denison, "How to Use Objects as Illustrations," *Chautauquan* 27, no. 1 (April 1898): 34.

Moreover, the popularity of photographic illustration directly involved the technological capacities of the halftone process, becoming a dominant form by century's end. However, it is not this aspect of photography that I single out here but the spread of camera ownership and the growth of the snapshot. By the 1880s Americans and Europeans were growing accustomed to photographs as renditions of people and places, particularly when they were prominent or newsworthy. What was new was the ability of millions of people, with relatively little training or money, to create their own illustrated records, to prowl the countryside, to stalk famous personalities, to pose family members, to attend great events like inaugurals and expositions, all for the mere purpose of accumulating photographic facsimilies, which could then be displayed as evidence of artistic skill or personal daring to friends or interested amateurs. The success of George Eastman in marketing his Kodak meant that the habit of picture taking was now becoming as widespread, perhaps more widespread, than the habit of picture looking.[14]

Each person could now be his own artist. And it was not simply a printed text but the life that lay around him that he illustrated. Pictures were becoming personal documents, increasingly a substitute for words as instruments of expression. For although the camera fiend brought many annoyances, including invasion of privacy, destruction of rural peace and solitude, monomaniacal obsession with lenses and lighting and posing (at the risk of personal friendship and social tranquility), there were other, more profound problems associated with the democratization of picture making. One was analogous to the dilemma of illustrated inaccuracy: the possibility of staging photographs to make them more flattering or artistic. Because (whatever theorists have to say) photographs were popularly supposed to bear a special relationship to objective truth. A photograph that lied or exaggerated was more dangerous than a painting or an etching that did so. It was more dangerous because it seemed more convincing.

[14] For more on the new pictorialism, see Neil Harris, "Iconography and Intellectual History: The Half-Tone Effect," in *New Directions in American Intellectual History*, ed. John Higham and Paul K. Conkin (Baltimore and London: Johns Hopkins University Press, 1979), pp. 196–211. For more on Eastman, Kodak, and the marketing revolution involved in the spread of the

Photographs, moreover, could be—and were—retouched in the late nineteenth century, and this occasioned considerable debate in amateur circles. But most important, perhaps, photographs could substitute for verbal description, and increasing reliance on them could impoverish both the imagination and the vocabulary.

It was difficult to make this argument in dealing with something as simple and innocent as family albums and casual snapshots. But once the photograph had been mounted on a piece of cardboard and sent through the mail, an entirely different sensibility stood revealed, one that could be effectively attacked. The rise of the picture postcard during the 1890s spelled just such an instance of a vulgarizing pictorialism to its many critics. Picture postcards could be assaulted from different directions. Many, of course, were simply illustrations, comic or sentimental, and could be derided on the grounds of their crudity, their sentimentality, or their silliness. But the increasing use of cards with photographed landscapes and architectural views suggested, on the one hand, an atrophy of descriptive powers and, on the other, dependence on standardized conceptions of the physical world. At one time the travel letter was a lengthy and fascinating document, highly personalized, filled with social commentary and extensive descriptions. These observations formed the basis of many books. Although much of the language, particularly the description of views, was highly standardized, the act of writing such letters forced a degree of self-consciousness, an attention both to what was being observed and to the letter's recipient. Written description seemed to demand more extended and more concentrated observation than did the selection of a small card, on which just a few lines could be scribbled, the picture substituting for more individualized responses. The picture postcard and the snapshot were, from one point of view, somewhat different eruptions of pictorialism. The postcard was anathema because of its easy standardization of response, the casual, nonthinking, passive approach to correspondence and to confronting experience that it

---

camera, see Reese V. Jenkins, *Images and Enterprise: Technology and the American Photographic Industry, 1839–1925* (Baltimore and London: Johns Hopkins University Press, 1975).

suggested.[15] The snapshot was more personal and aggressive, since it involved a set of decisions and framing acts. But what they shared was a reliance on an image to make a point that had previously been made by words. Both involved a challenge to traditional devices of transmitting attitude and information, substituting the authority of the commerical entrepreneur, the postcard shop, and the tourist industry on the one hand, and a subjective, sometimes aggressively eccentric view of people and objects on the other. Neither form of pictorialization was content to accept the older, verbal canons. They were challenges to the rules.

A second large area of challenge involved the increasing dependence on pictures to sell products and experiences, in the form of commerical advertisement in newspapers and magazines and, more distressing perhaps, in the development of the poster. With our new regard for art nouveau and for fin de siècle graphic design, we look back fondly on the great age of Chéret, Steinlen, Beardsley, Klinger, Klimt, Mucha, Moser, and their American counterparts. Certainly the reputations of Bradley, Penfield, Leyendecker, and Parrish have never stood higher. But in fact, there were those who found the lurid colors, the distorted drawing, the sometimes grotesque juxtapositions of the new poster art to be disorienting, dangerous, and disturbing. Admittedly European artists were more radically subjective than Americans, but the American posters could still challenge the cause of careful draftsmanship and artistic propriety. This, along with other forms of pictorial advertising, was mercenary art in the service of selling products.[16] At one time art had been suspect because of its eager service to the cause of church and state, a willing prop to tyranny and superstition. Now, the cause was commercial rather than political, but the prostituting role of pictures and of artists was unmistakable. Advertis-

[15] A convenient summary of attitudes to picture postcards, as well as bibliographic references, can be found in George Miller and Dorothy Miller, *Picture Postcards in the United States, 1893–1918* (New York: Clarkson N. Potter, 1976). For one complaint about the growth of snapshots and postcards, and the contrast with earlier methods of recording one's travels, see [W. A. Bradley], "The Lost Art of Sketching," *Nation* 90, no. 2343 (May 26, 1910): 530–31.

[16] The poster literature is vast. One recent article that refers to hostile comments about poster art is Michael Patrick Hearn, "An American Illustrator and His Posters, Part One," *American Book Collector* 3, no. 3 (May–June 1982): 11–18. A useful summary and bibliography is in Victor Margolin, *American Poster Renaissance: The Great Age of Poster Design,*

ing design could be charged, then, not only with challenging the conventions of drawing, coloring, and composition and with demeaning public taste but also with selling its services to the highest bidder. In its appeals to irrationalism, fed by psychological analyses of human motivation which began to appear regularly shortly after the turn of the century, the new pictorialism spelled a regression and an abandonment of the protections that verbal expression had brought with it to a credulous humanity.

A second aspect of the growth of a debasing and demoralizing pictorial art lay in the response to comic strips which, in Sunday supplements to newspapers, were beginning to attract attention in the 1890s and were perceived as a national menace not too long thereafter. Critics of the comics, like Ralph Bergengren writing in 1906, declared them to be a mechanistic, market-oriented menace, with "a confusing medley of impossible countrymen, mules, goats, German-Americans and their irreverent progeny, specialized children with a genius for annoying their elders . . . policemen, Chinamen, Irishmen, negroes, . . . boy inventors," a cast of characters without "respect for property, respect for parents, for law, for decency, for truth, for beauty, for kindliness, for dignity, or for honor." They were violent, brutal, coarse, and vulgar. "Physical pain is the most glaringly omnipresent of these *motifs*; it is counted upon invariably to amuse the average humanity of our so-called Christian civilization" with a "saturnalia of prearranged accidents." They were worse, in fact, than another target of conservative assault, the dime novel. That at least propped up certain ideals of bravery and chivalry. "The state of mind that accepts the humor of the comic weekly," Bergengren insisted, might well be the same as that which shuddered at Ibsen, yet the immorality caused by the Sunday comics was, in fact, far greater. There were exceptions like Peter Newell, or the inventor of Little Nemo, artists of taste, genuine humor, and wit, but the comics seemed, for the most part, an example

---

1890–1900 (New York: Watson-Guptill Publications, 1975). For a typical series of attacks on posters and billboards, see *Chautauquan* 51, no. 1 (June 1908): 18–81, featuring photographs of the offensive advertisements as well as speeches and manifestos. The assault on billboard art blended in with other areas of municipal and environmental reform which attracted progressive activists.

of the bad driving the good out of circulation, a reduction of the mass audience to its lowest common denominator.[17]

It was the pernicious influence of the comics on the manners and morals of the young that seemed most bothersome, and this applied as well to the illustration of children's books. Walter Taylor Field, crying "better give him no pictures at all than wrong ones," condemned the example of the comic-strip youth who "shampooed his sister's hair, and annointed the poodle, with a mixture of ink, glue, and the family hair-tonic." This suggested an artist who had little sympathy with children. What he meant, presumably, was an artist who had little sympathy with parents. The "picture is as important as the printed page in forming taste and influencing character," Field argued. The comics aided what Annie Russell Marble, writing in the *Dial* in 1903, called the "Reign of the Spectacular" in American art, a "craze for pictures and pageants apart from their essential or even relative value." The commercial demand for illustration spared no calling or sphere of activity, from the pulpit to the presidency. And even great lecturers, she added, were startled by the question, Haven't you some talks with lantern slides?[18]

Snapshots, postcards, illustrated periodical articles, comics—these were joined, at century's end, by still another, even more powerful and potentially debasing form of pictorialism, the rise of the motion picture. The nineties were, of course, the formative decade for the early, primitive efforts of filmmakers, but soon after the turn of the century, about 1905, their efforts began to bear fruit with the rise of the store-front nickelodeon theaters and the rash of one-reelers filled with action-oriented adventure stories and sentimental romances. The cry of concern and anxiety coming from teachers, clergymen, public officials, social workers, law and order groups, and moralists in general about the menace of the motion pictures has been documented by a generation of film historians. Immediately studies were launched to

[17] Ralph Bergengren, "The Humor of the Colored Supplement," *Atlantic Monthly* 98, no. 586 (August 1906): 270–73.

[18] Walter Taylor Field, "The Illustrating of Children's Books," *Dial* 35, no. 420 (December 16, 1903): 460; Annie Russell Marble, "The Reign of the Spectacular," *Dial* 35, no. 417 (November 1, 1903): 297.

demonstrate the pernicious effect the films were having on youthful morals, on the unhealthy impact of the crowded, germ-infested, fire-trap theaters which lured the young away from more vigorous outdoor play or even from gainful employment. Surveys attempted to establish that motion pictures gained a kind of hypnotic suggestive power over the minds and eyes of viewers, that things presented on the screen, even the commission of violent crimes, were imitated by those who had little conception of the magnitude of their actions. A variety of schemes were launched, the better to control this new and powerful force.[19] Suggestions included closing down the theaters, creating local boards of review and censorship, and obtaining the cooperation of filmmakers in the production of less subversive and more uplifting films. In certain places and at certain times, these interventions succeeded in reorganizing the flow of films to a mass audience, at least for a period of time. As the financial stakes of picture making and distribution grew more massive, self-policing on the part of the industry became more effective. But the appeal of film was too fundamental, too elemental to do much with. That they were silents only made their challenge to the word more emphatic. Despite the occasional titles, the films were dependent not on dialogue, or literary referencing, or verbal wit, but on pictorialism pure and simple, for narrative, continuity, and persuasiveness. Quotation, if there was any, would have to be visual. In the end this meant that many of the traditional aspects of the theater, and their heavy reliance on literary skills, both for playwrights and authors, could be abandoned.

It is, to be sure, a lengthy jump from the illustrations of Abbey, Pyle, Reinhart, and Gibson to the pictures of Griffith, Chaplin, and Fairbanks. It would be exaggerated in the extreme to say that many contemporaries saw the connections between an expanded pictorialism in mass culture and the power of illustrated literature basking in its golden age. Nonetheless, there are parallels and continuities in these apparently disconnected areas: the publishing of serious fiction,

---

[19] Convenient summaries of these responses can be found in Garth Jowett, *Film: The Democratic Art* (Boston and Toronto: Little, Brown, 1976), chaps. 4–5; and Robert Sklar, *Movie-Made America: How the Movies Changed American Life* (New York: Oxford University Press, 1975), pp. 30–32.

history, and biography, all in illustrated form, and the appearance and astonishing development of cartoons and caricatures, snapshots, postcards, comic strips, and motion pictures. What all of these forms of expression shared was a diversion of authority away from its orthodox sources and traditional methods, in favor of new and apparently untried techniques. Ingenious, aggressively original, or incompetent illustrators could challenge the authority of the storyteller, as letter writers pointed out; cartoonists could challenge the honesty, patriotism, and, even more seriously, the dignity of pillars of the establishment, and so undermine their authority as setters of standards; movies could challenge the very persuasiveness of the written text as their translations of classics, scripture, or even modern stories held mass audiences in a thralldom that was as novel as it was intense. The new pictorialism was powerful precisely because an expanding range of techniques and a growing market permitted a degree of individuation. It no longer needed stock cuts, so inexpensively inserted alongside a written text. Formulas, of course, would develop with a vengeance, in every area of this new culture, but the formulas were complex enough to include considerable variety and to disguise their structure beneath a mass of arresting details.

But pictures were subversive, most of all, because they presented a new and apparently uncontrollable set of sources to the larger public. Guardians of the word had developed over the previous centuries: lexicographers, grammarians, rhetoricians, orthographers, rulemakers, critics, codifiers. The spread of reading and writing was accomplished, to a large extent, with their guidance and leadership. The rise of literacy was accompanied, of course, by bitter debates about the appropriate national, linguistic, and aesthetic models. There were furious cries of vulgarization attending the increased circulation of cheap novels, daily newspapers, and sentimental magazines. But control of the word remained in the hands of writers, publishers, editors, and teachers who were remarkably effective in demarcating the boundaries separating the acceptable and the unacceptable. The pictorial revolution, however, was too sudden, too comprehensive, and too appealing to be handled within just a few decades. Painters, photographers, caricaturists, filmmakers, and commerical printers had agendas of their own and pursued dreams different from those of the traditional establishment. In stylistic terms alone, fin de siècle art raised various problems for conservatives, but when to these challenges was added the further issue of image distribution on a scale and with a variety never before attempted, the consequences seemed profound and disquieting. Many, if not most American illustrators of the last century did not mean to challenge cultural authority as such. Their values may well have been as traditional as those of most of the authors they illustrated but were part of a larger movement which assumed a direction they could not control, or always understand.

By challenging the relationship between form and content, the new pictorialism appeared to subvert the hard-won discipline of verbal mastery. In the nineteenth century, still a handmaiden, a helpmate to the arts and sciences, an instrument spreading the results of other investigations, pictorial illustration was now launched on a career of its own. As we calibrate its rise to influence, we must not ignore the pangs of uncertainty and pain that accompanied its growth.

.

Dobson's *Encyclopaedia*

A Precedent in American Engraving

Judy L. Larson

THE ENCYCLOPEDIA, a compendium of knowledge, was the natural issue of the eighteenth century, the Age of Enlightenment. The intellectual achievements and scientific advancements of the eighteenth century promoted the belief that human reason could bring man to perfectibility. The concept of an encyclopedia, the attempt to encompass universal knowledge, was a vehicle for that progression.

Ancient civilizations had attempted to record comprehensive knowledge, but the first modern encyclopedia—a work that drew on the knowledge of many and then arranged the collected information in an alphabetical sequence—was compiled by John Harris. His work was called the *Lexicon Technicum* and was published in England in 1704. This was followed by Ephraim Chambers's *Cyclopedia* published in London in 1728. The French encyclopedists originally planned to translate Chambers's encyclopedia, but the project changed course when Denis Diderot and Jean le Rond d'Alembert became involved in 1751. An entirely new work was compiled, called the *Encyclopédie*. Problems of censorship, adverse propaganda, and a lack of funding stretched out publication for twenty-one years, but in the end it was a work that would change the course of history.[1]

---

[1] For a detailed examination of the *Encyclopédie*, see Robert Darnton, *The Business of Enlightenment: A Publishing History of the Encyclopédie, 1775–1800* (Cambridge, Mass.: Harvard University Press, Belknap Press, 1979).

Many encyclopedias were published in the last half of the eighteenth century; one with long-lasting influence was the *Encyclopaedia Britannica*. Published first in Edinburgh as a three-volume set in 1771, it was revised in 1778 into a ten-volume set with more than 200 plates. It is the American edition of the *Encyclopaedia Britannica* with which this paper is concerned—the edition published in Philadelphia by Thomas Dobson (1751–1823), referred to simply as Dobson's *Encyclopaedia*.

At the end of the eighteenth century the publishing industry in America was struggling to outgrow its infancy. Each major city had presses, most of which were publishing pirated books from England and the Continent, periodicals which were short lived, local newspapers, and almanacs. Many of the books were illustrated with either woodcuts or copper engravings. But American engravers were merely copyists, materials were in short supply and expensive, and training was limited if available at all. To earn a living solely as a copperplate engraver was difficult at best. Engravers usually advertised under several professions—printers, booksellers, clock repairers, silversmiths.

Given the risks and problems of publications, it was a brave endeavor for Thomas Dobson of Philadelphia to advertise in 1789 a new, proposed publication—an American edition of the *Encyclopaedia Britannica*. It would be issued in ten volumes and greatly improved, the errors of former editions carefully corrected and omissions supplied, with alterations and improvements to the whole and thousands of additional articles. Dobson noted: "The present Publisher has only to add, . . . he flatters himself he shall be able to execute the American Edition of this important work in such a manner as to give universal satisfaction. The undertaking is arduous and extensive; he begs . . . to solicit the patronage and encouragement of all lovers of science and literature, and friends to American manufactures, in the United States, to promote a work of such general utility."[2] No work on such a grand scale had ever been attempted before. Obviously, its success was a matter of patriotic pride.

[2] Thomas Dobson, *A New Edition . . . Volume III of Encyclopaedia* (Philadelphia: Thomas Dobson, April 1791), p. [2]. (Broadside on Readex, Evans no. 46160, filmed from New-York Historical Society copy.)

Dobson's first problem was securing suppliers, editors, engravers, and printers. John Baine, a fellow Scotsman, made a new typeface especially for the *Encyclopaedia*. Likewise, the paper was made in America and described as superfine. There is no printed record of who edited the different sections. The *Encyclopaedia* was divided into broad topics so that a reader would search for a subject under its broadest classification, such as chemistry or medicine, and then read a lengthy article. Dobson added many new articles to the American edition. We know that Jedidiah Morse wrote the section on American history because the section was later published as a book. The sections on chemistry and anatomy were also separately published.[3] Philadelphia in 1789 had its share of literary intellectuals, scientists, and theologians. It was the aim of the *Encyclopaedia* to highlight the talent in America and to show, with pride, that Americans could compete intellectually with the British.

The demand for engravers was truly a problem, for Dobson would require more engraved plates for this single work than had heretofore been published in all Philadelphia imprints. In the British edition, all the plates had been done by one engraver, a partner in the British publishing company, Alexander Bell. Perhaps Dobson thought one engraver could accomplish the same for him when he commissioned Robert Scot (ca. 1745–1823) as engraver of the plates. Scot was born in Edinburgh, and early in his life he left college and immigrated to Virginia. He was an instructor in mathematics in Richmond and had an interest in heraldry. This interest prompted Scot to apprentice himself to an engraver and start a business of engraving heraldic emblems, medals, coins, certificates, and bank notes. In the early 1780s he relocated to Philadelphia where he advertised himself as "Late Engraver to the State of Virginia." In 1789 Scot advertised in the *Maryland Journal*, "Engraver Wanted Immediately, A Journeyman Engraver, who understands his Business—Such . . . will meet with suitable Encouragement, a long and constant Employment, from Robert Scott,

---

[3] Dobson, *New Edition*, p. [1]. The separately published books are [Jedidiah Morse], *The History of America* (Philadelphia: Thomas Dobson, 1790); [Andrew Fyfe], *A Compendious System of Anatomy* . . . (Philadelphia: Thomas Dobson, 1790); and *A System of Chemistry Comprehending the History, Theory and Practice* . . . (Philadelphia: Thomas Dobson, 1791).

Engraver, at Philadelphia."[4] The response came not from one but two engravers, a partnership, John Vallance and James Thackara. Both men had only recently finished apprenticeships with James Trenchard.

In January 1790, 1,000 copies of part 1, volume 1, were issued. Only 246 subscribers had agreed to terms whereby the patron would pick up weekly numbers, ten numbers making one part, each volume having two parts. There was an option to subscribe in parts or volumes, which proved to be more practical, and soon the weekly numbers were dropped. On receipt of a volume, it was required that the following volume be purchased. This insured Dobson the capital to continue as well as the encouragement for patrons to pick up work for which they had already paid. Dobson was encouraged by a liberal patronage of the *Encyclopaedia*, so much so that after the second volume he doubled the number of copies to 2,000. It was not until the eighth volume, however, that the original subscription of 1,000 was reached. As the *Encyclopaedia* progressed, the cost of the volumes escalated, partially in an effort to secure early subscribers. When the publication was complete, the set cost $156 in boards and between $187 and $250 bound, depending on the quality of the binding.

The British edition of the *Encyclopaedia Britannica* had 200 plates, whereas the American edition had 543 plates. This increase was not necessarily due to new and original material, but rather to a reorganization of the subjects from the British plates. The British edition often cluttered the plates with many different subjects. For example, in one British plate (fig. 1), we are given an elevation, a ground plan, and a perspective view of a floating bridge. And then, quite awkwardly, in the upper right-hand corner, there emerges the head of a bull. Scot copied this plate, eliminating the background details and substituting marine life for the bull's head. His composition obviously works much better (fig. 2). Also, by eliminating the background details, the engraver communicates only the essential information that the reader needs to know. The British plates are done in the technique

[4] *Pennsylvania Packet* (Philadelphia) (May 29, 1781) as cited in Alfred Coxe Prime, *The Arts and Crafts in Philadelphia, Maryland, and South Carolina, 1721–1785: Gleanings from Newspapers* (n.p.: Walpole Society, 1929), p. 27; *Maryland Journal and Baltimore Advertiser* (Baltimore) (April 10, 1789).

of etching which allows for a freer, more open style. Etching in America at this time was only experimental. All the *Encyclopaedia* plates in Dobson's edition are engraved. But the neat, clean line of an engraving seems fitting for the didactic nature of encyclopedia illustrations.

With the exception of a map engraved by James Smither, all 182 plates in the first six volumes were engraved by Scot, Thackara, and Vallance. Of the signed plates, 122 were engraved by Scot, accomplished in only three years. In 1792, issuing the seventh volume, Scot and Dobson advertised for an apprentice to the engraver's trade. The advertisement read, "Wanted, a youth about 14, . . . none need apply who has not the taste for drawing and the advantage of a good education." Samuel Allardice, a young man of seventeen, was taken on as apprentice. He was the fourth son of a Scotsman, and, as was common for younger sons, he had immigrated to America. We do not know if he had already received training as an engraver in Scotland, but he did begin to sign plates during the first year of his apprenticeship. These were, however, not signed in the normal way. Allardice either signed his initials after the master's name or camouflaged either his name or his initials within the composition (figs. 3, 4).[5] The signing of plates by apprentices was not the normal practice in America. It seems to have been unique to the workshop of Scot.

By 1793 Allardice was signing plates under his own name. The plate of an insect with magnified details is a neat, precise design showing his talent in rendering a variety of textures, including the transparent quality of insect wings (fig. 5). He has been described by David Stauffer as "an indifferent engraver," which simply is not so. Perhaps he is so judged because of the limited number of plates he produced in his lifetime. In 1793, Allardice was made a full partner to Scot, and the two engravers jointly signed plates until Allardice's untimely death from a lingering illness in 1798 at the age of twenty-three.[6]

[5] *Pennsylvania Packet* (Philadelphia) (May 14, 1792). The plates that Allardice signed in this manner are 32, 45, 55, 92, 100, 107–11, 115, 119, 121, 125, 126, 129, 134, 135, 138, 141, 149, 151, 159, 162, 163, 165, 171, 172, 175, 183, 204, 240, 243, 245, 248, 249, 260, and 263.
[6] David McNeely Stauffer, *American Engravers upon Copper and Steel*, vol. 1 (New York: Grolier Club, 1907), p. 8; *The Allardyce Family* (San Antonio, Texas: Martin and Allardyce, 1923), p. 10; *Claypoole's American Daily Advertiser* (Philadelphia) (August 28, 1798).

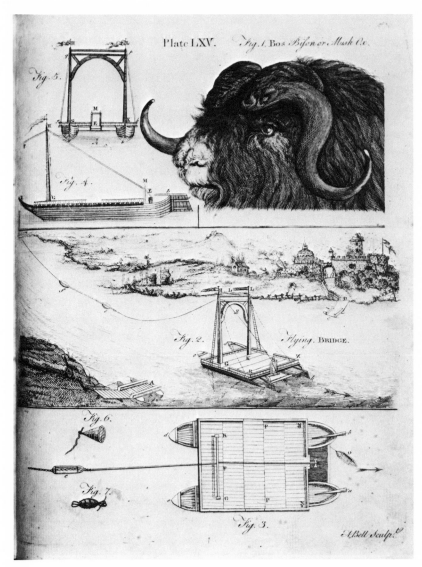

Fig. 1. A. Bell, plate 65, *Encyclopaedia Britannica* (2d ed.; Edinburgh, 1778–83). Engraving; H. 10½″, W. 8″. (Beinecke Rare Book and Manuscript Library, Yale University.)

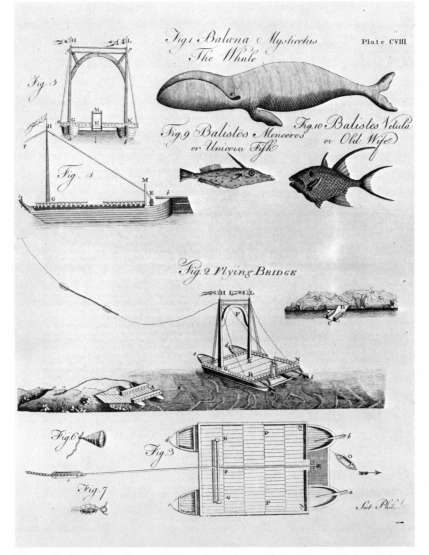

Fig. 2. Robert Scot, plate 108, *Encyclopaedia; or, A Dictionary of Arts, Sciences, and Miscellaneous Literature*, vol. 3 (Philadelphia: Thomas Dobson, 1798). Engraving; H. 10⅝″, W. 8¼″. (Winterthur Library.)

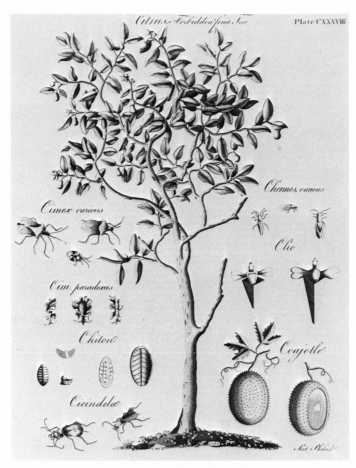

Fig. 3. Samuel Allardice, plate 138, *Encyclopaedia; or, A Dictionary of Arts, Sciences, and Miscellaneous Literature*, vol. 5 (Philadelphia: Thomas Dobson, 1798). Engraving; H. 10⅝″, W. 8¼″. (Winterthur Library.)

Fig. 4. Detail of figure 3, showing camouflaged initials of engraver Samuel Allardice.

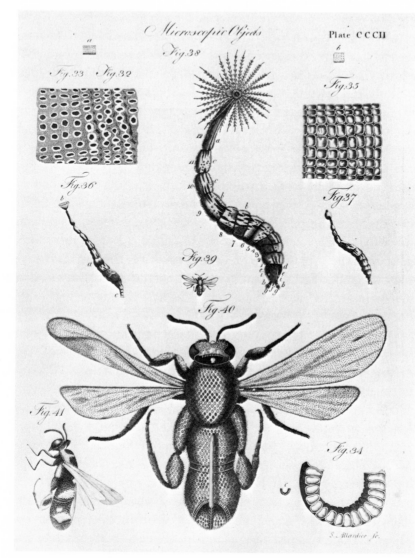

Fig. 5. Samuel Allardice, plate 302, *Encyclopaedia; or, A Dictionary of Arts, Sciences, and Miscellaneous Literature*, vol. 11 (Philadelphia: Thomas Dobson, 1798). Engraving; H. 10⅝", W. 8¼". (Winterthur Library.)

The year 1793 was a difficult one for production of the *Encyclopaedia*. There was the yellow fever epidemic in Philadelphia, the worst the city had ever experienced. Most businesses suspended production of any kind. It was also in 1793 that Dobson had a fire in the printing office.[7] The logarithmic tables, scheduled for the tenth volume, melted in the fire and needed to be reset. (The engravers were not affected by the fire, having their workshops elsewhere.) It was also in 1793 that President Washington made provisions for a United States mint to be established in Philadelphia. Thomas Jefferson offered his services in the task of finding an engraver for the mint. His aim was to find the best craftsman available; however, he did not look to indigenous talent. He failed to persuade a European engraver to relocate to America and wrote to David Rittenhouse, head of the mint, that Rittenhouse should do the best he could to find an engraver himself. Scot was chosen as engraver, and it seems logical to assume that the choice was based on the high quality of engraving that he had demonstrated in the *Encyclopaedia*.

Scot agreed to the appointment on the terms of a $1,200 annual salary and an open hand at working on outside assignments. This meant that Scot could finish the plates for the *Encyclopaedia*. Allardice was made a full partner to lessen the work load. Other engravers were added to the *Encyclopaedia*—James Trenchard, Joseph H. Seymour, James Akin, James Smither, Thomas Clarke, W. Ralph, Joseph Bowes, Henry Weston, and Alexander Lawson. In fact, Dobson employed so many Philadelphia engravers that other publishers had difficulty securing engravers for other books. Complained one publisher, "I . . . cannot yet find a good engraver who is disengaged. Dobson keeps them hard at work." Scot and Allardice took on three new apprentices. These engravers signed their plates in the same way Allardice had signed as an apprentice: "JD" was John Draper (figs. 6, 7); "BJ" was Benjamin Jones (figs. 8, 9); and "FS" was Francis Shallus (figs. 10, 11).[8]

[7] Charles Evans, *American Bibliography*, vol. 8 (Chicago: Columbian Press, 1915), pp. 27–28.

[8] *Collections of the Massachusetts Historical Society*, 5th ser., vol. 5 (Boston: Massachusetts Historical Society, 1878), p. 250, as cited in Rollo Silver, *The American Printer, 1787–1825*

Alexander Lawson arrived in America in 1794 and moved to Philadelphia where he secured employment with Thackara and Vallance as a journeyman engraver. The earliest contributions Lawson made to American engraving were plates for the *Encyclopaedia*. Lawson's comments were less than complimentary about his employers. He wrote: "Thackara and Vallance were partners when I came to Philadelphia. I engraved with them two years. They thought themselves artists, and that they knew every part of the art; and yet their art consisted in copying, in a dry, stiff manner with the graver, the plates for the Encyclopedia, all their attempts at etching having miscarried." Trenchard, said Lawson, made scratches on the plate. But Vallance, wrote Lawson, "was certainly the best engraver at this time . . . in the United States; and had he been placed in a more favorable situation, he would have been a fine artist."[9]

Dobson obviously agreed with Lawson's opinion, for when it came to choosing an engraver for the frontispiece, Vallance was selected. It was a great compliment to Vallance since other publishers were trying to lure subscribers with the promise of a frontispiece by an "eminent European artist."[10] The frontispiece was issued with the last volume, and as this plate is unique to the American edition, it seems likely that Vallance both designed and engraved the plate (fig. 12). It is an emblematic representation of the encyclopedia. The format is that of an ancient school where architecture, landscape, figures, instruments, tools, books, and so forth represent the complete knowledge of man in the arts and sciences.

Dobson had promised to adapt the *Encyclopaedia* to the American people, and this applied to the plates as well. Most of the changes were subtle. Usually it was a matter of changing a foreign flag to the

(Charlottesville: University Press of Virginia, 1967), p. 153. Plates signed in this manner are Draper's 392, 488, and 588; Jones's 385 and 393; and Shallus's 206, 252, 253, 258, 259, 280, 281, 287, 288, 297, 300, 308, 314, and 369.

[9] Lawson quoted in William Dunlap, *A History of the Rise and Progress of the Arts of Design in the United States*, 3 vols. (1834; reprint, Boston: C. E. Goodspeed, 1918), 2:123–24, 1:382, 2:122.

[10] *Pennsylvania Gazette* (Philadelphia) (July 8, 1789). Dobson proudly announced in his proposal that the whole of the plates would be done by American artists. See *Maryland Journal and Baltimore Advertiser* (Baltimore) (May 22, 1789).

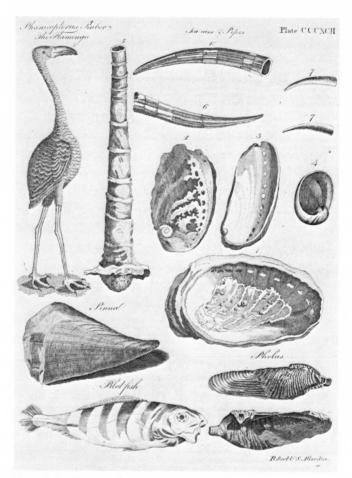

Fig. 6. John Draper, plate 392, *Encyclopaedia; or, A Dictionary of Arts, Sciences, and Miscellaneous Literature*, vol. 14 (Philadelphia: Thomas Dobson, 1798). Engraving; H. 10⅝″, W. 8¼″. (Winterthur Library.)

Fig. 7. Detail of figure 6, showing initials of engraver John Draper.

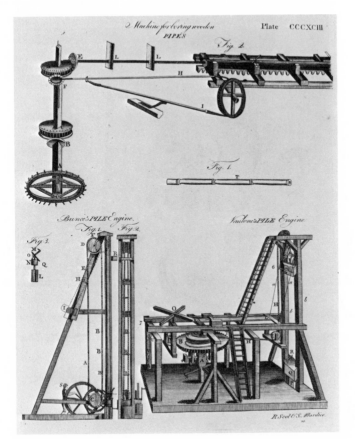

Fig. 8. Benjamin Jones, plate 393, *Encyclopaedia; or, A Dictionary of Arts, Sciences, and Miscellaneous Literature*, vol. 14 (Philadelphia: Thomas Dobson, 1798). Engraving; H. 10⅝″, W. 8¼″. (Winterthur Library.)

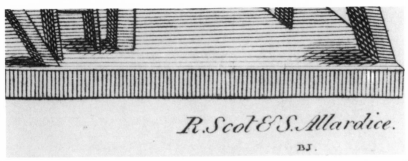

Fig. 9. Detail of figure 8, showing initials of engraver Benjamin Jones.

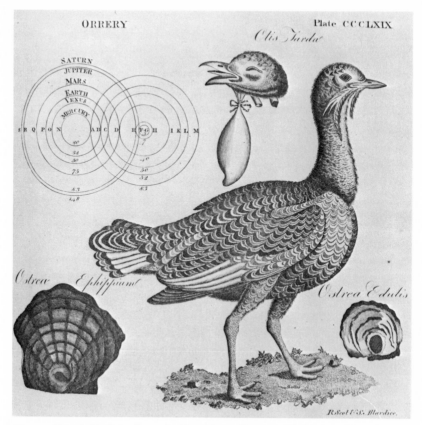

Fig. 10. Francis Shallus, plate 369, *Encyclopaedia; or, A Dictionary of Arts, Sciences, and Miscellaneous Literature,* vol. 13 (Philadelphia: Thomas Dobson, 1798). Engraving; H. 10⅝″, W. 8¼″. (Winterthur Library.)

Fig. 11. Detail of figure 10, showing camouflaged surname of engraver Francis Shallus.

ENCYCLOPÆDIA

Philad? *Publish'd by* T.Dobson N.º 41 S.º 2.ª *Street* 1798.

Fig. 12. John Vallance, frontispiece, *Encyclopaedia; or, A Dictionary of Arts, Sciences, and Miscellaneous Literature*, vol. 1 (Philadelphia: Thomas Dobson, 1798). Engraving; H. 10⅝″, W. 8¼″. (American Antiquarian Society.)

American flag or a foreign symbol to the American one. There were articles and illustrations in Dobson's *Encyclopaedia* that did not appear in the British edition. Much of the new material was drawn from the scientific and literary periodicals and journals of learned societies. For example, the section on polytheism is unique to the American edition. The source of the illustration of Saxon gods appeared in the eighteenth volume of *Gentleman's Magazine* published in London in 1748 (figs. 13, 14). The sources for new material were not always foreign. An illustration from the *Massachusetts Magazine* of 1790 captioned "Bird Catching at Orkney" also appears in the *Encyclopaedia* (figs. 15, 16). The same is true of the plate from *Select Essays; Containing the Manner of Raising and Dressing Flax and Hemp* published in Philadelphia in 1777. The objects from that plate are copied in the *Encyclopaedia*.

Dobson's *Encyclopaedia* was eighteen volumes long with a three-volume supplement published between 1800 and 1803. Begun in 1789, it had taken fifteen years to bring the entire project to fruition. Engraver David Edwin observed, the *Encyclopaedia* "was thought a rash undertaking; and General Washington, on being asked to subscribe to the work, declared, that 'he thought Mr. Dobson a bold man.'"[11] It had been an arduous task indeed and a success story that encouraged other publishers to follow his lead. As a pioneer in encyclopedia production, Dobson had set an example of excellence and elegance—a work that compared favorably with the British efforts.

In the two decades that followed the publication of Dobson's *Encyclopaedia*, six major illustrated encyclopedias were published in America. In fact, the *Encyclopaedia* was still in production when two of Dobson's own engravers, Thackara and Vallance, announced in the *Aurora* their plans to publish a folio-size encyclopedia to be called the *New Encyclopedia*. It never materialized. In 1804 James Mease edited an American edition of Anthony Willich's *Domestic Encyclopedia*. Its emphasis was on topics of animal husbandry and farming plus other practical applications of scientific advancements to domestic life. There were 31 plates shared by engravers Shallus, Weston, Lawson

[11] Edwin quoted in Dunlap, *History of the Arts of Design*, 2:203.

(who had worked on Dobson's *Encyclopaedia*), Benjamin Tanner, and S. Folwell. *The New and Complete Encyclopedia*, edited by John Low, was the only encyclopedia where the American edition originated from New York. Low, in the preface to his encyclopedia, describes Dobson's *Encyclopaedia* as "too voluminous and too expensive . . . to answer the beneficial purposes of a General circulation."[12] The Low encyclopedia was published between 1805 and 1811; it cost approximately $40 to $60, less than a quarter of what Dobson's had cost. The illustrations were numerous; in fact, many were copied directly from Dobson's *Encyclopaedia*. But the low production costs are clearly reflected in crude, hastily done plates. In 1806 Samuel Bradford began the American edition of Abraham Rees, *The Cyclopaedia; or, Universal Dictionary of Arts, Sciences, and Literature*; it was completed in 1822. There were forty-one volumes in eighty-three parts with four extra volumes of plates. *The New Edition of the Edinburgh Encyclopedia* was published by Edward Parker and Joseph Delaplaine between 1812 and 1831. There were eighteen volumes, each with two parts. This was an excellent encyclopedia, although like most others it had great financial difficulties in meeting production costs. The proposal for the work took great pride in noting that the contributing editors were all American and included such eminent persons as David Hosack, John Redman Coxe, John Syng Dorsey, Benjamin Smith Barton, and Benjamin Latrobe. *The New and Complete Dictionary of Arts and Sciences* by George Gregory was published in America by Isaac Pierce in 1816. It was a folio-size, three-volume set which was intended to be only a quick reference book. There were 54 plates by about seventeen different engravers. Finally, there was the American edition of the *British Encyclopedia*, often referred to as *Nicholson's Encyclopaedia*, published in 1815 and 1816. Its chief selling point was the quarto-size volumes which would fit easily onto any library shelf. William Kneass was commissioned to do the plates, and he formed a company of engravers, Kneass, Young, and Company, to complete the 153 plates. All the plates had a similar format, and using one engraving company insured a stylistic unity.

---

[12] *Aurora* (Philadelphia) (October 12, 1796); *The New and Complete American Encyclopedia . . .*, vol. 1 (New York: John Low, 1805), p. [iii].

Fig. 13. John Vallance, plate 411, *Encyclopaedia; or, A Dictionary of Arts, Sciences, and Miscellaneous Literature*, vol. 15 (Philadelphia: Thomas Dobson, 1798). Engraving; H. 10⅝″, W. 8¼″. (Winterthur Library.)

Similar problems of producing an encyclopedia were shared by all American publishers. The first problem, like Dobson's, was locating enough engravers and printers. Many engravers from other cities were attracted to Philadelphia because of the assurance of constant employment. But even so, much of the engraving was jobbed out to engravers in other cities. Probably the biggest concerns were keeping to a publication schedule and maintaining consistent subscribers to pick up their volumes. Dobson avoided this problem by publishing an encyclopedia that was complete when he began the American edition. But with Rees's *Cyclopedia*, for example, Bradford was obliged to wait, often for months, until the next British volume was released. These delays were bothersome both to subscribers who had been promised issues that were not ready and to publishers who needed the constant work. An encyclopedia was a major investment for the subscriber and the

Fig. 14. "The Principal Idols of the Saxons, worship'd in Britain," *Gentleman's Magazine and Historical Chronicle* 18 (November 1748): facing p. 512. Engraving; H. 8⅜″, W. 5″. (American Antiquarian Society.)

publisher. In a note from one book dealer to another, Philip Fisher wrote to Benjamin Warner, "I find great difficulty in delivering the Edinburgh Encyclopedia and much greater difficulty after it is delivered to collect the money even from the wealthiest of [patrons] and all classes of subscribers are anxious to get shut of this work. I am fully of the opinion it prevents many people from purchasing that otherwise would." When an encyclopedia took fifteen, sixteen, even seventeen years to complete, it was very difficult to maintain the original subscribers. Dobson had announced that he was doubling the number of issues after the second volume, but most others found it was necessary to cut back. The announcements of *Cyclopedia* in the newspapers began with advising, then pleading, and then begging or even threatening subscribers to pick up and *pay* for their issues. When the last issue of Rees's *Cyclopedia* was released in 1822, the notice in a weekly

Fig. 15. Samuel Hill, "Bird Catching at Orkney," *Massachusetts Magazine* 2, no. 12 (December 1790): facing p. 707. Engraving; H. 8¾", W. 5½". (Winterthur Library.)

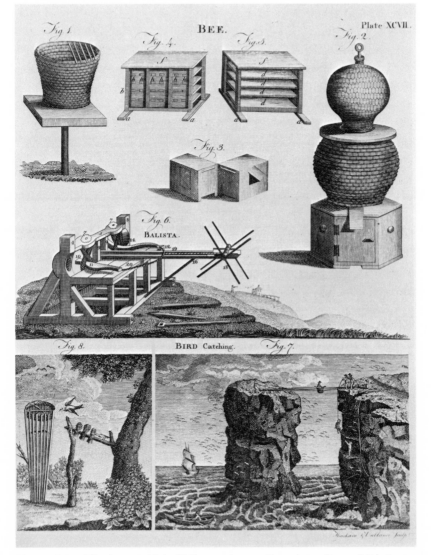

Fig. 16. James Thackara and John Vallance, plate 97, *Encyclopaedia; or, A Dictionary of Arts, Sciences, and Miscellaneous Literature*, vol. 3 (Philadelphia: Thomas Dobson, 1798). Engraving; H. 10⅝″, W. 8¼″. (Winterthur Library.)

newspaper tried to shame patrons into believing that it had been unpatriotic to let this project run at a loss to the publishers.[13]

Encyclopedias also seemed to take abuse from the reviewers and critics. Rees's *Cyclopedia* had already received bad publicity even before Bradford released the first issue. To defend the publication, an anonymous man from Princeton published a column in the *Gazette*, saying, Bradford's American edition of Rees's *Cyclopedia* "succeeds the old encyclopedia [Dobson's] by much in elegance and being of more modern date it furnishes contemporary information, which, is always most interesting, and generally most useful, for it may be said of sciences as Chesterfield has said of statesmen, it is better to be acquainted with one living than ten dead ones." Dobson, whose encyclopedia had been complete for two years at the time of this comment, took affront and answered the challenge in a half-page newspaper reply. He defended his encyclopedia as having a better and more logical order than Rees's. Rees's *Cyclopedia*, he claimed, is a mere book of references with diverse topics huddled together. He claimed as well to have better authorities than Rees. But his strongest point was that Dobson's was complete. Patrons could acquire the entire set if they wanted to do so.[14]

Bradford replied with his own half-page advertisement, his entitled "A reply to the attack on Dr. Rees' Cyclopedia." He began, "As the gauntlet is thus publickly thrown by the author of the advertisement, the editor is by the circumstances of the case imperiously called on to take it up." He defended Rees's as having the most recent information available on technologies, science, or any other subject. Dobson's, he claimed, had neglected biography, especially American, and Bradford promised to provide not only biographies but portraits as well.[15] The bickering back and forth via the newspapers did not hurt either publisher as far as publicity was concerned. Dobson had good reason to

[13] Jacob Johnson and Benjamin Warner account books, September 30, 1816, no. 74, Manuscripts Collection, American Antiquarian Society, Worcester, Mass. (hereafter cited as AAS); *United States Gazette* (Philadelphia) (May 13, 1806); *Aurora* (Philadelphia) (June 15, 1818, October 26, 1820, December 21, 1821); *Niles' Weekly Register* (Baltimore) new ser., 21, no. 23 (February 2, 1822): 353–54.

[14] *United States Gazette* (Philadelphia) (March 25, April 8, 1805).

[15] *United States Gazette* (Philadelphia) (April 19, 1805).

fear the popularity of Rees's *Cyclopedia*, for it did in fact contain the latest information on new technologies, scientific advancements, and historical occurrences. Although Dobson's encyclopedia had been a remarkable accomplishment in its day, the early volumes were now seventeen years old.

The success of Rees's *Cyclopedia* was due in large part to the brilliant editor of the English edition, Abraham Rees (1743–1825). He was a celebrated theologian, scholar, and member of the Royal Academy in England. In fact, he leaned heavily on his fellow academicians—leading scientists, doctors, artists, architects, historians, and antiquarians who contributed firsthand knowledge of their specialties. Earlier encyclopedias had been criticized for the sketchy information they contained. Said one critic, "Encyclopedias . . . are generally more likely to excite the smile of the merchant or manufacturer than to extend his knowledge or lead to useful improvements."[16] The contributors to Rees's spoke with the authority of knowing firsthand.

Bradford had planned an American edition of Rees's since 1802 when the English edition first appeared. The American edition was first issued in 1806. He recruited American editors for the various general topics but would not release their names. The *Monthly Anthology* was very critical of this omission, stating, "Bradford kept their names . . . from the publick, and thus screened [them] from all manner of responsibility." But on one favorable note all reviewers agreed: the engravings were excellent. The *Monthly Anthology* stated, "We take pleasure in imparting to our readers how much satisfaction we felt on the first view of the American edition, at the decisive and honourable testimony which it bore to the flourishing state of the arts of printing and engraving in our country. It is one of the few American editions, which, we can with truth say, is not surpassed by the English." The *Portfolio* reported, "The plates are *superior* to the British engravings."[17] In the final count, there were fifty different engravers who worked for Rees's *Cyclopedia*, and well over 1,000 plates.

[16] Robert Bakewell, *Observations on the Influence of Soil and Climate on Wool* (London, 1808), p. v, as cited in N. B. Harte, "On Rees's Cyclopaedia as a Source for the History of the Textile Industries in the Early Nineteenth Century," *Textile History* 5 (October 1974): 124.

[17] *Monthly Anthology and Boston Review* 5 (April 1808): 213, 3 (August 1806): 423; *Portfolio* (Philadelphia), new ser., 4 (October 31, 1807): 281.

The quality of the plates for Rees's *Cyclopedia* was consistently high. The plates are quite similar to the British copy, but the paper used in the American edition is much finer, giving the prints a richer appearance. By this time, mechanical devices were available to aid the engraver—lathes, ruling machines, and so on. Without the aid of these labor-saving instruments, the number of plates generated for this work would have proved impossible.

Scientific and technological plates were carefully annotated with descriptive information. Each plate dealt with only one subject, which minimized confusion. Similar subject matter was assigned to engravers who were best with those topics. Hugh Anderson, for example, dominated the technological subjects. Machinery was carefully drawn with elevations, plans, perspectives, and details of working parts (fig. 17). George Murray was used as a natural-history engraver; his plate of lions was described by William Dunlap as Murray's finest work (fig. 18). Cornelius Tiebout is represented most often by architectural subjects. His plate of the west door of the Cathedral of Carrara was described by the *Portfolio* as showing uncommon beauty and spirit (fig. 19).[18] The first soft-ground etchings in America were published in Rees's *Cyclopedia*. They were engraved by William Charles and intended to reproduce drawings by Gaspard Poussin (fig. 20).

By 1815 Bradford had invested $200,000 in Rees's *Cyclopedia*. He was on the verge of bankruptcy when three of the engravers who had done plates for Rees's took over as publishers. These three were partners in Murray, Draper, Fairman, and Company. The senior partner was George Murray, a Scotsman and immigrant to America. He originally settled in the South where he failed in the mercantile business. He had experience as an engraver in England and was able to find work in Philadelphia, engraving some of the plates for Alexander Wilson's *American Ornithology*. John Draper, the second in the partnership, has already been discussed as an apprentice to Scot and an engraver for several encyclopedia publications. Gideon Fairman was born in Connecticut but moved to Albany to apprentice himself to

---

[18]Dunlap, *History of the Arts of Design*, 2:285; *Portfolio* (Philadelphia), new ser., 4 (October 31, 1807): 281.

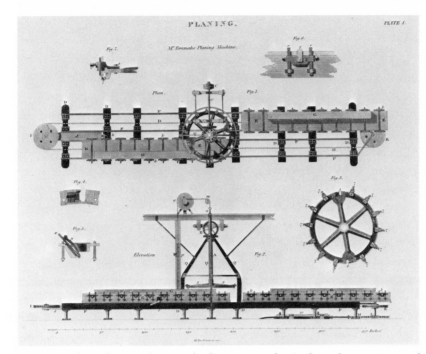

Fig. 17. Hugh Anderson, plate 1, Abraham Rees, *The Cyclopaedia; or, Universal Dictionary of Arts, Sciences, and Literature*, vol. 45 (Philadelphia: Samuel F. Bradford and Murray, Fairman, 1810–24). Engraving; H. 10¹¹⁄₁₆″, W. 8¼″. (Winterthur Library.)

jewelers and engravers. He showed talent and in 1800 established his own business in that city. His wife died in 1811, and he moved to Philadelphia. The company was formed primarily to do bank-note engraving. According to Dunlap, the firm did quite well; Murray kept his own carriage and wore a tie pin valued at $700.[19]

Murray, Draper, Fairman, and Company took over the publication of Rees's *Cyclopedia* in 1815 and in two years published twenty-five parts, seventeen of which were done in the same year. It was necessary to raise the price of half volumes from $3 to $4, $5 to nonsubscribers.

[19]Robert Bald and Thomas Underwood were the two other partners in the company in 1820. Commonwealth of Pennsylvania, *Acts of the General Assembly of the Commonwealth of Pennsylvania* (Harrisburg, 1820), p. 13; Dunlap, *History of the Arts of Design*, 2:285.

Fig. 18. George Murray, plate 1, Abraham Rees, *The Cyclopaedia; or, Universal Dictionary of Arts, Sciences, and Literature*, vol. 46 (Philadelphia: Samuel F. Bradford and Murray, Fairman, 1810–24). Engraving; H. 10¹¹⁄₁₆″, W. 8¼″. (Winterthur Library.)

Fig. 19. Cornelius Tiebout, plate 40, Abraham Rees, *The Cyclopaedia; or, Universal Dictionary of Arts, Sciences, and Literature*, vol. 42 (Philadelphia: Samuel F. Bradford and Murray, Fairman, 1810–24). Engraving; H. 10^{11}/$_{16}$″, W. 8¼″. (Winterthur Library.)

Fig. 20. William Charles, plate 9, Abraham Rees, *The Cyclopaedia; or, Universal Dictionary of Arts, Sciences, and Literature*, vol. 43 (Philadelphia: Samuel F. Bradford and Murray, Fairman, 1810–24). Engraving; H. 10¹¹⁄₁₆″, W. 8¼″. (Winterthur Library.)

Patrons were given the option to cancel their subscriptions; the publishers even offered to buy back issues. By 1818 the publication had caught up with the British edition. Between 1818 and 1820 the volumes were published directly as they were received from England. The last issue arrived in October 1820, and the publishers promised to have it ready for delivery by November. Between 1815 and 1817 an extra volume of prints was issued, labeled A. In 1820 with the last issue, two more extra volumes of plates were issued, B and C. Finally, in 1822 another volume of plates, D, was released. All four extra volumes were given gratis to subscribers.[20] The publishers claimed that this issue alone had cost them $11,000.

Murray, Draper, Fairman, and Company made no profit; in fact, the financial failure of the *Cyclopedia* was partially responsible for the ruin of the company. In 1819, Draper's name was dropped from the imprint. Fairman had left America to join Jacob Perkins in England in competition for a counterfeit-proof method of engraving. They lost the competition, but Fairman remained in England to form a partnership with Perkins and Charles Heath. Murray was left to manage the company, and he tried to raise money by investing in real estate. He also tried to make up for the severe losses of the *Cyclopedia* by holding a lottery to clear out the storehouses. In 1819 tickets were sold at $12.50 apiece for prizes: 200 sets of Rees's *Cyclopedia* fully bound; 100 sets elegantly bound; 250 imperfect sets; 250 sets of all engravings making 22 bound volumes; 300 ancient and modern atlases; 700 plain atlases; 1,000 of a number of portraits of American characters given in the work; one prize of all the copperplates used in the work. This last prize alone was valued at $10,000. There were 2,801 prizes and 8,000 tickets. It was a unique effort to raise capital lost in a publishing endeavor, but one that failed. Murray lost not only his own fortune but also the capital of the engraving firm. Fairman returned to Philadelphia unaware of the financial losses of the company. A friend rode out to greet him as he arrived and tell him of his losses. Fairman sneaked into Philadelphia thinking he might be able to undo what Murray had done. But the losses proved too much of a strain on both men. Murray died in 1822, the date of the final issue of Rees's *Cyclopedia*, and Fairman died five years later.[21]

The publishers wrote in the advertisement for the last issue, "[it is our] hope, that this vast fund of useful knowledge, spread over the United States, will materially contribute to call into active operation

[20]Samuel F. Bradford, broadside, Philadelphia, October 2, 1815, AAS. Bradford indicates that many back volumes were burned by the British at French-town; therefore, it was necessary to buy back unwanted sets or single volumes to fill the gaps. For reference to buy-back policy, see also *Aurora* (Philadelphia) (October 26, 1820).

[21]Commonwealth of Pennsylvania, *Acts of the Assembly*, pp. 13–15; Dunlap, *History of the Arts of Design*, 2:178–79.

the inexhaustible resources of this widely extended country; advance agriculture and internal improvements; promote the manufacture of the raw material into useful fabrics, and give a powerful stimulus to that national industry which is the basis of general prosperity and real [independence]." Americans had recognized the need to be financially and commercially independent from the English since the Revolution. But this need for independence had become poignant with the Embargo Act of 1807, the Non-Intercourse Act of 1809, and the War of 1812. The young country needed specialized knowledge to make advancements chiefly in industry and science. In a prospectus for *The Emporium of Arts and Sciences*, John Redman Coxe stated, "Ingenuity is so conspicious in the American character. Few nations can boast of more important improvements in labour saving machinery than have been discovered in the progress of the mechanical arts among us. We are, however, but young in practical information on numerous points, in which our highest interests are concerned. To aid our researches we still need that solid information arising out of extensive operations and experience, which European contemporaries are continually affording."[22] The ingenuity was there. Americans simply needed the basic information.

Could an American in 1820 actually construct a mechanical device, learn the principles of civil engineering, or perfect a surgical procedure based on the articles and plates of an encyclopedia? Most likely the encyclopedia was a good starting place in that process, combined with other specialized publications, a model of the machine or apparatus or instrument, and a knowledgeable mechanic, craftsman, or professional. There are, in fact, several contemporary references to encyclopedia articles. Engraver Alexander Anderson, for example, learned etching and aquatint from information in an encyclopedia article. Benjamin Dearborn, writing on improving locks and canals, cited Rees's *Cyclopedia* as having 150 pages devoted to "very extraordinary, if not Utopian" ideas on the subject. Thomas Cooper,

[22]*Aurora* (Philadelphia) (December 31, 1821). Prospectus for *The Emporium of Arts and Sciences*, published by Joseph Delaplaine, with editorial comments by John Redman Coxe, April 1, 1812, pasted onto back cover of *New Edinburgh Encyclopedia*, vol. 1 (Philadelphia, 1812), pt. 2, AAS.

in *A Practical Treatise on Dyeing and Callicoe Printing*, stated in the preface, "It is very singular that in the voluminous publication, Rees's Cyclopedia, I can find nothing on dyeing generally and only two articles relating to the subject of printing. Can this be a willful omission in the common jealous manufacturing spirit of the country?"[23] Cooper referred here to the English laws against the exportation of machinery to foreign countries. Other countries were forced to sneak out drawings and models and rely on emigrating craftsmen to reconstruct, as best they could, the needed equipment. Cooper saw his book as his patriotic contribution of practical knowledge to America.

The early nineteenth-century encyclopedias differ from modern encyclopedias in that the information they provide was the most current information available on any given topic. Rees's *Cyclopedia*, for example, is still considered the single richest source for the study and understanding of technological and scientific advancements in the nineteenth century. They are also a useful guide to the state of knowledge in early American society. Issues of theology, philosophy, art, and literature are discussed and reflect the subjective opinion of a particular editor. Overall, the encyclopedia in early nineteenth-century America functioned as a stimulus toward the pursuit of the arts and sciences.

If the encyclopedias were to be beneficial, they needed accurate plates demonstrating a high degree of artistic achievement. It was Dobson's *Encyclopaedia* that set a high standard of quality, proving that Americans would support a book trade that concentrated on elegance and excellence. The need for such a great number of plates had alone established the engraver's profession in America. Dobson's and other encyclopedias brought with them new, innovative graphic processes and mechanical devices to meet the demands of encyclopedia illustration. These improvements, of course, were not limited to the encyclopedias alone. Dobson had set a precedent of elegance in engraving which raised the general standards of quality in all book illustration.

---

[23] "Notebook written by A. Anderson containing riddles, receipts, notes on the Portable Camera Obscura, Etching, mezzotinto, Engraving, Aquatinta and Poetry," Alexander Anderson Papers, miscellaneous mss., New-York Historical Society. Benjamin Dearborn, *A Proposal, for Removing the Inconveniences Incident to Locks and Inclined Planes, in Transferring Canal-Boats from One Level to Another* (Boston, May 1814), broadside, AAS. Thomas Cooper, *A Practical Treatise on Dyeing and Callicoe Printing* (Philadelphia: Dobson, 1815), p. [v].

The Publication of Illustrated Natural Histories in Philadelphia, 1800–1850

Georgia B. Barnhill

THE ILLUSTRATED BOOK was the format chosen for much of the transmission of scientific and technical information during the nineteenth century, although journals also published scientific illustrations, as Charles B. Wood III explained in his "Prints and Scientific Illustration in America."[1] Until the late eighteenth century, scientific material relating to America's flora and fauna was printed in Europe. Naturalists from abroad accumulated information in the colonies and published it on their return or depended on specimens received from American correspondents. The earliest products of this process included John Josselyn's *New Englands Rarities Discovered* (London, 1672). Later naturalists such as Mark Catesby and George Edwards produced lavish works for which they have received much acclaim.

Although the earliest American natural-history publication was issued before the American Revolution,[2] the compilation and publica-

The author would like to express her gratitude to the following individuals for their assistance: Stephen Catlet and Willman Spawn, American Philosophical Society; Carol Spawn and Ellen E. Hopman, Academy of Natural Sciences; Peter Parker, Historical Society of Pennsylvania; Anne Blum, Museum of Comparative Zoology, Harvard University; Marcus A. McCorison and Audrey T. Zook, American Antiquarian Society.

[1] Charles B. Wood III, "Prints and Scientific Illustration in America," in *Prints in and of America to 1850*, ed. John D. Morse (Charlottesville: University Press of Virginia, 1970), pp. 161–91.

[2] Bernard Romans, *A Concise Natural History of East and West Florida* (New York, 1775).

tion of books of this genre by Americans did not occur with frequency until later. William Bartram published his illustrated *Travels through North and South Carolina, Georgia, East and West Florida* in Philadelphia in 1791. After the turn of the century, interest in natural history flourished, and the number of illustrated books increased dramatically. Philadelphia was the publishing center for this genre just as that city was the center for the study of science and medicine during colonial times.

It was in Philadelphia that the first American learned society devoted to the support and study of science was founded. The American Philosophical Society was founded in 1743. Although it floundered for a generation, it was reinvigorated late in the 1760s. Foremost among the early interests of this society was the study of natural history—plants and animals. Geography, astronomy, agriculture, mathematics, chemistry, and the useful trades were of lesser interest. Moreover, a long and cordial relationship existed between the city's intellectual elite and their counterparts in Great Britain. Cambridge and Boston had been settled by dissenters and populated by their descendants. Relationships between individuals in New England and Great Britain were fewer. Naturalists in Philadelphia corresponded with their peers in England, exchanging plant and animal specimens as well as information. Through the English members of this transatlantic circle, information spread to interested people on the Continent. George H. Daniels has commented, "Specimens were characteristically sent to Europeans as rapidly as they could be collected, where . . . they were to be assimilated with collections coming from other parts of the world." Philadelphia also led the other intellectual centers during the colonial era in establishing a medical school in 1766.[3] The presence of the medical faculty and students had a positive impact on the study of natural history.

Another factor in the primacy of Philadelphia as the center for natural-history studies was the presence of John Bartram, his son William, and the garden that John Bartram established along the banks

[3] Brooke Hindle, *The Pursuit of Science in Revolutionary America* (Chapel Hill: University of North Carolina Press, 1956), p. 69; George H. Daniels, *Science in American Society* (New York: Alfred A. Knopf, 1971), p. 131; Hindle, *Pursuit of Science*, p. 116.

of the Schuylkill River south of Philadelphia. Bartram served as a collector of plant specimens for Peter Collinson in England and for Collinson's friends. Although he was not traditionally educated, in the 1730s and later he provided an important intellectual stimulus to those around him, including his son William Bartram. He in turn provided the same kind of focal point for a new generation of naturalists including Alexander Wilson.

With this introduction to the importance of Philadelphia as the intellectual center for this literary genre, it is appropriate to discuss the publications that were produced in Philadelphia from 1800 to 1850. Despite the growing sentiments of nationalism and pride in American manufactures after the Revolution and the War of 1812, there was insufficient patronage for most of these publications. This difficulty persisted throughout the first half of the nineteenth century and was not alleviated until the federal and state governments began to support the scientific publications of the explorers and the investigations into the natural properties of each state. This movement did not begin until the late 1830s with the publication of the geologies of the states of Massachusetts, Maine, and New York. The publication of federally financed exploring expeditions was haphazard until the 1840s. The scientific findings of the Lewis and Clark expedition of 1804 were never fully published, and the fullest narrative of Maj. Stephen H. Long's expedition to the Rocky Mountains was published by Carey and Lea in Philadelphia in 1823—not by the federal government.

The pioneer American botanical work was compiled by Benjamin Smith Barton (1766–1815). Barton was the son of an Episcopalian clergyman whose avocation was the study of botany and mineralogy. His parents died before he was fifteen, at which time he moved from Lancaster to Philadelphia. He studied medicine at Edinburgh, London, and Gottingen, where he received his degree in 1789. He returned to Philadelphia where he practiced medicine and taught natural history and botany at the University of Pennsylvania. Tragically, he died of tuberculosis at the age of forty-nine.[4]

---

[4] *Dictionary of American Biography*, s.v. "Benjamin Smith Barton."

The Elements of Botany was published in an edition of about 500 copies for Barton in 1803. Containing thirty plates, this two-volume work was a departure from previous natural histories printed in the United States. In the preface, Barton explains his motives in compiling and publishing such an ambitious project.

I have never ceased to look forward, . . . to the time, when Natural History shall be taught as an indispensible branch of science, in our university: when it shall cease to "yield its laurels to languages which are withered or dead, and to studies, that are useless or ignoble." That period has not yet arrived. I have, however, the satisfaction of observing, that these sciences are making some, nay even great, advances among us; and I still flatter myself, that the directors of our principal American universities, . . . will see the propriety, and even necessity, of giving more substantial encouragement for the extension of Natural History among us. It was with the view of contributing something to this desirable end, that I undertook the arduous task of composing these Elements of Botany.[5]

Despite the lack of some basic reference works and the difficulties in publishing the work himself, Barton persevered and saw his work to completion. Although he was responsible for the text, he turned to William Bartram (1739–1823) for drawings for all but three plates (6, 7, and 30).

In addition to being a close and careful observer of nature in his written journals, Bartram was an artist, as his drawings (now located at the American Philosophical Society) of both flora and fauna attest.[6] Transforming Bartram's drawings into engravings was a fairly easy task. His style was linear, and he did not use washes which would obscure details on his sketches. Even in the deeply shaded areas of the drawings, it is possible to understand the forms. Many of the engraved plates consist of details of plants—roots, flower parts, seeds, and so forth. Bartram provided the drawings, but he did not compose them on the plates—that was apparently the responsibility of the author. Some of the drawings do not, therefore, have a finished appearance.

The plates were not terribly expensive to engrave. Joseph H.

[5] Wayne Hanley, *Natural History in America* (New York: Quadrangle/New York Times Book Co., 1977), p. 25; Benjamin Smith Barton, *The Elements of Botany; or, Outlines of the Natural History of Vegetables*, vol. 2 (Philadelphia, 1803), pp. v–vi.
[6] See Joseph Ewan, *William Bartram, Botanical and Zoological Drawings, 1756–1788* (Philadelphia: American Philosophical Society, 1968).

Seymour received $8.50 for engraving the "Venus's Fly-Trap" (fig. 1). Several of the extant receipts are dated 1801 and 1802, which indicates that bringing the project to fruition was a lengthy and difficult task.[7]

A reviewer in the *Medical Repository* wrote at length about the plates. In particular he noted, "The drawings are correct, natural and easy, and the engravings are handsomely executed."[8] The plates were engraved by at least seven different hands: Francis Shallus (six), Benjamin Tanner (six), Cornelius Tiebout (three), Benjamin Jones (three), Seymour (three), Gilbert Fox (one), and Alexander Lawson (one). Seven of the plates were unsigned. In spite of the number of hands working on the plates, there is a remarkable uniformity of style, so that the natural and lively qualities of Bartram's drawings were not lost in translation. The names of these engravers, particularly Tanner, Tiebout, and Lawson, will reappear with some frequency. These engravers excelled in this type of engraving which required close attention to detail.

Not having live specimens at hand to compare with the engravings, it is not possible to attest to the accuracy of the engravings; however, Barton's nephew, William P. C. Barton, who made some drawings of specimens for his uncle, wrote a biographical sketch of his uncle in which he discussed his attitudes toward the drawing of specimens. "I have frequently painted these subjects for him [Benjamin Smith Barton], and can therefore speak with the more certainty of the fact. In all my drawings made for him, whether of plants, animals, bones, &c., I learnt the absolute necessity (to please his eye) of adhering very faithfully to my models. . . . Those who painted the subjects of natural history for him know, and those who have multiplied those paintings by the graphick art also know, and can verify the statement I have given, of his uncommon perception of errors, in drawings and engravings."[9]

An indication of the success of this pioneer botanical work is its subsequent publishing history. An edition was issued in 1804 in Lon-

[7] Receipts, Benjamin Smith Barton Papers, Manuscript Department, American Philosophical Society.

[8] Review of Barton, *Elements of Botany*, in *Medical Repository* 7, no. 1 (May–July 1803): 48.

[9] William P. C. Barton, *A Biographical Sketch [of] . . . Professor Barton* (Philadelphia, 1816), pp. 7–8.

Fig. 1. "Venus's Fly-trap (*Dionaea Muscipula*)." Engraved by J. H. Seymour.
From Benjamin Smith Barton, *The Elements of Botany; or, Outlines of the
Natural History of Vegetables*, vol. 2 (Philadelphia, 1803), pl. 7. H. 8″, W.
5⅛″. (American Antiquarian Society.)

don. The plates are similar to the 1803 Philadelphia edition except
that the few folding plates in the earlier edition were reduced in size.
An edition with ten additional plates was printed for the author in
1814. One of the new plates was dated 1809, which might mean that
the revision had started at that time or earlier. Robert Desilver issued
another edition in 1827 with the same plates used in the earlier printings. By that time they looked very worn indeed.

Contemporary comments on *The Elements of Botany* are another
indication of its value to its readers. A review in the *Medical Repository*
stated: "Upon the whole, when we consider the learning and practical
researches of the author, we consider his work as a substantial addition
to the number of valuable publications. It is calculated to render easy
and familiar one of the most charming departments of natural knowledge; and, for this purpose, we hope it will be consulted, not only by
the gentlemen who devoted themselves to professions, but by others
of liberal minds and easy fortunes."[10]

Barton sent one copy of *The Elements of Botany* to Joseph
Priestley who wrote in return thanking him for the volume. He went
on to say, "I shall read and study it with care, tho at my time of life,
it cannot be in your power, or that of any man, to make me a good
botanist." In July 1803, Priestley wrote again: "I have read with great
satisfaction your *Elements of Botany* and have learned from it much
more than I ever knew before, especially by a careful attention to your
well chosen and well engraved *Plates*."[11]

Barton's work was still of interest as late as 1825 when William
Jackson Hooker, professor of botany in the University of Glasgow,
wrote, "[Barton] has the credit of publishing an elementary work on
Botany, which, though rather diffuse in style, is full of entertaining
anecdotes; . . . it must have done much towards recommending the
study of botany in that country."[12] From these comments it is evident
that Barton achieved his goal.

---

[10] Review of Barton, *Elements of Botany*, in *Medical Repository* 7, no. 2 (August–October
1803): 165–66.

[11] Joseph Priestley to Benjamin Smith Barton, May 18, July 12, 1803, Benjamin Smith
Barton Collection, Historical Society of Pennsylvania.

[12] William Jackson Hooker, "On the Botany of America," *American Journal of Science
and Arts* 9, no. 2 (1825): 263–64.

The most ambitious scheme for the publication of a natural history was conceived by Alexander Wilson (1766–1813), a weaver by trade and a poet by avocation. Born in Scotland, he arrived in Philadelphia in 1794 practically penniless. Over the next ten years he taught school near Philadelphia and explored the wilderness of his newly adopted country. In 1804 he journeyed to Niagara Falls on foot and later composed "The Foresters," a poem about his trip. He was befriended by Bartram who encouraged him in his hobby of observing and collecting birds. Sometime around 1804 Wilson began to work seriously on describing and drawing the birds of North America.

I am not going to review Wilson's life, nor will I retrace his steps in his travels in search of information on the habits of birds or for subscribers.[13] The former pursuit was, however, far easier than the latter. What is of interest here is the production of the plates, of which there were seventy-six, on which there are 320 figures of birds representing 262 species.

American Ornithology was issued on a subscription basis with 200 set as the minimum number of subscribers acceptable to the publisher, Samuel Bradford. In the end Wilson obtained more than double that number, but that effort required long, strenuous journeys during which he also collected information on the birds he was including in his work.

In addition to obtaining the subscribers and writing the text, Wilson was responsible for the production of the plates. Several naturalists, including Mark Catesby and Bernard Romans, attempted to produce their own book illustrations with varying degrees of success. Wilson also tried, receiving much coaching from engraver Alexander Lawson and from William Bartram, who drew the illustrations for Barton's *Elements of Botany*. Lawson even taught Wilson to etch, and at least one example of his experimentation is extant (fig. 2). The most notable attribute of Wilson's etching is the overall impression of softness. The outlines are not starkly delineated, and Wilson's plate prob-

---

[13] A most enjoyable biography of Wilson and his various activities is Robert Cantwell, *Alexander Wilson, Naturalist and Pioneer* (Philadelphia and New York: J. B. Lippincott Co., 1961). Another excellent summary of Wilson's *American Ornithology* was prepared by Gordon Marshall for *Philadelphia: Three Centuries of American Art* (Philadelphia: Philadelphia Museum of Art, 1976), pp. 206–11.

ably would not have withstood the printing of 400 impressions. The lightly etched lines provide a guide to the colorist, but the published plate of the blue jay engraved by Lawson provides more distinct lines (fig. 3). Both styles, however, follow one guideline established by Catesby in his *Natural History of Carolina* printed in London in 1731. To avoid the cost of having the plates engraved, Catesby learned to etch. He explains in his preface: "I have not done [it] in a graver-like manner, choosing rather to omit their method of cross-Hatching, and follow the humour of the Feathers, which is more laborious, and I hope has proved more to the purpose."[14]

One recent naturalist, Donald C. Peattie, wrote of Wilson, "great ornithologist as Wilson was, he was no artist. When he was woefully out of drawing, he sensed it no more than a poor singer off key. His birds are flat, two-dimensional, and all too obviously dead." Another naturalist made a similar criticism of Catesby, but explained that his "goal was a flat representation to be studied for its accuracy rather than its artistic merit." Unlike John James Audubon a generation later, Wilson did not attempt to set his birds in a natural landscape, although he did try to capture characteristic poses. Wilson was capable of producing finished watercolors that rival Audubon's, but generally he was making drawings with his publication in mind. And he was most interested in creating drawings "made with the most scrupulous adherence to nature," as he announced in a prospectus printed in April 1807.[15]

There are more than seventy drawings by Wilson for *American Ornithology* that survive. The drawings are instructive for they indicate the contributions of the engravers to this project. Alexander Lawson, the engraver whose name is most often associated with this work, engraved fifty plates; John G. Warnicke executed twenty; George Murray, who was the chief engraver of natural-history subjects for Rees's

---

[14] The Academy of Natural Sciences, Philadelphia (hereafter cited as ANS), has in the Lawson Collection a hand-colored etching of a blue jay signed by Wilson. Catesby cited in William M. Smallwood, *Natural History and the American Mind* (New York: Columbia University Press, 1941), p. 26.

[15] Donald C. Peattie, *Green Laurels: The Lives and Achievements of the Great Naturalists* (New York: Simon and Schuster, 1935), p. 229; Hanley, *Natural History*, p. 6; Alexander Wilson, *To the Lovers of Natural History . . . Proposals for Publishing by Subscription . . . American Ornithology* (Philadelphia: Samuel Bradford, April 6, 1807).

Fringilla tristis. Goldfinch.   Cervus cristatus, Blue Jay.   Oriolus Baltimore. Hanging Bird.

Fig. 2. Alexander Wilson, "*Fringilla tristis*, Goldfinch. *Cervus cristatus*, Blue Jay. *Oriolus Baltimore*, Hanging Bird," ca. 1808. Etching; H. 13¾", W. 9½". (Library, Academy of Natural Sciences of Philadelphia.)

Fig. 3. "1. *Corvus cristatus*, Blue Jay. 2. *Fringilla Tristis*, Yellow-Bird or Goldfinch. 3. *Oriolus Baltimorus*, Baltimore Bird." From Alexander Wilson, *American Ornithology; or, The Natural History of the Birds of the United States*, vol. 1 (Philadelphia: Bradford and Inskeep, 1808), pl. 1. H. 13⅝", W. 10". (Winterthur Library.)

Cyclopaedia, did five plates, and Benjamin Tanner engraved one.[16]

Wilson's preparatory drawings for the plates varied in degree of finish. The drawing of the fox sparrow is typical of the more finished designs (fig. 4). Generally the engravers and the colorists had both a sketch (watercolor or pencil) and a stuffed or, on occasion, a live specimen. Some of the stuffed specimens are still at Harvard University.

Some of the preparatory drawings for the later volumes of *American Ornithology* are highly finished with some indication of landscape and with the birds arranged in a composition. The sketches for the earlier parts are drawn on stiff paper and cut into odd shapes. Lawson and the other engravers apparently cut the drawings into these odd shapes so that they could arrange them on the plates. Most of the extant sketches are of the same size in which they appeared on the engraved plates. A comparison of the sketches with the engravings suggests that much of the success of *American Ornithology* is due to the skills of the engravers and to the colorists.

It was Wilson's responsibility to arrange for the coloring of the plates. A small memorandum book covering Wilson's payments to colorists, engravers, and plate printers from January 9, 1810, to January 15, 1811, has survived. Among those who were paid during that period for coloring plates were Alexander Rider (a recent immigrant from Germany), John H. Beck, Prosper Marin, Anna Peale, Eliza Leslie, John H. Hopkins, and Louise Adelersterren. They received 25¢ for each plate. The coloring must have been tedious, but it was relatively lucrative. Hopkins, then a youth of eighteen years, received $235 for his labors in a year. In a biography of Hopkins (1792–1868), his son wrote at length about his father's experiences:

Wilson the ornithologist had begun the publication of his *Birds of America*; but, in the infancy of the arts among us at that time, he was unable to find anyone competent to color the splendid plates of that great work from Nature. My Father was at length induced to attempt it. The price paid was lucrative,

---

[16]Frank N. Edgerton, "Notes Chiefly on the Plates of Wilson's *American Ornithology*," *Journal of the Society for the Bibliography of Natural History* 4, pt. 2 (January 1963): 125–37, describes the sixty-two drawings owned by the Museum of Comparative Zoology at Harvard University (Houghton Library Deposit MCZ 869.15a) and the eight located in the Lawson Collection at ANS. An additional drawing is at the Historical Society of Pennsylvania, Philadelphia (hereafter cited as HSP).

Fig. 4. Alexander Wilson, *Fox Sparrow,* ca. 1807–8. Drawing; H. 3¾″, W. 4¾″. (Library, Academy of Natural Sciences of Philadelphia.)

to him: and his proficiency in the art of painting, his delicacy and accuracy of both eye and hand in observing and imitating the hues and the forms of Nature, ensured him a degree of success which delighted his employer, besides being for a time, very agreeable to himself. Mr. Wilson always shot a fresh bird for his colorist, so that there should be no chance of the fading or changing of the brilliant tints of life. But constant repetition at length brought weariness, where the work had been begun with so much of zest and conscious self-improvement; and when other assistants had been sufficiently well trained, the task-work was willingly transferred to humbler hands.[17]

Rider earned a total of $436 during that year; Wilson was earning $900 a year as editor for the encyclopedia Bradford was publishing.

[17]MCZ 1, 6 Ms 52.42.1, Museum of Comparative Zoology, Harvard University; John Henry Hopkins, Jr., *The Life of the Late Right Reverend John Henry Hopkins* (New York: F. J. Huntington, 1837), p. 29.

Wilson had problems finding enough colorists for the duration of the project. For a while, Charles Robert Leslie colored plates, but he was so talented that Bradford and some other Philadelphians sent him to London to study art. In the end, Wilson colored most of the impressions in the volumes that appeared in the two or three years before his death in 1813. Although Wilson's *American Ornithology* was successful, both financially and critically, the effort cost him his life. Work on parts 8 and 9 was completed by George Ord, who in the 1820s reprinted the entire work.[18]

Hand coloring the plates for the illustrated natural histories continued to be a problem. Wilson proved, with his single-minded dedication, that such a project could attract enough subscribers to be a financial success, even at the cost of $12 a volume. The problem was one of execution. Barton's *Elements of Botany* was basically a textbook, and the plates were incorporated into the work only to explain plant parts and functions. For the identification of specific species of animals or plants, color was considered to be integral to the function of the plates. The problems encountered by Wilson were shared by William Paul Crillon Barton in the publication a decade later of the *Vegetable Materia Medica*.

William P. C. Barton (1786–1856) was trained as a physician and served as a surgeon in the United States Navy from 1809 to 1815, at which time he became professor of botany at the University of Pennsylvania. He descended from a distinguished Philadelphia family and was Benjamin Smith Barton's nephew.

Barton began work on his *Vegetable Materia Medica* in 1814. By July 1, 1817, his work was advertised by Mathew Carey: "The object of this work is to present the public with faithful representations of the many important medicinal plants of our country, most of which are as yet known only by name, to our physicians. The engravings will be executed in the best style after the author's drawings, in which the greatest accuracy will be studied. The plates will be coloured by his own hand; and are promised to be true imitations of nature." The

---

[18] James E. DeKay referred to *American Ornithology* as a "great work" in his *Anniversary Address on the Progress of the Natural Sciences in the United States* (New York: T. and C. Carvill, 1826), p. 43.

work was to appear in two quarto volumes, with twenty-five plates each. The total cost was to be \$27 with delivery in early 1820.[19]

Because Jacob Bigelow had the same idea at the same time in Boston, the plans were changed. To meet the competition, the work was issued in eight parts, rather than appearing in two volumes, in 1820. Both Bigelow and Barton encountered the same problem: coloring the plates by hand was slow, tedious work. Bigelow's publisher turned to the innovative process of printing the plates in color; Barton persisted in presenting hand-colored plates (fig. 5).[20] The history of this publication is well documented by surviving manuscript accounts and letters.

In the preface to part 1, Barton remarked, "even botanists are sometimes perplexed with the close alliances in the habit and structure of plants ... to enable every one to identify the precise plants described, good coloured engravings of them are indispensable." To be satisfied with the accuracy of the drawings, he drew them himself. "In all the drawings, many of which are already finished, the greatest accuracy will be studied; and with a view to render the work as correct as possible, the author encounters the laborious task of colouring all the plates in his own hand. Since faithful colouring is nearly as important in a work of this nature, as correct drawings, he trusts that the usefulness of the undertaking will be enhanced by this part of his labour."[21]

In a letter dated October 31, 1817, to the publisher, Mathew Carey, Barton reports the death of his father and the need of the family for additional income. He wrote, "My sisters paint extremely well, and have already coloured many of the plates of the first number of Vegetable Materia Medica. It is equally my duty, as it is certainly my inclination, to contribute all in my power, to the support of my mother & sisters and I cannot in any way do this, but by employing the latter to assist me in colouring the work you are now publishing."[22]

---

[19] M. Carey and Son, List of New Works, and of New Editions, Philadelphia, July 1, 1817, broadside, American Antiquarian Society (hereafter cited as AAS).

[20] Richard J. Wolfe, *Jacob Bigelow's American Medical Botany* (North Hills, Pa.: Bird and Bull Press; Boston: Boston Medical Library, 1979).

[21] William P. C. Barton, *Vegetable Materia Medica of the United States*, vol. 1 (Philadelphia: M. Carey and Son, 1817), pp. xii–xiv.

[22] William P. C. Barton to Mathew Carey, October 31, 1817, Lea and Febinger Collection, HSP.

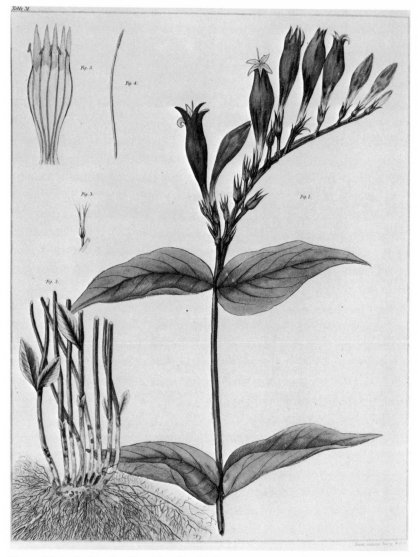

Fig. 5. "*Spigelia Marilandica*. (Carolina Pink-root)." From William P. C. Barton, *Vegetable Materia Medica of the United States; or, Medical Botany*, vol. 2 (Philadelphia: M. Carey and Son, 1818), pl. 31. H. 10⁹⁄₁₆", W. 8". (Winterthur Library.)

As the publication progressed, the coloring of the plates proceeded piecemeal. Barton submitted bills to Carey which are interspersed through the Carey account books. One bill might cover the coloring of six plates for parts 2 and 3; another bill will cover the coloring of 350 plates at one time. The coloring continued after the year of 1818 which appears on the title page of volume 2. As late as July 31, 1819, Barton wrote to Henry Carey that he had three people coloring for him. Barton apparently received all the money for the coloring and then paid his colorists. The rate was 75¢ for coloring the plates for each part. Later the reimbursement was 8¼¢ per print. In the preface to volume 2, Barton refers to the "tediousness of the colouring" and admits that up to six people were coloring the plates, including members of his family.[23]

The Carey account books also include the bills for engraving and printing the plates. Tanner, Vallance, Kearny, and Company engraved all but eight of the plates; the cost of each, including the copperplate, was $15. The engravers later raised the price to $20. Printing the impressions was an additional cost, as was pressing the plates. The cost of producing the illustrations was approximately $3,862.

Apparently all that Barton received from the publication of his work was the money for coloring the plates. In January 1819 he offered to convey the copyright to M. Carey and Son for $600. On July 26, 1819, he wrote, "this is the only pecuniary reward I received for my original drawings & labour. You must be sensible of this when I remind you, that unless you do this, I shall have toiled for two years past without any pecuniary reward. This toil I was willing to encounter in the beginning, till the work was tried. By the colouring I can make very little; and that little is obtained as payment for the services of an artist, & heretofore, at the Expense of Mrs. Barton's industry."[24]

Also on July 26, 1819, he wrote outlining his plans for a third volume to be issued in four numbers, each containing six plates and sixty pages of letterpress. The conditions he laid out were stringent

[23]Mathew Carey account books, vols. 30, 31, AAS; Barton to Henry Carey, Mathew Carey account books, vol. 32, no. 5658, AAS; Barton, *Vegetable Materia*, 2:xv.

[24]Barton to M. Carey and Son, January 19, July 26, 1819, Mathew Carey Papers, Edward Carey Gardiner Collection, HSP.

and demanding. It seems that Carey turned it down. The copyright for all three volumes would total $1,000. Barton would be paid for all coloring. The volume would be completed in one year, with the first issue appearing October 1, 1819. Barton would receive a copper-plate press and twenty-five copies of each issue. Volumes 1 and 2 would be reissued with corrections which Barton would be paid to make, and no copies would be sold with uncolored plates. Finally, a monopoly on coloring the plates would go to him, his wife, or his sisters.[25]

Was all the work of hand coloring the plates worth it? Walter Channing wrote, "the figures were drawn and partly colored by the author; many of them very correctly and elegantly, but many others so badly as to indicate great haste both in the coloring and the designs."[26]

The strongest criticism of Barton's and Bigelow's works came from Constantine S. Rafinesque who commented in his *Medical Flora* on the cost of the two works. He wrote, "Works of general utility ought to be accurate, complete, portable and cheap." He continued, "The popular knowledge of the natural sciences has been prevented in the United States, by the first works published on them, having followed the model of the splendid European publications intended for the wealthy."[27] Instead of the costly hand-colored engraved plates, Rafinesque recommended simpler cuts, such as relief cuts printed in green which appeared in his work. Such plates are adequate for recognition. Moreover, Rafinesque's two-volume octavo work is portable. No botanist would have carried Barton's or Bigelow's volumes into the field. The incorporation of inexpensive cuts into the texts of natural histories is one solution that was found to combat the expense and slowness of producing colored plates. An alternative solution was to print engraved plates in color. Barton's next book published by Carey, *A Flora of North America*, made use of plates printed in green ink

[25] Barton to M. Carey and Son, July 26, 1819, Mathew Carey Papers, Edward Carey Gardiner Collection, HSP.

[26] Walter Channing, "Botany of the United States," *North American Review* 13, no. 1 (July 1821): 120.

[27] Constantine S. Rafinesque, *Medical Flora*, vol. 1 (Philadelphia: Atkinson and Alexander, 1828), p. vii.

with hand coloring applied separately. Those plates were engraved by Cornelius Tiebout, and the same technique appears in *American Entomology* compiled by Thomas Say.

Say's *American Entomology* was published in Philadelphia by Samuel A. Mitchell in three volumes from 1824 to 1828. Thomas Say (1787–1834), a druggist by profession, was the son of a prominent Philadelphia physician. He served as the zoologist of Long's expeditions to the Rocky Mountains in 1819/20 and to the Minnesota River in 1823. For several years, he served as professor of natural history at the University of Pennsylvania. In 1826, he arrived at New Harmony, Indiana, with William Maclure and Charles Alexandre Lesueur. Tiebout and his daughter may have arrived there with them.[28] He died at the age of forty-seven, having published widely on insects and shells.

In 1817, Say issued a specimen for his projected work. In the preface he pointed out, "almost nothing has yet been done in the United States" on the subject of insects. He continued:

The variety of systems, the obscurity of the distinctive characteristics, and often the great requisite nicety of discrimination upon which some of those systems are founded, the want of a guide such as would be afforded by good books of plates, all conspire to retard the progress of the student. To these obstacles we may also add, the difficulty of procuring the many splendid and costly works of European authors—our booksellers being unwilling to incur the risk of importing them unless expressly ordered. Attributable to these causes is the absence of knowledge of this science and of taste for its cultivation.[29]

It was not until after his return from the two exploring expeditions that Say's work began to appear. In the preface to volume 1, Say wrote, "he enters upon the task without any expectation of remuneration, and fully aware of the many obstacles by which he must be inevitably opposed. The graphic execution of the work will exhibit the present state of the arts in this country, as applied to this particular department of natural science, as no attention will be wanting."[30]

[28] William E. Wilson, *The Angel and the Serpent: The Story of New Harmony* (Bloomington: Indiana University Press, 1964), pp. 138–39.
[29] Thomas Say, *American Entomology; or, Descriptions of the Insects of North America* (Philadelphia: Mitchell and Ames, 1817), pp. iii–v.
[30] Thomas Say, *American Entomology*, vol. 1 (Philadelphia: Samuel A. Mitchell, 1825–28), p. v.

Volume 1 opens with an emblematical frontispiece designed by Lesueur, a French naturalist who traveled through the northeast in 1816 with Maclure. Lesueur collected specimens for a projected work on the fish of America, while Maclure made observations relevant to the geology of the country. From 1817 until 1825, Lesueur lived in Philadelphia, teaching art and providing illustrations for scientific publications. He traveled widely from his base at New Harmony between 1826 and 1837, when he returned to Le Havre, France, where he died in 1846 at the age of sixty-eight. In addition to designing the frontispiece, Lesueur provided drawings for ten of the plates.

Thirty-two of the plates were drawn by Titian Ramsay Peale (1799–1885), one of the talented sons of Charles Willson Peale. He was precocious, for at the age of seventeen he was elected to the Academy of Natural Sciences and joined an expedition that year to procure specimens from the Sea Islands and coastal Georgia and Florida. Other members of the expedition were Maclure, Say, and Ord. The next year Peale was appointed assistant naturalist on Long's expedition. He later was commissioned by Charles Lucien Bonaparte to make drawings for his continuation of Wilson's *Ornithology*. A biographical sketch of Peale states that he colored the plates for Say's *American Entomology*, but I have not been able to verify this. In fact, several of the plates are printed in brown or green ink to eliminate some coloring by hand. Peale worked as a naturalist through the 1840s. In 1848, he became an examiner in the United States Patent Office where he worked until 1873. He then returned to Philadelphia and to a work he had started in 1833 on the butterflies of North America. Lack of financial support had prevented his work from being published in the 1830s. The publication in 1868 of the first series of William Henry Edwards's *Butterflies of North America* rendered Peale's project obsolete.[31]

All but four of the plates were engraved by Cornelius Tiebout. In these plates, Tiebout uses a variety of techniques—stipple, aquatint, and line work (fig. 6). Jared Sparks commented, "The letter-press of Wilson's Ornithology and of the famous edition of the Columbiad, is

---

[31] Albert C. Peale, "Titian R. Peale, 1800–1885," *Bulletin of the Philosophical Society of Washington* 14 (December 1905): 317–26.

Fig. 6. [*Smerinthus Geminatus.*] Drawn by T. R. Peale; engraved by C. Tiebout. From Thomas Say, *American Entomology; or, Descriptions of the Insects of North America,* vol. 1 (Philadelphia: Samuel Augustus Mitchell, 1824), pl. 12. H. 9″, W. 5½″. (Winterthur Library.)

executed in a more finished style; but in the exquisite delicacy of the drawings and beauty of the engravings, as well as in the marks of taste indicated in the external attractions of the volume, the American Entomology is much superior to either of them. . . . The specimens of their labours here furnished are in the highest degree creditable to these artists. . . . We hope the author will meet with the full measure of encouragement, which the extent of his labors, and his zeal in the cause of knowledge, so justly deserve." On the other hand, James E. DeKay expressed his chagrin that the "expensive form [put] it beyond the reach of most private individuals." The cost of each volume was $5. There were a total of fifty-three plates depicting 133 species. Of these, 112 were described for the first time, making this a very significant publication. Although this book seems to have been accomplished without great difficulties, biographers of Say have suggested that the lack of additional volumes was "due probably to the indifference of the public on account of its high price, and to the distance which separated the author and the publisher."[32] Moreover, Say began to publish his *American Conchology* in New Harmony in 1830.

John Godman (1794–1830) was the author of *American Natural History*, published by Carey and Lea from 1826 to 1828 in three volumes. Godman's career as a physician did not begin until 1818 when he was twenty-four years old. Until that time he had been apprenticed to a printer and had served in the navy during the War of 1812. He served as professor of anatomy at Rutgers in 1826 and 1827 but resigned because of a fatal case of tuberculosis. He was extremely prolific, and it was, perhaps, too much work that made him succumb to his disease so early in life.

Godman's contemporaries encouraged his work. DeKay wrote in 1826, "Has Zoology, or the history of animals, been cultivated with the same success as botany, or geology and mineralogy? The answer must be in the negative. . . . It has had to contend against the unjust views which have been taken of its relative importance, and to a want of concert in nomenclature and systematic arrangement between the

[32] Jared Sparks, "American Entomology . . . ," *North American Review* 21, no. 48 (July 1825): 251–52; DeKay, *Anniversary Address*, p. 52; Harry B. Weiss and Grace M. Ziegler, *Thomas Say, Early American Naturalist* (Springfield, Ill.: Charles C. Thomas, 1931), p. 191.

labours in the different subdivisions of this science." DeKay looked forward with impatience to Godman's work.[33]

Godman and DeKay were not the first men to respond to the inadequate coverage of the mammals of North America. Benjamin Smith Barton issued a prospectus for *Elements of Zoology* in 1806. He envisioned a two-volume work with at least 256 pages per volume and ten plates. The cost was to be $5, and he needed 300 subscribers before publication could begin. After Barton's death, Ord found that only 56 pages of text had been completed.[34]

In 1825 Carey and Lea had published Godman's *Contribution to Physiological and Pathological Anatomy*. It is not surprising that Godman turned to the same publisher for his *American Natural History*. Unfortunately, information on this title does not appear in the publisher's cost book.

American Natural History contains forty-three uncolored plates, in addition to engraved title pages and a frontispiece, and Lesueur provided drawings for fifteen of them (fig. 7). Rider, who worked as a colorist for Wilson soon after his arrival in Philadelphia in 1810 from Germany, also drew fifteen plates. Titian Peale drew the plate of the great mastodon which his father had exhumed in 1801 and assembled in his museum in Philadelphia. There are several other plates relating to the mastodon and to other fossil remains in the second volume. The other men who supplied drawings for the plates were W. W. Wood, Charles Burton, and W. Scoresby, Jr. Another plate was designed by T. Landseer, and Charles Willson Peale drew two plates of "Wistar's Fossil Ox." The engravers included Peter Maverick, Francis Kearney, George B. Ellis, and William E. Tucker, one of Kearney's students. Despite the diversity of artists and engravers, the plates are remarkably uniform in style.

Sparks commented on the plates in his review of the first volume in the *North American Review*: "The drawings, with which the book abounds are executed with great beauty and spirit; some of them would do no discredit to [English artist Thomas] Bewick. The engrav-

[33] DeKay, *Anniversary Address*, pp. 37, 42.
[34] Jeannette E. Graustein, "The Eminent Benjamin Smith Barton," *Pennsylvania Magazine of History and Biography* 85, no. 4 (October 1961): 427.

Fig. 7. "1. Black Bear. 2. Grizzly Bear." Drawn by C. A. Lesueur; engraved by F. Kearney. From John D. Godman, *American Natural History*, vol. 1 (Philadelphia: H. C. Carey and L. Lea, 1826), facing p. 131. H. 8⁵⁄₁₆", W. 5". (Winterthur Library.)

ings are highly finished. The fame, which the Philadelphia artists have acquired in delineating and engraving specimens of natural history, is fully sustained in this work."[35]

Godman, however, wrote a conclusion at the end of the third volume which seems to express some disappointment about the way in which the publication appeared. He apologized too for the many delays that he caused, but pleaded, "it has been frequently necessary to suspend it for weeks and months, in order to procure certain animals, to observe their habits in captivity, or to make daily visits to the woods and fields for the sake of witnessing their actions in a state of nature."[36] And, of course, he was suffering from tuberculosis which must have contributed to the slowness of publication. At least, it was not the execution of the plates that caused delays.

This volume is far less lavishly produced than the other natural histories under consideration. Nor can it compare with the *Viviparous Quadrupeds of North America* compiled by John Bachman and John James Audubon and published from 1845 to 1853. Yet, this work, meant to be a popular natural history rather than a work concerning nomenclature and classification, was reprinted five times between 1828 and 1860.

Samuel Stehman Haldeman (1812–80) was born in Lancaster County, Pennsylvania. He attended Dickinson College for three years but did not graduate. In the late 1830s he worked on the geological survey of Pennsylvania. He later lectured at Franklin Institute and became a professor of natural history at the University of Pennsylvania. For many years he resided on the banks of the Susquehanna River. His interest in freshwater shells derived from his living in a location rich in various examples. This interest eventually culminated in the publication of *A Monograph of the Freshwater Univalve Mullusca.*

In January 1840, Haldeman sent to members of the scientific community a specimen of his proposed work which contained two plates and sample text. One plate was drawn and engraved by Law-

[35] Jared Sparks, review of Godman, *American Natural History,* in *North American Review* 24, no. 55 (April 1827): 468.
[36] John D. Godman, *American Natural History,* 3 vols. (Philadelphia: H. C. Carey and L. Lea, 1828), 3:246, 1:v–vi.

son's son, Oscar A. Lawson. The price as advertised was to be $1 for each number, which was to contain five colored plates.

One of his friends, on hearing of the proposed work, wrote to Haldeman expressing his interest and offering to help in any way possible. After he had received the specimen, John G. Anthony wrote, "Your prospectus and Specimen No. came to hand one week after your letter. I am much pleased with the work and particularly so with your describing the animal as well as his habitation and food. All such items are extremely interesting and too much overlooked generally by those who study shells."[37]

Such words must have encouraged Haldeman, for he issued the first part of his *Monograph of the Freshwater Univalve Mullusca* in July 1840 with only fifty-nine subscribers from many cities. Obtaining subscribers for a scientific work was no easier in 1840 than it had been for Wilson thirty years earlier. One correspondent in Boston could come up with suggestions of only eight names for Haldeman's subscription list.[38] Interest in these publications was still limited to the small scientific community of amateurs and professionals.

Eight parts of this work were issued. The first six came at regular, six-month intervals. A year elapsed between parts 6 and 7. Part 8 was issued in June 1845. The whole was reissued with a ninth part in 1871. Amos Binney might have had some premonition of the tardiness of the parts when he wrote to Haldeman in 1841: "During a recent visit to Philadelphia, I obtained from Mr. Dobson the 2d number of your monograph. I am very much pleased with the execution of it and I hope you will press forward to complete it as soon as possible."[39]

Haldeman's *Monograph* contained thirty-nine plates, thirty-six of which were drawn and colored by Helen E. Lawson, the talented daughter of Alexander Lawson, Wilson's engraver. Benjamin F. Nutting, a landscape and portrait painter, drew one plate, and A. Lawson drew two plates. The plates are beautifully executed with a heavy reliance on the use of watercolor to provide a sense of roundness to the shells (fig. 8). A comparison of engraved proofs with the finished plates indicates that the engravings served as guides for the colorist.

[37] John G. Anthony to S. S. Haldeman, January 21, 31, 1840, Haldeman Collection, ANS.

[38] Augustus Addison Gould to Haldeman, January 28, 1840, Haldeman Collection, ANS.

[39] Amos Binney to Haldeman, April 20, 1841, Haldeman Collection, ANS.

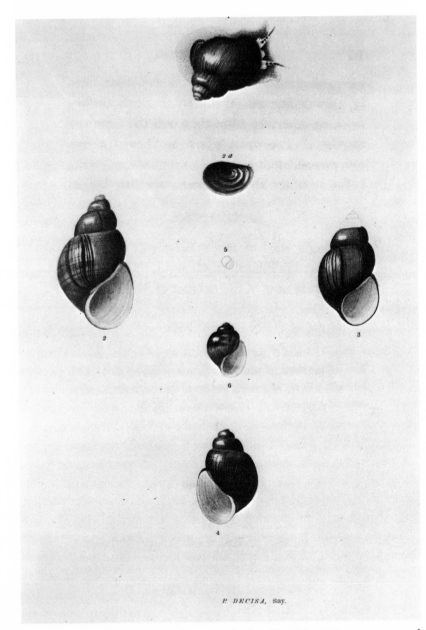

Fig. 8. "*Paludina. P. Decisa*, Say." Drawn and colored by Helen E. Lawson; engraved by Oscar A. Lawson. From S. S. Haldeman, *A Monograph of the Freshwater Univalve Mollusca of the United States* (Philadelphia: J. Dobson, 1842), pl. 1. H. 7¾", W. 4¼". (American Antiquarian Society.)

Moreover, since the original artist and the colorist were the same person, it is no surprise that the illustrations as published are so close to the original drawings.[40]

Silliman's *American Journal of Science and Arts* had two notices about this work. In a review of the first number, they commented: "The plates are executed in fine style, on copper, drawn by Miss Lawson, and colored very beautifully, with five or six examples of each species." In a review of the fifth part, they noted: "The illustrations of this work are on copper, by Alex. Lawson, drawn and colored by Miss Lawson and are so perfect as certainly to leave nothing to be desired." In September 1840, Anthony wrote to Haldeman, "Your No. 1 reached me safely and the plates are well done, indeed they are extremely well done and strikingly correct. In fact the whole, text and all is such as to do credit to all concerned. I have seldom seen any works of the kind which pleased me so much in its whole execution as this. If your other plates keep up with this you will make a work worth having and one which I very much wish to see."[41]

The perfection and the subsequent expense of these plates might well have caused the demise of Haldeman's *Monograph*. Writing in 1854, John Livingston noted that the early parts of the *Monograph* were reprinted in Paris in a work called *Illustrations conchyologiques* by J. C. Chenu. In 1847, Haldeman sent his *Monographie du genre leptotis* directly to Paris to be published by Chenu, which means that he avoided the expense of commissioning illustrations. His biographer continues, "This also reduced the expense of his own, which fell short of paying for itself about a thousand dollars, although, if the plates had been in lithography and less care bestowed upon the whole, it would have paid its expenses." Another publication envisioned by Haldeman would have incurred the loss of $2,000 or $3,000, and Livingston doubted that it would "ever see the light," at least in the United States.[42]

[40]The original drawings and engraved proofs for Haldeman's work are in the Lawson Collection at ANS.

[41]Reviews of Haldeman, *A Monograph of the Freshwater Univalve Mullusca,* in *American Journal of Science and Arts* 39, no. 2 (July–September 1840): 393, and 43, no. 2 (July–September 1842): 391; Anthony to Haldeman, September 26, 1840, Haldeman Collection, ANS.

[42]John Livingston, *Portraits of Americans Now Living,* vol. 4 (New York: Cornish, Lamport; London: Sampson Low, Son, 1853–54), p. 96.

Another factor in the premature end to the *Monograph* was the author's wide-ranging interests. As the *Monograph* was being published, he developed interests in the noises made by insects and in philology and dialects. From 1851 to 1855, he lectured in zoology at the University of Pennsylvania and established an agricultural journal to which he contributed articles on scientific agriculture. The change in his interests is striking when we realize that he became the first professor of comparative philology at the University of Pennsylvania in 1868.

A third factor in the cessation of the *Monograph* might have been the retirement of Judah Dobson from the publishing business. The son of Thomas Dobson, a Philadelphia bookseller and publisher from 1786 until his death in 1823, Judah Dobson was the publisher of several important works on natural history including those by John Edwards Holbrook, Thomas Nuttall, and François André Michaux. He retired in 1846, the same year in which Alexander Lawson died at the age of seventy-three. All these elements probably contributed to the end of Haldeman's *Monograph*. Economic factors and Dobson's retirement might have been overcome if Haldeman had had a single-minded devotion to the work, but his interests strayed elsewhere.

As Livingston indicated in his observations about Haldeman's publications, lithography was an option for the production of plates. Judah Dobson, the publisher of Holbrook's monumental work on reptiles and amphibians, *The North American Herpetology*, did turn to this medium when he began this publication in 1836. Holbrook, born in Beaufort, South Carolina, but raised in New England, was a physician in Charleston, South Carolina. During the colonial era, Charleston was a center of active naturalists; that interest remained into the 1830s.

As early as 1826, Holbrook conceived his plan for publishing a work on reptiles and amphibians, for he engaged the services of an Italian artist, J. Sera, whom Anna Wells Rutledge characterized as a "scene, decorative and fancy painter." Among his works was the design and execution of the decorations at the theater in Charleston for the ball honoring the visit of LaFayette in 1825. Rutledge also recorded two landscapes by Sera as well as a transparency painting of Mazeppa.

According to Thomas L. Ogier, another Charleston physician, "This excellent artist had a particular fancy for drawing reptiles. We have often heard him say that he could never be satisfied with his work unless he gave the particular expressions of his subject. He was as enthusiastic about giving the peculiarly hard, cruel expression of the alligator's eye, or the bright deceitful look of the eye of the black snake, as if his subjects belonged to the highest order of creation; and his drawings are indeed *fac similes* of the animals he intended to represent and monuments of his talent."[43] Holbrook noted in the preface to his work that Sera was Italian by birth, but had long been a resident of the United States. Sera died about 1836, the year that the first edition of *The North American Herpetology* began to appear.

Four volumes were issued in 1836, 1837, and 1838. Complete copies of the first edition are rare. At that point, Holbrook stopped and decided to revise what he had already done and to rearrange the material. The first edition was arranged in the order in which the material was prepared, not in any scientific order. In 1842 the second edition was issued in five volumes by Judah Dobson, also the publisher of the first edition. To the 111 plates of the first edition were added an additional 36, making a total of 147.

Most of the plates were printed by Peter S. Duval of Philadelphia, although five bear the imprint of Lehman and Duval and one lacks the name of the lithographer. Each plate is credited to the artist who drew the illustration of the specimen. Occasionally the delineator and lithographic draftsman are the same person. Sera provided drawings for thirty-seven of the plates. Albert Newsam, James Queen, and George Lehman also drew several of the plates from nature and put them on stone. Other draftsmen who worked on the first edition were S. Cichowski, Lewis Brechemin, Heiman, Stocking, and Charles C. Kuchel.

A name that appears frequently on the plates is John H. Richard. Richard was born in Germany about 1807. Between 1841 and 1843 he and Duval experimented with the lithotint process and produced

[43] Anna Wells Rutledge, *Artists in the Life of Charleston* (Philadelphia: American Philosophical Society, 1949), p. 148; Theodore Gill, "Biographical Memoir of John Edwards Holbrook 1794–1811," *National Academy of Sciences Biographical Memoirs* 5 (1905): 54.

the "Grandpapa's Pet" in *Miss Leslie's Magazine* for April 1843. Although this plate has been called the "first specimen of this art ever published in America," three lithotints by Richard were published in this work by Holbrook, including a plate of a turtle (*Emys guttata*) in the first volume issued in 1842 (fig. 9). Although a specimen of the same name appeared in the first edition, I suspect that the lithotint was newly prepared for the second edition. The publisher did note, "many of the Plates have been re-engraved and improved."[44]

Since there are only three lithotints in the five-volume set, the technique was obviously experimental, but its use indicated that hand-coloring the plates was potentially disruptive to the publication of such lavish productions. Another attempt at replacing the laborious hand coloring was to print the plate in color and apply additional touches of color only by hand. One example is the lizard (*Crotaphytus collaris*) drawn on stone by Richard. This plate was printed in blue and then hand colored. Holbrook promised in the preface, "The colouring of the plates may be fully relied on, as almost every one was done from life." In the description of this plate, Holbrook notes that the colors in this case were taken from a specimen preserved in alcohol, and the coloring was "not to be relied upon."[45]

Specimens for this work were sent to Holbrook from many people in various parts of the country. The lizard came from an unknown source, but the first person to identify one was Say during the expedition to the Rocky Mountains led by Long. The drawing of the specimen of the *Menobranchus maculatur* was sent to Holbrook from the bishop of Vermont, the Reverend John Henry Hopkins. As a student many years before in Philadelphia, Hopkins had colored plates for Wilson. The circle of naturalists and interested amateurs evidently remained a close one.

With Thomas Nuttall's *North America Sylva*, a different set of circumstances is encountered. This three-volume work was published in Philadelphia in 1842, 1846, and 1849 and contained 121 lithographed plates. The plates in the first two volumes were lithographed

[44] "The New Art of Lithotint," *Miss Leslie's* 1, no. 2 (April 1843): 113.

[45] John Edward Holbrook, *The North American Herpetology*, 5 vols. (Philadelphia: J. Dobson, 1842), 1:lx, 2:83.

Emys guttata.

Fig. 9. "*Emys guttata*." Lithotinted by J. H. Richard; lithographed by P. S. Duval. From J. S. Holbrook, *North American Herpetology*, vol. 1 (Philadelphia: J. Dobson, 1842), pl. 11. H. 8¼", W. 4⅞". (American Antiquarian Society.)

by Thomas Sinclair; only one plate in the third volume bears his imprint, the others being anonymous.

Nuttall (1786–1859), born in England, was apprenticed to a printer and came to the United States in 1808, already interested in the study of natural history. He became a professional naturalist, writing and lecturing widely. In these activities he was encouraged by Benjamin Smith Barton. Nuttall's work is a supplement to *The North American Sylva* compiled by Michaux. First published in Paris in 1810, a translation was issued in Philadelphia from 1817 to 1819 by Thomas Dobson, who apparently purchased the plates from the French publisher. In 1841 Judah Dobson began to reissue Michaux's work with restrikes from the original plates, engraved by various French engravers after drawings by P. J. Redouté. The hand-colored, lithographed plates in the first volume of Nuttall's work compare quite favorably in appearance to the stipple plates of the 1810 French edition (fig. 10). The plates in the later volumes are not of the same quality. What happened? A review by Asa Gray in the *North American Review* indicates that the first volume was issued in two parts, and he notes that the text was committed to the publisher in 1842 or earlier. Gray reported, "the paper and typography are good, and the plates which are colored lithographs, are respectable."[46] That is hardly a rave review, but the renowned Gray had his own standards and was familiar with the finest publications in this field.

An 1841 letter from Nuttall to John K. Townsend suggests that Nuttall was actively supervising the production of this work. Explaining why he could not leave Philadelphia for Washington, he wrote: "Another reason, if no other remained, for wishing the plants to be sent on here [Philadelphia] is that I am now engaged with the additional volume of the *Sylva Americana*, of which I have nearly finished the writing part, but must superintend the engravings and drawings, as they have to be made from dried specimens and require my immediate supervision."[47]

---

[46] Asa Gray, review of Nuttall, *North American Sylva*, in *North American Review* 59, no. 124 (July 1844): 194.

[47] Thomas Nuttall to John K. Townsend, April 7, 1841, American Scientists Collection, case 7, box 24, HSP.

Fig. 10. "*Quercus Densiflora* (Dense Flowered Oak)." Drawn by G. West; lithographed by Sinclair. From Thomas Nuttall, *The North America Sylva; or, A Description of the Forest Trees of the United States, Canada, and Nova Scotia* . . ., vol. 1
(Philadelphia: J. Dobson, 1842), pl. 5. H. 10″, W. 6″. (American Antiquarian Society.)

Volume 2 was published by Townsend Ward in 1846, and volume 3 appeared under the imprint of Smith and Wistar in 1849. Two events occurred before the publication of volume 2. First, Judah Dobson retired from active business. Second, Nuttall inherited an estate near Liverpool, England, and the terms of the bequest required him to take up residence there. While the plates for the second and third volumes were being prepared, Nuttall was not in Philadelphia to supervise the work. The subsequent lack of quality in the final product is evident. An advertisement placed by the publisher appeared in the *American Journal of Science*. Typically, it was complimentary to the whole work: "The figures in these three additional volumes comprise one hundred and twenty-one plates, finely coloured, mostly of new subjects, or such as have not before been published in the Sylva, executed with the strictest fidelity to nature, under the eye of the Author."[48]

The plates were drawn by five different draftsmen: John T. French, J. B. Butler, E. D. Long, G. West, and George Worley. Nothing is known about these draftsmen, although we can probably assume that they were apprentices or had just finished their apprenticeships at the time of the publication of the work.

Although the plates are far from beautiful, they were probably adequate for the amateur. The price was reasonable — $21 for the three volumes with colored plates, $15 for uncolored plates. Twenty years earlier, Say's *American Entomology* sold for $5 per volume, but each volume had only eighteen plates instead of forty. It is impossible to determine if the plates in *The North American Sylva* would have been more carefully produced if Nuttall had been on hand to supervise the work and if Dobson had not retired. With his family's long association with the project, his dedication to it might well have ensured higher quality.

At the conclusion of the period from 1800 to 1850, the observer of the publishing scene might assume that the publication of illustrated natural histories might have become easier, perhaps through changes in financing, publicizing, or technology. Yet, the problems of issuing these deluxe volumes remained constant.

[48] Advertisement for Nuttall, *North American Sylva*, in *American Journal of Science*, n.s., 9, no. 27 (May 1850).

By 1850, thanks to the efforts of the naturalists whose works we have considered, the publication of natural histories with colored illustrations in Philadelphia and elsewhere had made their research available to Americans. There still was, however, competition from European presses, and the cost and technical problems of reproduction had not been solved. These would not be overcome until the development of chromolithography and four-color printing at a later time.

The works that were published did have an impact on the progress of American science and were well received by critics here and abroad. A professor of botany at the University of Glasgow wrote of Wilson's *American Ornithology*, for example, that it was "one of the most valuable works on science that was ever published in any country."[49]

It was unfortunate that publishers were unwilling to risk their own money for the production of these works. Haldeman in the late 1840s was still struggling with a financial burden, as Barton had in 1817. The theme that binds these publications together was the expense of the plates. It was not until the state and federal governments began to publish works on natural history that the problem was resolved. There is a remarkable parallel to today's world as we look to various programs of the federal government to support research and publications.

[49]William Jackson Hooker, "On the Botany of America," *American Journal of Science and Arts* 9, no. 2 (1825): 271.

"Messengers of Love, Tokens of Friendship"

Gift-Book Illustrations by John Sartain

KATHERINE MARTINEZ

IN THE NINETEENTH CENTURY the gift book, or keep-sake, represented a significant aspect of book illustration. Gift books were anthologies of genteel literature with elaborate title pages and lavish steel-engraved illustrations. The paper and printing were of excellent quality, the volumes were leather bound, and the covers were stamped with pictures from the book. Altogether, gift books represented a considerable advance in book illustration. What was unique about a large body of these illustrated books was that frequently the engraved plates, rather than the text, were the primary element of the book. It was not uncommon for a publisher to pay more for the illustrations than for the text and for an author to be commissioned to write a text that would complement a particular set of plates. The steel-engraved illustrations were often lavishly detailed copies of famous paintings by American and European artists (fig. 1). The popularity of gift books encouraged illustrators to do more and better work, and Americans who bought them "learned to look at a book in a way only the elite had done before—that is, as something to treasure, like a work of art." Such beautiful books were often the centerpiece in the nineteenth-century parlor, displayed on a table like

The author wishes to acknowledge the assistance of Deborah Alterman, former librarian of Moore College of Art in Philadelphia, who brought the collection of John Sartain memorabilia owned by the college to her attention.

Fig. 1. John Sartain after Samuel Cousins, *Lady and Children* (1831), after Sir Thomas Lawrence, *Countess Grey and Her Daughters* (1805). From *The Christmas Blossom* (Philadelphia: E. H. Butler, 1852). Mezzotint and engraving; H. 4¼", W. 3½". (Rare Book and Manuscript Library, Columbia University.)

a precious object, and handled only with great care. A passage from one such book highlights this attitude: "To describe the delight of Amelia on receiving this elegant present, is impossible. She spread a clean handkerchief over her lap before she drew the book from its case, that it might not be soiled in the slightest degree, and she removed to a distance from the fire lest the cover should be warped by the heat. After she had eagerly looked all through it, she commenced again, and examined the plates with the most minute attention. She then showed them to her little brother and sister."[1]

Although publishing illustrated books was expensive, the potential for significant profits attracted many publishers and engravers. The career of John Sartain (1808–97), one of the most productive engravers during the nineteenth century (fig. 2), is an excellent example of one such profitable venture into the business of publishing illustrated books.

Sartain's American career began in 1830 when he arrived in Philadelphia from London at the age of twenty-two. He was already an experienced engraver, specializing in mezzotint, with years of training in London. Thomas Sully, Philadelphia's preeminent portrait painter, convinced the young engraver to settle in Philadelphia, and the city remained Sartain's home until his death in 1897. Throughout his life Sartain was immensely active and successful. In addition to managing a lucrative engraving business, he was for many years on the board of directors of the Pennsylvania Academy of the Fine Arts and an officer of both the Artists' Fund Society and the Art Union of Philadelphia.

---

[1] John W. Tebbel, *A History of Book Publishing in the United States*, vol. 1, *The Creation of an Industry, 1630–1865* (New York: R. R. Bowker, 1972), p. 254. Other sources on gift books include: Frederick W. Faxon, *Literary Annuals and Gift Books* (1912; reprint, London: Private Libraries Assn., 1973); "Annuals and Gift Books" in *The Cambridge History of American Literature*, vol. 2 (New York: Macmillan, 1931), pp. 170–74; E. Bruce Kirkham and John W. Fink, *Indices to American Literary Annuals and Gift Books, 1825–1865* (New Haven: Research Publications, 1975); Ola Elizabeth Winslow, "Books for the Lady Reader, 1820–1860," in *Romanticism in America*, ed. George Boas (Baltimore: Johns Hopkins University Press, 1940), pp. 89–109; Ralph Thompson, *American Literary Annuals and Gift Books, 1825–1865* (1936; reprint, New York: Archon Books, 1967); David S. Lovejoy, "American Painting in Early Nineteenth Century Gift Books," *American Quarterly* 7, no. 4 (Winter 1955): 345–61; Benjamin Rowland, Jr., "Popular Romanticism: Art and the Gift Books, 1825–1865," *Art Quarterly* 20, no. 4 (Winter 1957): 365–81. Passage from E. L., "The Souvenir," *Affection's Gift* (New York: J. C. Riker, 1832), p. 55.

Fig. 2. John Sartain, *Self-portrait*, after a daguerreotype by Marcus Aurelius Root. From *Nineteenth Century* 1 (1848). Mezzotint; H. 6½″, W. 4½″. (Columbia University Libraries.)

In 1867 he was appointed art director of the International Centennial Exhibition and in his later years was vice-president of Philadelphia's School of Design for Women (now Moore College of Art).

Soon after his arrival in Philadelphia, Sartain began to make the acquaintance of several of the city's publishers, who were delighted with what the new engraver from London had to offer. Thomas T. Ash commissioned Sartain to copy the engraved illustrations after the well-known designs done by J. M. W. Turner and Thomas Stothard for the London edition of Samuel Rogers's *Italy* (1830). Like many other competitive American publishers, Ash gained considerable profits from his pirated American editions of popular English literary works. The energetic Ash also published gift books, and he commissioned Sartain to illustrate many of them. Gift books were not new to Sartain. In London he had engraved illustrations for gift books published by Rudolph Ackermann in the 1820s, so he was familiar with the subjects, style, and spirit that Ash required. Throughout the 1830s Sartain engraved numerous illustrations for Ash's gift book *The Pearl*, based on his own designs (fig. 3), or those of other artists. Sartain's engraving of John Neagle's painting *Brother and Sister* (fig. 4) is fairly typical of the style and subject matter of most gift books. As one publisher described them, gift books were "messengers of love, tokens of friendship, signs and symbols of affection, luxury, and refinement," and certainly Sartain's soft mezzotint version of Neagle's painting epitomized these characteristics.[2]

Gift books were expensive to produce. Publishers competed with each other to include the best engravings by America's best engravers, who might be paid up to $250 for a plate, depending on its size and the status of the engraver. Despite such expenses, publishers were encouraged by the public's enthusiastic response to gift books. Between 1825 and 1865 more than a thousand gift books were published in the United States.[3] During this time, Sartain's engravings appeared in more than sixty gift books published in Boston, New York, and Philadelphia (see Appendix). For many he provided all the engravings

[2] Samuel Griswold Goodrich, *Recollections of a Lifetime; or, Men and Things I have Seen* (New York: Miller, Orton and Mulligan, 1856), p. 182.

[3] Thompson, *Annuals and Gift Books*, preface.

Fig. 3. John Sartain, *The Sail Boat*. From *The Pearl* (Philadelphia: Thomas T. Ash, 1837). Mezzotint and engraving; H. 2¾", W. 3⁵⁄₁₆". (Rare Book and Manuscript Library, Columbia University.)

in a single volume. During the peak of his career he engraved most, if not all, of the illustrations for five to eight annuals per year.

The period of Sartain's greatest activity coincided with a dramatic increase in literacy, particularly among women and children, and a shift in public taste toward books intended for family reading. Such popular books, including gift books, reflected the public's concern for the moral and spiritual life of the family. America's family life was being radically altered in the nineteenth century, buffeted by the effects of an increasingly urban and industrial society. That a growing number of men worked away from home, frequently for long hours, was a matter of great public concern. "Paternal neglect is at the present time, one of the most abundant sources of domestic sorrow. The father, eager in the pursuit of business, toils early and late, and finds no time to fulfill duties to his children."[4]

[4] John S. C. Abbott, "Paternal Neglect," *Parent's Magazine* 2 (March 1842): 148, as quoted in Anne L. Kuhn, *The Mother's Role in Childhood Education: New England Concepts, 1830–1860* (New Haven: Yale University Press, 1947), p. 4.

Fig. 4. John Sartain after John Neagle, *Brother and Sister.* From *The Pearl* (Philadelphia: Thomas T. Ash, 1840). Mezzotint and engraving; H. 3¹¹⁄₁₆″, W. 3″. (Rare Book and Manuscript Library, Columbia University.)

Women, particularly mothers, assumed a greater responsibility during the nineteenth century for upholding the family's piety, purity, and domesticity. They were the guardians of all that was good in the family. "When our land is filled with virtuous and patriotic mothers, then will it be filled with virtuous and patriotic men."[5] Such attitudes are clearly evident in Sartain's book illustrations (figs. 5, 6).

The joys of family life were important elements in nineteenth-century American literature. "The mere sentiment of home," wrote Andrew Jackson Downing in his study of domestic architecture, "is like a strong anchor, saving many a man from shipwreck in the storms of life." This attitude was also voiced by Congregationalist minister Horace Bushnell, whose sermons and lectures upheld the virtues of home education, home life, and home religion. "The home, having a domestic spirit of grace dwelling in it, should become the church of childhood. . . . The manners, personal views, prejudices, practical motives, and spirit of the house is an atmosphere which passes into all and pervades all as naturally as the air we breathe." Instructions for the practical application of such ideas as those voiced by Downing and Bushnell were provided by domestic textbooks for women. The most famous of these was *The American Woman's Home* by Catharine Beecher and her sister Harriet Beecher Stowe, published in 1869. The frontispiece for the book shows a family gathered around a lamp-lit table, looking at a book together.[6]

Illustrated books were considered to be important tools in the moral and religious education of a family. Reading was hardly a leisure activity, but rather a crusade to nurture and safeguard certain values. Since beauty was equated with goodness, it was considered important to begin to foster a love of beauty at an early age.

William H. Furness, the pastor of Sartain's church in Philadelphia, noted the importance of illustrated books in the home when he wrote:

[5] John S. C. Abbott, *The Mother at Home; or, The Principles of Maternal Duty* (Boston: Crocker and Brewster, 1833), p. 148.

[6] Andrew Jackson Downing, *The Architecture of Country Houses* (New York: D. Appleton, 1850), p. iv; Horace Bushnell, as quoted in David Handlin, *The American Home: Architecture and Society, 1815–1915* (Boston: Little, Brown, 1979), p. 10; Catharine Beecher and Harriet Beecher Stowe, *The American Woman's Home; or, Principles of Domestic Science* (New York: J. B. Ford, 1869).

"One of the characteristics of childhood is the open and eager sense of the beautiful, the sentiment which so kindles the imagination and inspires the activity of the young, which makes a book of pictures an all-sufficing balm for the heaviest sorrows of infancy, transforms a slate and pencil into a magician's tools and prompts to endless innovation. It is the deep, unrecognized, sacred hunger of the soul after the true, the beautiful, the perfect, and if we lose it as we grow old, Time can make us no compensations." The artist who participated in the creation of a picture book was an ally for those who wished to instill a love of beauty and goodness in society. "Happy is he," continued Furness, "who has a mind filled with all noble and beautiful images, and who by the chisel or the brush can help us to participate in the glory and blessedness of his good thoughts, and make them our own!"[7]

Illustrated books thus functioned as "wish books." The pictures suggested an attitude toward life that the viewers could seize upon as emblematic of their own natures and goals. Such attitudes, in common with those espoused by Downing, Bushnell, and the Beecher sisters, toward beauty and its importance in the home are reflected in Sartain's engravings. One editor wrote, in referring to a gift book illustrated by Sartain, "All the pieces in this volume are of the purest moral character, [and] . . . a good number of them contain in an uncommon degree, the religious and poetical spirit united. The importance of having books of this nature, sweet and chaste in their moral influence, as well as refined in their intellectual and poetical character is not enough appreciated."[8]

Sartain relied on European paintings available through reproductive prints as models for many of his engraved illustrations. In choosing an image to engrave as a book illustration, the emphasis was on the choice of an appropriate image; that it was borrowed from another painter or even engraver's original did not seem to matter much to Sartain's contemporaries. There is ample evidence to indicate that Sartain owned a large collection of European reproductive prints. For example, Thomas Sully noted in his diary soon after the engraver's

---

[7] William H. Furness, "Fine Arts," in *The American Gallery of Art*, ed. John Sartain (Philadelphia: Lindsay and Blakiston, 1848), pp. 18–20.

[8] George B. Cheever, *The Poets of America* (New York: Levitt and Allen, 1857), p. 5.

Fig. 5. John Sartain after Thomas Webster, *The Bubble Blowers*. From *Christmas Blossoms* (Philadelphia: E. H. Butler, 1852). Mezzotint and engraving; H. 4¼", W. 3⁷⁄₁₆". (Rare Book and Manuscript Library, Columbia University.)

Fig. 6. John Sartain after Samuel Cousins (1835) after Fanny Corbaux, *The Pet Rabbit*. From *The Pearl* (Philadelphia: Thomas T. Ash, 1840). Mezzotint and engraving; H. 3⅝″, W. 2¹⁵⁄₁₆″. (Rare Book and Manuscript Library, Columbia University.)

arrival in Philadelphia that Sartain had lent a scrapbook of prints to Cephas G. Childs, another Philadelphia engraver. Sartain was forced to sell his collection of prints in 1857 when his periodical, *Sartain's Union Magazine of Literature and Art*, failed. Later photographs of the interior of his home, however, show a lavish abundance of prints, paintings, and books, indicating that he quickly rebuilt his collection.[9]

During the 1840s Sartain engraved illustrations for a series of religious gift books published by the Philadelphia firm of Lindsay and Blakiston. Presley Blakiston had originally been employed by Carey and Lea, the distinguished publishing firm that had produced Philadelphia's first gift book, *The Atlantic Souvenir*, in 1825. Robert Lindsay was a successful bookbinder. Initially the firm specialized in religious works and gift books, and it was only natural that eventually they decided to publish a series of religious gift books. It was a unique approach to gift books. The firm's attempt to publish a series with an emphasis on scenes from the Bible was possibly due in large part to Sartain's access to European religious images in his collection. The series began in 1845 with *Scenes in the Life of the Savior*, followed in 1846 with *Scenes in the Lives of the Apostles*, and in 1847 by *Scenes in the Lives of the Patriarchs and Prophets*. Sartain engraved all the illustrations, each volume having a frontispiece, a title-page vignette, and six plates (fig. 7).

Sartain's extensive collection of European prints and illustrated books must have attracted many such commissions to him. Although little correspondence between Sartain and his publishers has survived, it is likely that they approached him with ideas for illustrated books knowing that he could easily rely on his large visual reference collection for just the right image. It is also likely that Sartain suggested potential publication topics to publishers, in effect operating as a salesman for commissions. It was faster, cheaper, and easier for the publishers to rely on Sartain for an appropriate image than it would be for them to locate a painting, with all the inherent headaches of requesting permission to copy it, guaranteeing safe transportation to Sartain, plus returning it on time as promised. Sartain was in effect a Bettmann Archives

---

[9] The collection included 20,000 prints, according to the *Evening Item* (Philadelphia) (October 25, 1897), p. 12. It is presently owned by the Moore College of Art Library.

Fig. 7. John Sartain after Karl-Joseph Begas, *Christ Weeping over Jerusalem.* From *Scenes from the Lives of the Apostles* (Philadelphia: Lindsay and Blakiston, 1846). Mezzotint and engraving; H. 4¼", W. 5¹¹⁄₁₆". (Rare Book and Manuscript Library, Columbia University.)

for nineteenth-century publishers. He had access to a large collection of images, and more significant, his obviously superior technical skill allowed him to copy any image with ease.

Copies of European paintings were immensely popular in nineteenth-century America because they allowed the viewers to link themselves with a more culturally advanced world. Even such supporters of American art as Henry Tuckerman noted the advantages when he recommended reproductive prints "as ornaments to a drawing room or subjects of habitual contemplation. A first rate copy of Raphael, Claude or Leonardo, one of Landseer's animal groups, a cattle scene by Rosa Bonheur . . . appeal to the purse and eye of the judicious infinitely more than the average crude efforts of the native art."[10]

[10] Henry T. Tuckerman, *American Artist Life* (New York: Putnam, 1867), p. 36.

Sartain's mezzotint illustrations were lavish, unlike anything previously available from American illustrators. He was able to translate rich colors, textures, and shadows with great skill (figs. 8, 9). His admirers were enthusiastic in their response to his work.

In America the early history of the art of mezzotint is inseparably associated with the name of John Sartain of Philadelphia. . . . In his hands it underwent a change in its application and consequently in its methods, in adapting it to the production of small book embellishments for which it had not been used before. From the broad effects of large framing prints it was forced down to the expression of the most minute details, on the diminutive scale of pictorial books; and we count by hundreds the steel plates engraved in his style during the period referred to, all the product of one prolific hand. The facility of its execution, its inexpensiveness, the richness and softness of its effects, all tended to extend its popularity. And its use . . . hastened the diffusion of that rapidly growing taste for prints in this country.[11]

There are several pertinent points in this quotation that emphasize the reasons for Sartain's fame and infamy. The art of mezzotint did indeed undergo a change in its application and methods in Sartain's hands. For example, he could use it to show off the rich texture of fabrics (fig. 10). In adapting mezzotint to mass production, Sartain adopted the mixed method, a technique whereby mezzotint is reinforced with etching, line engraving, and aquatint to facilitate larger editions. The mixed method was faster, and therefore cheaper, much to the delight of the publishers. While the mixed method was most heavily used in the production of framing prints published by the art unions in England and America, Sartain was responsible in large part for introducing the method to American book illustration. The richness of the mixed method was entirely appropriate for lavish gift books, and the public responded by showing its willingness to buy the annual publications year after year.

While it was evidently easier for Sartain to rely on European sources for much of his work, he also attempted to support American artists by copying their work. One such effort was *The American*

---

[11] Edwin T. Freedley, *Leading Pursuits and Leading Men* (Philadelphia: Lippincott, 1854), p. 174.

Gallery of Art, published in 1848 by Lindsay and Blakiston. Sartain acted as both editor and illustrator for the volume, which he intended to be "a complete epitome of American art, a record of works by American artists for Europeans who, heretofore, have had no means of forming a correct estimate of the general character of American art."[12] The engravings in the volume were mostly historical scenes or figural paintings after those by Peter Rothermel, Thomas Sully, Joshua Shaw, James Hamilton, John Neagle, and Russell Smith. Considering that the artists of the Hudson River school were evolving a uniquely American attitude toward landscape when Sartain was orchestrating this record of American painting, it is noteworthy that only two mezzotints in the book were after landscape paintings. This selection does not indicate that Sartain was unaware of the artists of the Hudson River school; rather, the works he chose to illustrate indicate the degree of difficulty he must have experienced in trying to locate and borrow original works of art to copy. He had to rely on what was available locally in Philadelphia, and therefore most of the works in *The American Gallery of Art* are by Philadelphia artists, who, for the most part, were not focusing on landscape as the inspiration for their art. Certain compromises had to be made in his effort to promote American art if Sartain wished to bring the book to publication.

The American Gallery of Art serves to illuminate the two aspects of Sartain that must be understood in order to appreciate his importance. It is evident that Sartain considered his identity as a businessman to be just as important as his identity as an artist. If he had not been willing to compromise, he might not have remained such an active and successful artist. The business community respected his entrepreneurship, for Sartain's name frequently appears in nineteenth-century publications that eulogize the history and progress of American business, technology, and manufacturing, sources where one might least expect to find information about an artist, even an engraver.[13] It is quite possible that Sartain was included in some of these because he was a Mason and thus socialized with other businessmen.

---

[12] Sartain, *American Gallery*, intro.
[13] For example, Freedley, *Leading Pursuits*.

Fig. 8. John Sartain after Sir William Boxall, *Amelia*. From *The Snow Flake* (Philadelphia: E. H. Butler, 1851). Mezzotint and engraving; H. 4³⁄₁₆″, W. 3½″. (Rare Book and Manuscript Library, Columbia University.)

Fig. 9. John Sartain after Horace Vernet, *Judith and Holofernes*. From *The Boudoir Annual* (Boston: Phillips and Sampson, 1846). Mezzotint and engraving; H. 5½″, W. 3½″. (The Research Libraries, New York Public Library.)

Fig. 10. John Sartain after Sir David Wilkie, *The First Ear-ring*. From *The Snow Flake* (Philadelphia: E. H. Butler, 1851). Mezzotint and engraving; H. 4³⁄₁₆″, W. 3½″. (Rare Book and Manuscript Library, Columbia University.)

That Sartain may have perceived himself as a businessman should not detract from his importance as an artist. The 1973 Winterthur conference, "Technological Innovation and the Decorative Arts," dispelled the cult of the individual artist/craftsman. One speaker noted, "Far from being individualistic proprietors of simple firms, many master craftsmen, especially in cities, were masters, not of their crafts, but of the business skills necessary to survive in the bewilderingly complex world of colonial trade and finance. They were organizers and managers who had to deal with rapidly fluctuating currencies, to contract for labor and supplies, to oversee what was sometimes considerable specialization and subdivision of productive processes, and to arrange transportation, insurance, and sale of the finished product."[14] Certainly this attitude can be applied toward nineteenth-century printmakers. It is obvious that such successful printmakers as Sartain survived the numerous financial panics of the nineteenth century because they were good businessmen. Further, they did not see their roles as both artist and entrepreneur as incompatible, and therein lies the real challenge for many American artists. I suspect that many artists gave up their artistic careers in disgust not only because the climate for art was so unsympathetic in the early nineteenth century but also because they either were incapable of being good businessmen or could not resolve the contradictions of the two roles, one concerned with the higher realm of art, and one concerned with the practical problem of making a living.

Sartain was visibly successful. By the 1840s, ten years after his arrival in America, he was well established in Philadelphia. His home on Sansom Street just off fashionable Chestnut Street near Independence Hall guaranteed easy access to the city's art exhibition spaces: the Pennsylvania Academy of the Fine Arts, the Franklin Institute, Sully and Earle's Gallery, and the studios of other artists. Sartain owned a plate printing press and trained an English mechanic to be a plate printer to his exacting standards, thus freeing himself from the local printers whom he felt were technically inadequate. Sartain's children were trained to assist their father in his work, and from time to

[14]Polly Anne Earl, "Craftsmen and Machines: The Nineteenth-Century Furniture Industry," in *Technological Innovation and the Decorative Arts*, ed. Ian M. G. Quimby (Charlottesville: University Press of Virginia, 1974), p. 307.

time other young artists lived in his home, learning to be engravers.

Given the competitive climate among printmakers during Sartain's lifetime, it is not surprising to see that he often compromised high standards in favor of meeting deadlines. Nineteenth-century connoisseurs who clung to conservative attitudes toward engraving sometime reacted negatively to his work, because they did not admire his use of the mixed method, preferring instead the more time-consuming linework or pure mezzotint of previous generations. Sartain, in order to maintain his business, had to make compromises all the time, even if he too did not always agree as an artist that the resulting art was of the highest quality.[15]

One example of the reaction against Sartain's illustrations during his lifetime might suffice to show the kind of choices between art and business that often confronted him. In 1850 wealthy New York philanthropist and book collector James Lenox purchased the original manuscript of George Washington's Farewell Address and had it privately printed in an edition of 175 quarto and 54 folio copies for use as presents to his friends. He commissioned Sartain to engrave two portraits of George Washington, one after a 1778 portrait by James Peale, the other after Gilbert Stuart's Lansdowne portrait, for the book.

Sartain's engravings were done in the mixed method, mostly mezzotint with etching and engraving. The two prints indicate that a great deal of care was obviously taken with the plates, appropriate for the type of publication that they accompanied. But Lenox was not pleased with the final results. In a letter to John L. Sibley, tipped into the front of the copy of the book owned by the Houghton Library at Harvard, Lenox complained about the quality of Sartain's work: "The engraving from Stuart by Sartain, accompanying the Farewell Address of Washington, was so unsatisfactory that sometime after I had another engraved by Ritchie."[16] Lenox does not expand on the reasons for his discontent, but a comparison of the two engravings in the Houghton Library copy suggests the major reasons. A. H. Ritchie's version of the Stuart Lansdowne portrait is more clearly an aquatint with etched

[15] John Sartain, *A Brief Sketch of the History and Practice of Engraving* (Philadelphia: Privately printed, 1880).

[16] Letter tipped into *Washington's Farewell Address to the People of the United States of America* (New York: Privately printed, 1850) (Houghton Library, Harvard University).

outlines. Such a technique was probably considered by Lenox to be a more appropriate accompaniment for an eighteenth-century text published in a limited edition, rather than the more "modern" mixed method chosen by Sartain.

While connoisseurs such as Lenox clung to the traditional attitudes toward reproductive engraving, publishers who catered to a general public were more than happy with Sartain's use of the mixed method and its speed, which guaranteed that he could meet their deadlines.

Because Sartain's overtly sentimental gift-book illustrations do not reflect the reality of antebellum daily life as described in contemporary newspapers, letters, and diaries, the modern historian should not be led to dismiss them as an evasion of reality. Rather, when Sartain's concern with radical social reform and his participation in various movements furthering reform are taken into consideration, a more serious purpose behind his work for gift-book publishers becomes evident. He joined the radical Pennsylvania Anti-Slavery Society in the mid 1830s and later, during the 1850s, was associated with a utopian community, the North American Phalanx in Redbank, New Jersey. In light of this involvement, his illustrations can be interpreted as depictions of an alternative or utopian society, meant to counteract the violence, competition, and un-Christian behavior perceived by social critics. Direct reference to specific social ills was scrupulously avoided, in part because gift books were intended for family reading. In order to attract as wide an audience as possible, the publishers, editors, artists, and authors of gift books collaborated to depict a utopian society without reference to any particular religious, political, or economic point of view. Yet while Sartain might have been sincere in his desire to offer views of a more perfect society, there is no evidence that his publishers or editors attempted to disseminate the relatively expensive gift book to the very people considered in need of reform and refinement; on the whole, the families who could afford gift books were not posing a danger to social stability. As decorative elements in the home, gift books acted as signs of the owner's self-image, reinforcing already-held values. Sartain's illustrations, therefore, reveal his audience's concern about the present state and the future course of their society, but they were hardly the catalyst for actual social change.

Appendix

Gift Books Illustrated by John Sartain

1832   *The Pearl; or, Affection's Gift.* Philadelphia: Thomas T. Ash.

1833   *The Pearl; or, Affection's Gift.* Philadelphia: Thomas T. Ash.

1834   *The Offering.* Philadelphia: Thomas T. Ash.
        The Pearl; or, Affection's Gift. Philadelphia: Thomas T. Ash.

1836   *The Pearl; or, Affection's Gift.* Philadelphia: Thomas T. Ash.

1837   *The Pearl; or, Affection's Gift.* Philadelphia: Thomas T. Ash and
        Henry F. Anners.

1840   *The Pearl; or, Affection's Gift.* Philadelphia: Henry F. Anners.
        The Religious Offering. Philadelphia: William Marshall.

1844   *The Liberty Bell by Friends of Freedom.* Boston: Massachusetts
        Anti-Slavery Fair.

1845   *The Diadem.* Philadelphia: Carey and Hart.
        Friendship's Offering. Boston: Lewis and Sampson.
        The Rose of Sharon. Boston: A. Tompkins and B. B. Mussey.
        Scenes in the Life of the Savior. Philadelphia: Lindsay and Blakiston.

1846   *The Boudoir Annual.* Boston: Phillips and Sampson.
        Friendship's Offering. Boston: Phillips and Sampson.
        The Gem of the Season. New York: Leavitt, Trow.
        The Hyacinth or Affection's Gift. Philadelphia: Henry F. Anners.
        The May Flower. Boston: Saxton and Kelt.
        The Rose of Sharon. Boston: A. Tompkins and B. B. Mussey.
        Scenes in the Lives of the Apostles. Philadelphia: Lindsay and
        Blakiston.

1847   *The Boudoir Annual.* Philadelphia: Theodore Bliss.
        The Christian Keepsake and Missionary Annual. Boston: Phillips
        and Sampson.
        Christmas Blossoms and New Years Wreath. Boston: Phillips and
        Sampson.
        The Evergreen. Philadelphia: Carey and Hart.
        The Fountain. Philadelphia: William Sloanaker.
        Friendship's Offering. Boston: Phillips and Sampson.
        The May Flower. Boston: Saxton and Kelt.

The Mirror of Life. Philadelphia: Lindsay and Blakiston.
Scenes in the Lives of the Patriarchs and Prophets. Philadelphia: Lindsay and Blakiston.

1848 *The American Gallery of Art*. Philadelphia: Lindsay and Blakiston.
The Christian Keepsake and Missionary Annual. Philadelphia: Brower, Hayes.
Christmas Blossoms and New Years Wreath. Boston: Phillips and Sampson.
Friendship's Offering. Boston: Phillips and Sampson.
The Gem of the Season. New York: Leavitt, Trow.
The Mayflower. Boston: Saxton and Kelt.
The Mirror of Life. Philadelphia: Lindsay and Blakiston.
The Rose of Sharon. Boston: A. Tompkins and B. B. Mussey.
The Women of the Scriptures. Philadelphia: Lindsay and Blakiston.

1849 *The Christian Keepsake and Missionary Annual*. Philadelphia: Brower, Hayes.
Christmas Blossoms and New Years Wreath. Philadelphia: E. H. Butler.
Friendship's Offering. Boston: Phillips and Sampson.
The Gem of the Season. New York: Leavitt, Trow.
The Rose of Sharon. Boston: A. Tompkins and B. B. Mussey.

1850 *Christmas Blossoms and New Years Wreath*. Philadelphia: E. H. Butler.
The Drawing Room Scrap Book. Philadelphia: Carey and Hart.
Friendship's Offering. Boston: Phillips, Sampson.
Gallery of Mezzotints. New York: M. H. Newman.
Leaflets of Memory. Philadelphia: E. H. Butler.
The Snow Flake. Philadelphia: E. H. Butler.

1851 *Cabinet of Modern Art*. Philadelphia: E. H. Butler.
Christmas Blossoms and New Years Wreath. Philadelphia: E. H. Butler.
Christmas Tribute and New Year's Gift. Philadelphia: E. H. Butler.
Friendship's Offering. Boston: Phillips, Sampson.
The Irving Offering. New York: Leavitt.
Leaflets of Memory. Philadelphia: E. H. Butler.
The Snow Flake. Philadelphia: E. H. Butler.

1852 *Christmas Blossoms and New Years Wreath*. Philadelphia: E. H. Butler.
Friendship's Offering. Philadelphia: E. H. Butler.
Leaflets of Memory. Philadelphia: E. H. Butler.
The Snow Flake. Philadelphia: E. H. Butler.

1853   *Friendship's Offering*. Philadelphia: E. H. Butler.

1854   *Friendship's Offering*. Philadelphia: E. H. Butler.

1855   *Affection's Gift*. Philadelphia: E. H. Butler.
       Friendship's Offering. Philadelphia: E. H. Butler.
       The Gem Annual. Philadelphia: E. H. Butler.
       Leaflets of Memory. Philadelphia: E. H. Butler.
       The Snow Flake. Philadelphia: E. H. Butler.

F. O. C. Darley's Outline Illustrations

SUE W. REED

B Y THE MID NINETEENTH CENTURY, F. O. C. Darley was this country's foremost popular illustrator. He made literary and historical characters and events graphically visible to his contemporaries and helped to codify our image of America's past. Most of his enormous output was in the form of wash drawings to serve as models for wood or metal engravers. Four series of illustrations produced between 1847 and 1856, however, were drawn entirely in outline and printed as lithographs. Commissioned by the American Art-Union, Darley made twelve illustrations for Washington Irving's *Rip Van Winkle* and *Legend of Sleepy Hollow* and four for James Fenimore Cooper's *Leather Stocking Tales*. On his own initiative he produced thirty illustrations to a midcentury novel of reform, Sylvester Judd's *Margaret*. These outline illustrations have not been sufficiently investigated and will be considered here, along with the reasons for Darley's choice of an outline style for these particular subjects and a detailed look into the production of *Margaret*.[1]

The author would like to express her gratitude to the curators and staff of the collections she visited who so generously put their Darley material at her disposal.

[1]Books illustrated by Darley are listed in Theodore Bolton, "The Book Illustrations of Felix Octavius Carr Darley," *Proceedings of the American Antiquarian Society* 61, no. 1 (April 1951): 136–82; and Sinclair Hamilton, *Early American Book Illustrators and Wood Engravers, 1670–1870* (Princeton, N.J.: Princeton University Library, 1958), pp. 101–16, and vol. 2, *Supplement* (Princeton, N.J.: Princeton University Press, 1968), pp. 66–73. A second supplement in typed manuscript also contains Darley material. See also Frank Weitenkampf, "F. O. C. Darley, American Illustrator," *Art Quarterly* 10, no. 2 (Spring 1947): 100–113. Late in life Darley issued a final series of outline illustrations to Nathaniel Hawthorne's *Scarlet Letter* (Boston:

Born to actor parents in Philadelphia in 1822, Felix Octavius Carr Darley began his career there in the mid 1840s. He moved to New York City in 1848 where he had already established a reputation. A designer of illustrations for books, periodicals, and bank notes and of single prints, he befriended many important writers and painters and was made a full member of the National Academy of Design in 1853. He married in 1859 and moved to Claymont, Delaware, where he continued to pursue his career until his death in 1888.[2]

The context for Darley's midcentury outline illustrations is to be found in England and Europe beginning in the late eighteenth century. The work of two artists, Flaxman and Retzsch, may stand for a large and international body of work. English sculptor John Flaxman (1755–1826) made outline drawings to illustrate Homer's *Iliad* and *Odyssey*, plays by Aeschylus, and Dante's *Divine Comedy*. These extremely influential images were engraved and published between 1793 and 1802, and new and enlarged editions continued to appear throughout the nineteenth century. Flaxman's compositions were well known to American audiences. Henry James's biography of Hawthorne describes a New England parlor in winter with "a group of sensitive and serious people . . . fixing their eyes upon a bookful of Flaxman's attenuated outlines."[3] The popularity of Flaxman in nineteenth-century America can be explained in part by the prevalence of classical imagery, chosen to supply visual symbols for the New Republic. In both Europe and America there was an identification of purity and rejuvenation with the arts of ancient Greece and pre-Renaissance or "primitive" Italy.

In his compositions, Flaxman simplified settings, used a primitive perspective, and reduced his descriptive means to an outline of consis-

---

Houghton, Mifflin, 1879). No printmaker was involved, for in keeping with technological advances, the pen drawings were reproduced photomechanically. The choice of an outline style was appropriate to the subject, a romantic tale of seventeenth-century America.

[2] For additional biographical material, see ". . . *Illustrated by Darley*": *An Exhibition of Original Drawings* (Wilmington: Delaware Art Museum, 1978), pp. 1–2, 3–24.

[3] For other artists and their outline work, see Robert Rosenblum, *Transformations in Late Eighteenth Century Art* (Princeton, N.J.: Princeton University Press, 1967), pp. 173–75. Robert Rosenblum, *The International Style of 1800: A Study in Linear Abstraction* (New York: Garland Publishing, 1976), p. 159 n. 41.

tent width. All vestiges of texture or shadow were eliminated (fig. 1). Robert Rosenblum has provided a clear analysis of the relationship of Flaxman's outlines to both neoclassical and romantic tastes. Discussing the affinity of the outlines to the classics and to Dante, he noted: "In both cases a style of linear purity, evoking a remote and uncorrupted era, is used as a vehicle for the presentation of a mythical world of fantasy, heroism, and divinity that could not be properly recorded through the earthbound empiricism of most Renaissance and Baroque styles."[4]

That Darley knew Flaxman's outlines is proved by the existence of his pencil copy of Flaxman's "Burial of Hector" from the *Iliad*. Moreover, a humorous early drawing by Darley depicts an athletic angler dressed as one of Flaxman's Greek warriors and is inscribed: "This is my own *Composition*. It is intended for a man a fishing."[5]

The next generation of European artists to make pure outline drawings included the German romantics, among them Moritz Retzsch (1779–1857). They used the technique to illustrate Christian and medieval subject matter as well as scenes from the Greek and Roman classics. Their outlines tended to vary in width and thus suggest more substance. Settings, although simplified, provided space for the figures to occupy, and plants and flowers were drawn in meticulous detail. In general, their style was less abstract and more concrete and was undoubtedly more sympathetic to a broader American audience than Flaxman's austere style.

Retzsch executed outline illustrations to literary works by Shakespeare, Schiller, Goethe, and others that were extremely popular and frequently commented on in the American media, often in connection with Darley's work. His prolific output was published between 1810 and 1845 in various European cities and in New York. The outlines were accompanied by generous passages of text in several languages. His more than a hundred illustrations to Shakespeare incorporate closely observed details of medieval and Renaissance costume and both natural and architectural settings. While the etchings describe

[4] Rosenblum, *Transformations*, pp. 163–73, 169.
[5] Collection of the State of Delaware; see *Illustrated by Darley*, no. 126 illus. Sinclair Hamilton Collection, Department of Printing and Graphic Arts, Princeton University Library.

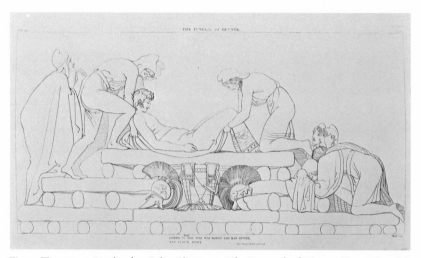

Fig. 1. Tommaso Piroli after John Flaxman, *The Funeral of Hector*. Engraving; H. 6⅝″, W. 13¼″ (borderline). From *The Iliad of Homer Engraved from the Compositions of John Flaxman* (London: Longman, Hurst, Rees & Orme, 1805), pl. 39. (Museum of Fine Arts, Boston, gift of Thomas Gaffield.)

neither shadow nor texture, the variation in the thickness of the line suggests greater volume and substance. Although no direct borrowing has been identified, it is difficult to conceive of Darley's being ignorant of these readily available volumes of Retzsch's work (fig. 2).[6]

The subject matter Retzsch illustrated in outline (romantic stories of heroic deeds, epics, narrative poems, adventure, and so forth) falls within the definition of Rosenblum's "mythical world," as do the subjects that Darley chose to illustrate in outline.

One of the most romantic of American subjects was its aboriginal inhabitant, the Indian. In 1843, when he was first becoming established as a professional illustrator, Darley made a series of fourteen outline lithographs for *Scenes in Indian Life* (Philadelphia: J. R. Colon,

---

[6] A prospectus of about 1843 for *Scenes in Indian Life* comments: "These etchings upon stone possess much of the spirit of Flaxman and Retch [*sic*] and are altogether superior to any specimens of linear outline as yet offered to the American public." From a Darley scrapbook of clippings, acquired in 1941, and from internal evidence compiled by a member of the family, possibly his wife, Jane, Library of Congress. For a discussion of Darley and Retzsch, see Richard Henry Stoddard, "Felix O. C. Darley," *National Magazine* 9, no. 15 (September 1856): 193–97.

Fig. 2. Moritz Retzsch, *Romeo and Juliet*. Etching; H. 6⅞″, W. 9⅛″ (borderline). From *Romeo and Juliet* (Leipzig: Ernest Fleischer, 1836), pl. 6. (Museum of Fine Arts, Boston, gift of Miss Ellen Bullard.)

1843). These were "drawn and etched on stone" by Darley and printed by Thomas Sinclair. Depicted were such subjects as buffalo and bear hunting (fig. 3), war parties, and the family life of Plains Indians, derived from textual and pictorial descriptions, for Darley never traveled to the West.[7] In the same year, Darley drew on stone a series of pen lithographs, *In Town and About*, that depict street life in Philadelphia. Significantly, the genre subjects are not presented in outline form, but are shaded with hatching (fig. 4).

[7]John C. Ewers, "Not Quite Redman: The Plains Indians Illustrations of Felix O. C. Darley," *American Art Journal* 3, no. 2 (Fall 1971): 88–98.

Fig. 3. F. O. C. Darley, *Indian Shooting a Bear*. Etched lithograph; H. 6¹⁵⁄₁₆″, W. 9″ (image). From *Scenes in Indian Life* (Philadelphia: J. & R. Colon, 1843), pl. 5. (Amon Carter Museum, Fort Worth, Texas.)

By the time he left Philadelphia for New York in 1848, Darley had already begun his self-initiated project to illustrate Judd's novel of reform, *Margaret. Outline Illustrations to Judd's Margaret* was not published until 1856 and was most probably worked on intermittently during this decade.

One of the reasons for the immediate success of Darley's illustrations to *Margaret* was surely the popularity of three projects undertaken for the American Art-Union between 1848 and 1851. Each of these was a series of outline illustrations to American authors. By 1848 the Art-Union was having difficulties providing an annual gift engraving to its more than 16,000 subscribers. Twelve months was not enough time to engrave a plate and print the required number of

Fig. 4. F. O. C. Darley, *The Boys that Run with the Engine*. Pen lithograph with tint stone; H. 7″, W. 9¾″ (image). From *In Town and About* (Philadelphia: Godey and McMichael, 1843), pl. 1. (Houghton Library, Harvard University, bequest of Evert Jansen Wendell.)

impressions.[8] In 1848 Darley was commissioned to produce six outline illustrations to Irving's *Rip Van Winkle*. These "engravings on stone" (actually etched lithographs) were distributed in 1849 to the members of the Art-Union. The project was undoubtedly facilitated by Darley's having just completed designs for wood-engraved illustrations to *The Sketchbook of Geoffrey Crayon, Gent.* (New York: G. P. Putnam, 1848), which contained the story.

Rip Van Winkle was a financial and popular success for the Art-Union. Darley was commissioned to make a sequel for the subscribers

[8] Jay Cantor, "Prints and the American Art-Union," in *Prints in and of America to 1850*, ed. John D. Morse (Charlottesville: University Press of Virginia, 1970), pp. 310, 313–16; *Illustrated by Darley*, pp. 14–15.

of 1849, illustrating *The Legend of Sleepy Hollow* (1850), another
Irving tale from *The Sketchbook*. These fanciful and humorous stories
of New York State's past by one of America's most beloved living
authors were issued with an abbreviated text between paper covers.
Some pressure was exerted on Darley to complete the series on time,
for in a letter of September 2, 1849, to Evert A. Duyckinck, he said,
"[I am sorry that the] Art Union will not give me a month longer than
last year for the completion of the etchings. I suppose I must make a
forced march of it."[9]

Five outline illustrations appeared in various issues of the *Bulletin
of the American Art-Union* for 1850 and 1851. In the December 1850
issue a preview of *Margaret* appeared in the form of a single plate, *A
Glimpse at the World*. Four scenes from Cooper's novels appeared
one at a time in issues of the *Bulletin* for 1851.[10]

Each of Darley's Art-Union illustrations bears the information
that he was the designer and printmaker. The illustrations to Irving
and Judd state, "Darley invent et sculpt.," while the title pages of the
two Irving tales state, "Designed and etched by Felix O. C. Darley."
The four Cooper illustrations state, "Designed & etched on stone by
F. O. C. Darley." On all but *A Glimpse at the World*, the stones include
the name of the printer, Sarony & Major.

Lithography answered the Art-Union's needs for a means of producing prints more cheaply and with greater speed than engraving.
The transition from copper to stone was eased by the use of the process
of lithographic etching (or engraving) which not only was eminently
suited to Darley's outline designs but also made it possible to refer to
these prints in terms evoking the more expensive metal intaglio
processes. Advertisements appear monthly in the *Crayon* for 1855 by
E. B. Clayton's Sons Printers that state, "Line Stone Engraving. A New
Style of Art, recently introduced into this country. . . . All the elegance
of the most finished steel engraving, and at a much less cost."

[9]New York Public Library, Duyckinck Collection (microfilm, Archives of American Art,
reel N6, fr. 907–29).

[10]The plates that appeared in issues of the 1851 *Bulletin of the American Art-Union* are
Leather Stocking, Paul Hover and Ellen, Concealing Themselves from the Indians (April), facing
p. 17; *Leather Stocking at the Grave of Chingach-gook* (July), facing p. 61; *The Treachery of
Mahotoree* (October), facing p. 101; and *The Warning* (December), facing p. 137. Each measures
7" x 9½" (borderlines).

To make an etched lithograph of high quality, fine-grained stone is sealed completely by means of a gum-arabic solution. The draftsman scratches through the sealing coat with an etching needle, exposing the bare stone. The lines are bitten with acid and can be stopped out, much in the way a copperplate is treated, to make them narrow or broad. The grooves are then rubbed with greasy matter to make them receptive to printing ink. After the grease and sealant are cleaned off the stone, the image is ready to print. The surface is dampened, ink is rubbed into the grooves then wiped off, and the stone is printed in a lithographic press under greater pressure than usual. The ink is raised on the paper surface. A stone, like a copperplate, can also be engraved with a burin. It is estimated that engraving on stone takes one-fifth to one-third the time of engraving on copper and that stones can be printed three times faster than copperplates and can stand up to longer runs. It is also possible to transfer the image from an etched or engraved stone to other stones to speed production time further. The lines printed from the transfer stones would be on the surface of the paper in a true planographic manner.[11]

On some impressions of Darley's outlines, especially those that can be identified as proofs, the ink is raised on the paper surface. Many of the published impressions do not have the qualities of intaglio lines, but those of planographic, and were probably printed from transfer stones. It seems almost a foregone conclusion that for the Art-Union editions of Irving multiple stones were employed to achieve the necessary 16,000 impressions of each of six images.

In etching the stones himself, Darley had not only the autographic freedom of line available to any etcher but also the freedom to make changes in the process of transferring his design. Two extant pencil drawings for *The Legend of Sleepy Hollow* are relatively complete designs, but neither shows signs of indentation for transfer or tracing. Each appears to be close to the final study. The minor changes in the finished lithographs are attributable to the author's change of mind while etching the stone (figs. 5, 6).

---

[11] Aloys Senefelder, *A Complete Course of Lithography* (London: Ackermann, 1819); Michael Twyman, *Lithography, 1800–1850* (London: Oxford University Press, 1970), p. 104.

Fig. 5. F. O. C. Darley, *Ichabod in the Schoolroom*. Graphite on paper; H. 11″, W. 14¾″ (sheet). (Museum of Fine Arts, Boston, gift of Benjamin A. and Julia M. Trustman.)

Fig. 6. F. O. C. Darley, *Ichabod in the Schoolroom*. Etched lithograph; H. 8½″, W. 11″ (borderline). From *The Legend of Sleepy Hollow* (New York: The American Art-Union, 1850), pl. 1. (Museum of Fine Arts, Boston.)

Not only could Darley make changes in transferring his model drawing to the stone; he could make changes on the stone itself. Two etched stones in the New-York Historical Society still preserve three of the Cooper illustrations.[12] Each stone bears signs of correction by means of scraping the surface to eradicate the intaglio lines. In some places the corrected areas have been left blank; in others alterations have been reetched. When Konrad Huber engraved after Darley's designs for *Margaret* he made corrections in the same way. A proof impression of *The Master* (pl. 2) in the New York Public Library shows the gentleman's wig differently shaped than in the published print, a change no doubt requested by the designer.

Darley's outline illustrations to *Margaret* occupied nearly a decade of his attention. Apparently the success of the Art-Union outlines encouraged Darley to continue his independent project, begun in Philadelphia in 1846 or 1847. The book, a contemporary novel of reform by the Reverend Sylvester Judd of Augusta, Maine, was first published anonymously in Boston in 1845 by Jordan and Wiley and entitled *Margaret: A Tale of the Real and Ideal, Blight and Bloom; Including Sketches of a Place not before Described Called Mons Christi.* Darley's *Compositions in Outline . . . from Judd's Margaret* was completed by 1856 when thirty lithographed plates accompanied by excerpts from the text were published in New York by J. S. Redfield. The plates for Darley's *Margaret* are divided equally between full-length vertical portraits of the main characters that alternate with horizontal narrative episodes from the story. Twenty-eight of the designs are contained within arched-top rectangles; two are oval in format. The arrangement of text and plates differs from the Irving tales—more familiar to their readers—and each plate of *Margaret* is preceded by a page of relevant text. Although Judd's "eccentric and original" tale was never to become an American classic, there was an 1851 revised edition and an 1857 reprint (perhaps in response to Darley's illustrations).[13]

---

[12] *The Warning* is on a stone 12″ x 15″; *Leather Stocking at the Grave of Chingach-gook* and *Leather Stocking . . . Concealing Themselves* are on a single stone 20″ x 14″.

[13] The sheet size of *Margaret* is 12½″ x 16½″. The illustrations vary in size from 7″ to 7½″ by 9″ to 10⅛″. *Athenaeum* (London), no. 1533 (March 14, 1857): 347.

The moral story tells of Margaret, an innocent child, whose religion is nature and whose education is the classics. After several failed attempts in childhood, as an adult she embraces Christianity through the efforts of a patient lover and her need for comfort after her brother Chilion's execution for murder. Throughout its absorbing story, the book maintains a constant call for temperance reform. The populace of a backwoods town in western Massachusetts in the last decades of the eighteenth century is vividly characterized, with regard to both physical appearance and patterns of speech and behavior. The author describes with care the natural surroundings and occasions such as a camp meeting, Sunday services, a husking bee, a murder, making maple syrup, gathering herbs and honey, and training militia. Its sharply drawn participants and uniquely local elements make *Margaret* an engaging and readable book and cloak its moral message in colorful regional garb. It is easy to understand Darley's attraction to the story.

As early as April 1848 Darley refers to *Margaret* as his "most successful effort." Articles on the illustrator in succeeding years occasionally mention the ongoing project, and when the outlines appeared in 1856 the reviews were lengthy and commendatory. An English critic stated: "This book of illustrations is the best thing American Art has yet produced."[14]

At least sixty drawings and a number of unpublished proofs for *Margaret* are preserved.[15] They bear witness to Darley's extended involvement and permit an examination of his working methods and the changes in his drawing style and choice of printmaking techniques that took place over the decade. A list of the plate titles and related drawings and proofs sums up the material from which the following discussion is drawn (see Appendix).

The preparatory drawings may be grouped into five categories. It is clear that at a relatively early date Darley had conceived seventeen

[14]Darley to Edward Duyckinck, April 3, 1848, New York Public Library, Duyckinck Collection (microfilm, Archives of American Art, reel N6, fr. 907–29). See Darley scrapbook, Library of Congress, where the most extensive review of *Margaret* is that in the *Athenaeum*, no. 1533 (March 14, 1857), from which the critic's quotation is taken.

[15]The majority of the drawings for *Margaret* are in the collection of the Delaware Art Museum, Wilmington. Unpublished proofs are in the New York Public Library and the Museum of Fine Arts, Boston.

designs in a style quite different from the published versions. For the early versions there are four small oval compositions in wash, six partial studies for five subjects, and fourteen finished designs in outline executed in pen and brown ink. For the published versions there are fourteen partial or preliminary studies for ten plates and twenty-two completed outline drawings, the majority in pen and black ink on tissue paper. In addition to various working proofs of the published lithographs, there are proofs of eight subjects from unpublished stones.

From this body of work it is possible to propose a reconstruction of Darley's working methods. The original concept, probably dating from 1846–47, was to present the illustrations in oval format, possibly in response to some of Retzsch's work. The four small, horizontal ovals, executed in brush and gray wash over graphite, set forth compositions for narrative subjects, *The Bee-Hunt, Chilion Played* (fig. 7), *A Glimpse at the World*, and *School-Keeping.* (The first three subjects were ultimately published as plates 5, 9, and 11; the last was not included in the final version.) These studies resemble Darley's preliminary drawings for wood engravings of the late 1840s. The arrangement of figures for *Chilion Played* differs from the published version in many details, most notably in depicting Chilion seated to play the violin, whereas in the final version he is standing (fig. 8). Darley must have made many more preliminary pencil studies than the eight known to me. Of these the two most significant are for the boy Chilion (fig. 9). They indicate the artist's concern to characterize the youth as refined and sensitive in contrast to his enrapt but countrified audience.

The fourteen finished drawings for the early version were drawn in outline with pen and a warm brown ink (fig. 10). Twelve of these are in oval format, horizontal for the five narrative subjects and vertical for the seven portraits. *The Husking Bee* is rectangular, and *The Arrest* octagonal.

The only print from this stage of the project to be published was *A Glimpse at the World.* It depicts the interior of a country store with two young ladies of the community selecting fabric while Margaret looks on. The print was published in the December 1850 issue of the *Bulletin of the American Art-Union.* The title is not printed on the plate, but is given in the table of contents as well as with the print's

Fig. 7. F. O. C. Darley, compositional study for *Chilion Played*. Brush and gray wash over graphite; H. 4″, W. 5½″ (oval image). (New York Public Library, Duyckinck Collection.)

placement on page 151. The print is an etched lithograph inscribed "Darley invent et sculpt." Other proofs of prints from this stage exist in the New York Public Library. The portraits of Margaret and Tony Washington have the appearance of engraved lithographs but are without any text, making an attribution to the printmaker difficult.

On the basis of the completed drawings and prints (published and unpublished), it seems likely that a good number of the illustrations for *Margaret* were completed by the end of 1850. Sometime during the next five years Darley extensively revised the existing designs and completed the project in an updated style. At least fourteen preliminary or partial studies for ten plates are known today, but one must assume the execution of many more drawings. The twenty-two finished outlines in pen and black ink (fourteen on tissue paper) were clearly meant as models for the engraver. Most indicate the arched-top rectangle that is the final format. Several sheets have instructions to the engraver

Fig. 8. Konrad Huber after F. O. C. Darley, *Chilion Played and They Were Silent*. Engraved lithograph; H. 7½″, W. 9⅞″. From *Compositions in Outline by Felix O. C. Darley from Judd's Margaret* (New York: J. S. Redfield, 1856), pl. 9. (Museum of Fine Arts, Boston.)

such as "engrave from this," "foreground from this," "engrave from this side."[16] These drawings and the completed lithographs are extremely similar, for the engraver followed Darley's models with precision.

Very little is known about Konrad (or Conrad) Huber who so skillfully engraved Darley's designs onto lithographic stones. His name occurs on these thirty plates as well as on one lithographic view and one portrait. He is listed in the New York City directories for 1855–56 and 1856–57, but not before or after.[17] The printer of the stones is

[16] Designs for *Hash*, *The Murder*, and *Camp Meeting*, Delaware Art Museum.

[17] See George C. Groce and David H. Wallace, *The New-York Historical Society's Dictionary of Artists in America, 1564–1860* (New Haven: Yale University Press, 1957), s.v. "Conrad Huber"; and Frank Weitenkampf, manuscript notes on Huber, print room, New York Public Library.

Fig. 9. F. O. C. Darley, studies of Chilion and a dog. Graphite; H. 8⅝", W. 10⅛".
(Delaware Art Museum, Permanent Collection.)

expressed as Sarony & Co. on eighteen of the plates and the title page,
and as Sarony, Major & Knapp on twelve plates. The ink is usually
dark brown, although occasionally a plate appears printed in red-
brown or black. Given Darley's popularity, a large edition was probably printed, making it likely that additional transfer stones were made
to speed production. Close examination of several copies of the book
reveals that the inked lines do not stand up above the paper surface,
but print as planographic lines. Unfinished proofs, on the other hand,
do show the raised lines characteristic of an intaglio process.

Several periods of work on the project are evidenced by unpub-

Fig. 10. F. O. C. Darley, *Chilion Played and They Were Silent*. Pen and brown ink; H. 7⅞″, W. 9¹¹⁄₁₆″. (Delaware Art Museum, Permanent Collection.)

lished proofs of the designs in both the early and the final versions and by experiments in different lithographic processes. Besides the engraved lithographic proofs in the early style of *Margaret* and *Tony Washington* mentioned above, there are two pairs of progressive proofs for *The Widow Wright* and *Brown Moll* that may be of a later date. One impression of *Brown Moll* was printed with a solid black background from the surface of the stone, while the intaglio printed figure was washed with red-brown watercolor, making it resemble a Greek red-figured vase, as do the printed board covers of some early copies of the book (fig. 11).

Four other unpublished prints are known: *The Widow Wright*, *Margaret and Obed Encounter the Master*, *Retrospection*, and *The Husking Bee*. Each of these is close in style to the prints published in

Fig. 11. Cover to *Compositions in Outline by Felix O. C. Darley from Judd's Margaret*
(New York: J. S. Redfield, 1856). Lithograph in black and red-brown; H. 12¾", W.
16¾". (Museum of Fine Arts, Boston, Sylvester Rosa Koehler Collection.)

1856 and drawn in outline. The technique for each, however, is pen
lithography. The images are drawn with great control and a sureness
and freedom that can come only from the designer's hand. Why Darley
rejected both this method and that of etching the stones himself is not
known. No documentary evidence has yet come to light regarding the
decision to have the plates for *Margaret* engraved professionally. The
prestige of the "engraving" process may have been a factor, as might
the demands on Darley's time.

The change in style between the early and final versions of *Margaret* can be seen by comparing the two versions of *A Glimpse at the
World*, one from 1850 (fig. 12) and the other from 1856 (fig. 13). In
the latter version the composition has been reversed, but there are no
changes to the setting or to the poses of the four figures. Each element

Fig. 12. F. O. C. Darley, *A Glimpse at the World*. Pen and brown ink; H. 8″, W. 9⅞″. (Delaware Art Museum, Permanent Collection.)

of the design, be it costume, flour sack, chair seat, or brush broom, has been drawn so as to appear more voluminous and weighty. Bodies have filled out and occupy more space in the crowded shop. Costume details add to the sense of completeness and concreteness; less is left to the imagination.

The final version of the portrait of Margaret (pl. 28) depicts a sturdy young woman with a brooding expression. She conveys little of the mystery implied in the attitude of the slender form of the earlier version (figs. 14, 15). A contemporary critic analyzed the weaknesses of the published image of the heroine. "Darley's conception of Margaret . . . [is] not in accordance with our estimate of what the author's ideal was. The individuality is strong; but neither strong enough for 'Margaret,' nor externally manifested with the intensity with which

Fig. 13. Konrad Huber after F. O. C. Darley, *A Glimpse at the World*. Engraved lithograph; H. 7¼″, W. 9″ (oval). From *Compositions in Outline by Felix O. C. Darley from Judd's Margaret* (New York: J. S. Redfield, 1856), pl. 11. (Museum of Fine Arts, Boston.)

she would have shown it. . . . She is too beautiful; the Margaret of the book was rather splendid than beautiful."[18] It is conjecture, but that critic writing in 1856 would probably have found the earlier version of the portrait neither beautiful nor strong. By the mid 1850s more solid and tangible realism had entered American painting, and Darley had kept abreast of these developments and reflected them in his changes to the designs for *Margaret*.

Despite the increased materialism of the final designs for the book, Darley retained an outline style. By using the well-known manner of

18 "Darley's Outline Illustrations of 'Margaret,'" *Crayon* 3, no. 12 (December 1856): 370.

Fig. 14. F. O. C. Darley, *Margaret*. Pen and brown ink; H. 9¹³⁄₁₆″, W. 8⅛″. (Delaware Art Museum, Permanent Collection.)

neoclassical and romantic European antecedents, he was able to idealize the story's earthy and imperfect characters and to remove to a more abstract time and place its dramatic incidents. Darley's outline illustrations to Judd's *Margaret* do, in fact, permit the "real and ideal" of the book's title to coexist successfully.

Fig. 15. Konrad Huber after F. O. C. Darley, *Margaret*. Engraved lithograph; H.
10⅛″, W. 7″. From *Compositions in Outline by Felix O. C. Darley from Judd's
Margaret* (New York: J. S. Redfield, 1856), pl. 28. (Museum of Fine Arts, Boston.)

Appendix

F. O. C. Darley's Outline Illustrations to Sylvester Judd's *Margaret*

		Type and number of studies					
		Early version			Later version		
Plate no.	Published title	Oval wash	Partial study	Pen in oval	Study or pencil	Pen and black ink	Proofs
1	Childhood	—	—	—	—	1	—
2	The Master	—	—	—	—	—	2
3	Margaret annoyed by her Brother	—	—	1	1	1	1
4	Hash	—	1	1	—	1	—
5	The Bee-Hunt	1	—	—	—	1	—
6	Obed	—	—	—	—	1	1
7	Margaret & Obed encounter the Master	—	—	1	—	1	1
8	Chilion	—	—	1	—	1	—
9	Chilion played and they were Silent	1	2	—	3	1	—
10	Pluck	—	—	—	—	1	1
11	A Glimpse at The World	1	—	1	—	1	2
12	M. M. Gisborne	—	1	1	1	—	—
13	Nimrod exhibits humor	—	—	—	—	1	1
14	The Widow Wright	—	—	—	—	1	3
15	Camp Meeting	—	—	—	2	1	2
16	The Preacher	—	—	—	1	—	—
17	Retrospection	—	—	1	—	—	2
18	Brown Moll	—	—	1	—	1	2
19	The Contest	—	—	—	1	1	—
20	Bethia Weeks	—	—	—	—	—	—
21	The Husking Bee	—	—	1	—	—	1
22	Tony Washington	—	1	1	1	1	1
23	The Murder	—	1	—	—	1	—
24	Rose	—	—	—	—	—	—
25	The Arrest	—	—	1	—	—	—
26	Deacon Ramdill	—	—	—	—	1	—
27	Margaret meets with Sympathy	—	—	—	1	1	1
28	Margaret	—	—	1	—	1	1
29	The Parting	—	—	—	2	1	—
30	Parson Wells & Wife	—	—	—	1	1	1
	Unpublished title						
	School Keeping	1	—	1	—	—	—
	Abel Wilcox	—	—	1	—	—	—
	Total plates	4	5	14	10	22	16
	Total objects	4	6	14	14	22	23

Tools of Persuasion

The American Architectural Book of the Nineteenth Century

NEVILLE THOMPSON

THE AMERICAN ARCHITECTURAL BOOK of the nineteenth century has attracted relatively little of the scholarly interest or collecting fervor of its contemporaries. Except among specialists in the work of one architect or one period's buildings, these books seldom appear in catalogues or are dismembered as sources of decorative prints. While a considerable literature is devoted to architectural drawings, much less has been written about the book as a book; in fact, in one recent survey of American architectural drawings, some of the "drawings" described were actually book illustrations, with little or no distinction having been made between two very different genres.

Why should this be so? Is it because we perceive architectural literature as too specialized or too technical to be of interest to nonarchitects? That would indeed be an ironic outgrowth of a century of professionalization and promotion on the part of American architects and might well puzzle the layman of the mid nineteenth century, at whom many of these publications were specifically aimed. After surveying the rich and well-rounded collection at Winterthur, I would

For their support and encouragement, the author would like to thank E. McSherry Fowble and Ian M. G. Quimby, organizers of the conference for which this paper was prepared; and her colleagues in the Printed Book and Periodical Collection, Winterthur Library.

137

have to admit that if people approach this type of literature expecting a visual equivalent of the great collections of ornament or works of natural history for which the period is so justly famous, they will probably be disappointed: many of these books seem at first glance to be rather ordinary. They tend to cannibalize each other's designs and are for the most part inexpensively printed and produced. These may well be reasons for their neglect, but I suggest that the disappointment the reader may feel at their pedestrian appearance can spring from a misapprehension of the purposes for which they were written, illustrated, and published. The last thing that most of these books were intended to be was an "art book." Their aim was different and, indeed, more dynamic: they were tools of persuasion. For a number of reasons, books that were simply illustrated, inexpensively produced, and widely sold would have been considered most effective in promoting the styles, products, and attitudes advocated by the book's author, very often himself an architect or a designer. Not for these books the passive role of existing to be looked *at*, but instead that of spurring their readers to rise and *do*—to build, buy, or adopt an aesthetic stance. These volumes were, in fact, active vehicles of salesmanship, aimed primarily at the middle classes and the "industrious mechanic," for whom such an easily accessible format seems to have been deliberately chosen. As always, exceptions existed, particularly in the latter part of the century. Luxury volumes were produced to appeal to an upwardly mobile readership or to impress their readers with the sophistication of the work of a particular architectural firm. As the century wore on, the scope and variety of output in the field in general broadened greatly, but the basic goals of this literature remained paramount throughout the period.

Three distinct motivations suggest themselves as the underlying reasons for the production of these books. First, there was the simple need to furnish technical information to those about to build, whether layman or professional. As the technology of building changed more and more rapidly and became more complex and specialized, so correspondingly did this type of manual. A second motivation was purely commercial. There were simply many more people with money to spend on building, and a developing system of publication and distribution enabled authors to bring books before this public more quickly and inexpensively than before. In a growing country, where new towns were continually being born and old ones rebuilt as they continued to expand, and where the population was encouraged to think of an ever-rising standard of living and a home of one's own as a natural right, the audience for suggestions on what to build was ready-made. Technological changes and the gradual passing of traditional craft methods of building meant that an increasing number of consumers felt that they needed advice from a book—a situation abetted by the spread of literacy and the example of parallel changes from custom to innovation in many other fields at the same time. A new self-consciousness about the propriety of aesthetic decisions occupied the minds of these consumers in a way that their grandparents would probably not have understood, and for each such consumer an author was ready to give advice. This leads directly to a third motivation for the spread of these publications, which I have called, as an umbrella phrase, the crusading instinct. Whether manifested as a belief in the need to develop a particularly "American" style of architecture or in the right of every hard-working family man to have a home of his own or in the fitness of a given style for a specific building situation, a strain of idealism runs through this literature. Examining the books with attention will show that many of them turn out to be a mixture of several of these strains—a different mix for each book. I imagine that this mixture is not exclusive to architectural books alone, but it does suggest that many of them may have had more in common with contemporary trade catalogues than with fine volumes of steel engravings. If not trade catalogues in actuality, they were a sort of trade catalogue of ideas, presented with fervor.

We can learn a great deal from these books, taken on their own terms. They have much to tell us about the goals and attitudes of their own period and can reveal much about the origins of the built environment that still surrounds us, in which a great deal of nineteenth-century architecture remains. Above all, they were quite influential in their time. A minority of the buildings of that period came directly from the drawing board of an architect. At first-, second-, or thirdhand, most had their origins in a book, whether copied directly from a plan in a volume belonging to the builder, built from a set of plans ordered by mail from another book/catalogue, assembled in great part from separate units ordered by mail from yet another catalogue, or copied by a builder from another building that might itself be a memory of a plate in a builder's guide. The succession of revival styles that swept the country during the nineteenth century was spread in great part through books and periodicals. Even in those cases where a building was designed by an architect, the architect himself was likely to have been inspired by the written word or the printed illustration.

It goes without saying that an architectural book demands to be illustrated (although a few were not). Throughout this period, changing graphic and illustrative techniques interacted in interesting ways with the styles they illustrated. The first books to appear, with their simple woodcuts, proclaimed the handiwork of their creators in a direct way, as did the buildings that they inspired. By the end of the period, photography, with its anonymity, had replaced other graphic methods, and, in many cases, the consumer of a building had no contact with the designer of the building he inhabited or worked in and often no idea of how it may have been built. Technology had outstripped the consumer, and the impersonal touch of the machine was overtaking the stamp of the hand. (One must be wary of generalizing: at the turn of the century, there was a blossoming of the decorative arts associated with architecture and, because of them, of craftsmanship; conversely, the earliest woodcut illustrations were, although simple, still "mass" produced.) The simplicity and linear delicacy of federal ornament seems well served by the copperplate illustrations of the early nineteenth century; later, lithography seems as well adapted to portray the more "romantic" Gothic-revival cottage in its natural setting. All this can lead to interesting "chicken-and-egg" debates as to the influence of illustrative styles on design, and on the visual consciousness of the users of the book, but it is undeniable that some illustrations are almost impossible to conceive in a different graphic medium.

A less apparent result of the influence of technique on illustration is the relationship of the original creator to the illustration itself as it finally appears in a book. In most cases several hands were involved in transmission of the artist's idea to its appearance on the printed page. Unlike many authors of this period, the architects themselves probably executed at least the first draft of their own illustrations but had to be resigned to seeing engravers and printers carry out the completed work, a process in which, undoubtedly, the author saw his original work changed to some extent. Signatures on such illustrations can tell us that while the artist may have been the architect/author, the engraver of a plate might well have been a generalist, whose signature might equally well appear on illustrations in a work of fiction or on advertisements in a periodical. This process was integral to the inexpensive production of books and periodicals, but because of it many plates of the period seem almost interchangeable from book to book. The emphasis is on the functional supplying of visual information. (This is not always true, however, particularly in the case of lithographs, where the ability of the artist to draw, if he so wished, directly on stone and the color effects that chromolithography could achieve often resulted in something less ordinary.)

When I began my overview of illustration in these books, I first consulted the bible for historians of American architecture, Henry-Russell Hitchcock's *American Architectural Books*, a bibliography that neatly spans the period under discussion here.[1] The subject index confirms what we might suspect: the subject most written about from the first publication of architectural books in this country until the end of the nineteenth century was domestic architecture—not surprising when one considers the continuing importance of home ownership in most of our lives and the relative abundance of space and opportunity to build during this period. A quick trip through the first century of architectural publication in America, focusing on books about the house and its construction and interiors, shows a progression of technological development, the appearance and disappearance of trends in taste, and an increasing diversity and complexity in the literature. But the persistence of the three basic motivations remains: furnishing of technical information, promotion for commercial gain, and propagandizing on behalf of a style or an idea.

[1] Henry-Russell Hitchcock, *American Architectural Books: New Expanded Edition* (New York: Da Capo Press, 1976).

Any chronological survey of this literature most handily begins in 1797 with two similar books. Both were published in the United States, but there is one important difference between them: William Pain's *Carpenter's Pocket Directory* (Philadelphia, 1797) is a republication of an earlier London edition; Asher Benjamin's *Country Builder's Assistant* is the first architectural work written and published in this country (fig. 1).[2] Both are typical of their genre—"builders' guides." Small, handy, and practical, they are meant to help the house carpenter achieve the requisite qualities of "strength and convenience" necessary for any building. They provide the builder with information on what we might call the "hard bits" of a building: staircases, roof framing, the proportions of the orders, and a few simple plans and elevations (fig. 2). Often both dimensions and specific room designations are absent; the builder is simply assumed to know the rest, as in any traditional craft.

Pain's and Benjamin's small books stand at the end of one publishing tradition and the beginning of another. The career of our first American architectural writer, Asher Benjamin (1773–1845), covered several decades of the early nineteenth century. Both the books he wrote and the buildings he designed had an influence on building in New England that is still visible. He probably will be best remembered for his popularization of the federal style through his early books (and the Greek revival in his later ones). Benjamin wrote seven books in all: the first was published in 1797, the last in 1843, and posthumous editions of some of his works continued to appear through the 1850s. His most popular book, *The Practical House Carpenter*, went through seventeen editions from 1830 to 1856—a respectable record for any author in any field.[3] The thousands of neat white houses that any visitor to New England sees are testimony to the ability of the printed word to help to spread an architectural idea: many of them can be traced to a plate from one of Benjamin's many books.

[2] William Pain, *The Carpenter's Pocket Directory: Containing the Best Methods of Framing Timber Buildings of All Figures and Dimensions* (Philadelphia: J. H. Dobelbower and L. Thackara, 1797); Asher Benjamin, *The Country Builder's Assistant, Fully Explaining, the Best Methods for Striking Regular and Quirked Mouldings* (Boston: Printed by Spotswood and Etheridge, 1798).

[3] These seventeen editions, as well as the rest of Benjamin's extensive output, are cited in detail in Hitchcock, *American Architectural Books*, pp. 9–13.

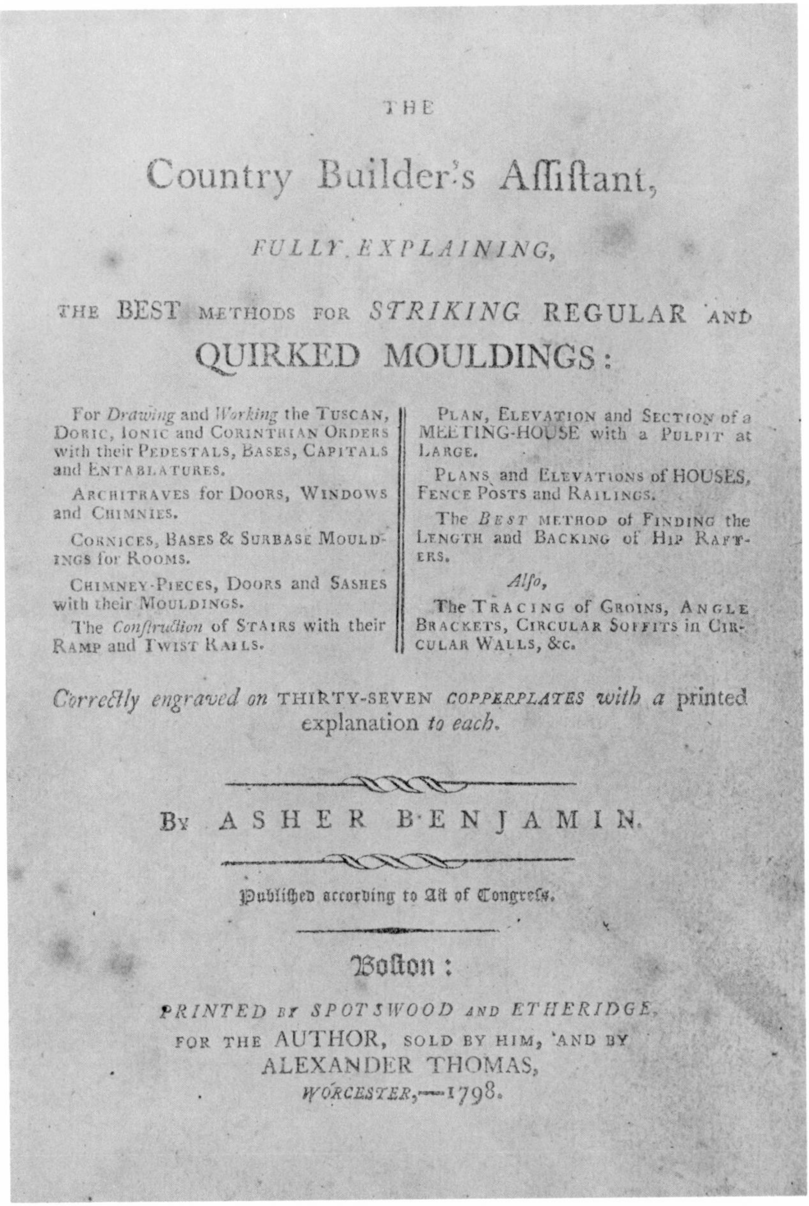

THE

Country Builder's Assistant,

FULLY EXPLAINING,

THE BEST METHODS FOR *STRIKING* REGULAR AND

QUIRKED MOULDINGS:

For *Drawing* and *Working* the TUSCAN, DORIC, IONIC and CORINTHIAN ORDERS with their PEDESTALS, BASES, CAPITALS and ENTABLATURES.

ARCHITRAVES for DOORS, WINDOWS and CHIMNIES.

CORNICES, BASES & SURBASE MOULDINGS for ROOMS.

CHIMNEY-PIECES, DOORS and SASHES with their MOULDINGS.

The *Construction* of STAIRS with their RAMP and TWIST RAILS.

PLAN, ELEVATION and SECTION of a MEETING-HOUSE with a PULPIT at LARGE.

PLANS and ELEVATIONS of HOUSES, FENCE POSTS and RAILINGS.

The *BEST* METHOD of FINDING the LENGTH and BACKING of HIP RAFTERS.

Also,

The TRACING of GROINS, ANGLE BRACKETS, CIRCULAR SOFFITS in CIRCULAR WALLS, &c.

Correctly engraved on THIRTY-SEVEN *COPPERPLATES with a* printed explanation *to each.*

By A S H E R B E N J A M I N.

Published according to Act of Congress.

Boston :

PRINTED BY SPOTSWOOD AND ETHERIDGE,

FOR THE AUTHOR, SOLD BY HIM, AND BY

ALEXANDER THOMAS,

WORCESTER,—1798.

Fig. 1. Title page from Asher Benjamin, *The Country Builder's Assistant* (Boston: Printed by Spotswood and Etheridge, 1798). H. 7¾", W. 5¾". (Winterthur Library.)

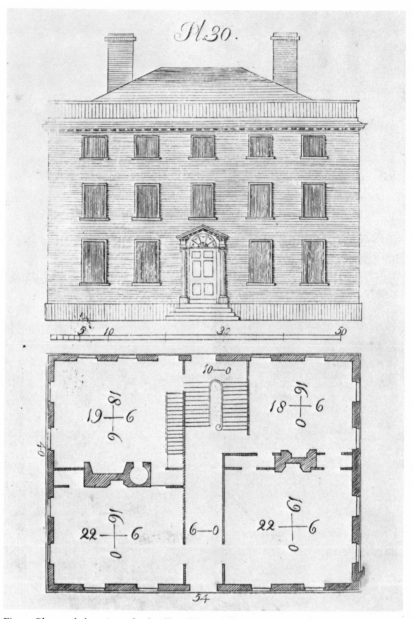

Fig. 2. Plan and elevation of a dwelling. From Asher Benjamin, *The Country Builder's Assistant* (Boston: Printed by Spotswood and Etheridge, 1798), pl. 30. (Winterthur Library.)

A similar early work, *The Young Carpenter's Assistant* by Owen Biddle (1774–1806), was published in Philadelphia in 1805 (fig. 3). Biddle described himself as both a house carpenter and a teacher of architectural drawing. In his preface Biddle states that as a teacher he had experienced "much inconvenience" for want of suitable books on the subject. "All that have yet appeared," he says, ignoring Benjamin, "have been written by foreign authors, who have adapted their examples and observations almost directly to the style of building in their respective countries, which in many cases differs materially from ours." He adds, "for my part, I can conceive of few objects of more consequence in a new and improving country like our own, as it regards health and convenience than the proper construction and building of our houses." Without excuse, however, he goes on to say that his plates of the orders were taken with little adaptation from Pain, and for some of the geometrical problems he was indebted to Peter Nicholson, another popular English author of architectural manuals.[4] (This is an early example of a tension that has existed until the present in American architecture: the search for an independent "style" as against dependence on foreign prototypes for inspiration.) In spite of his personal declaration of independence, Biddle seems to have come to terms with his own reliance on English architectural literature. We might assume, from his self-description as a teacher of architectural drawing, that Biddle executed the original drawings from which the copperplates were engraved, but this might not be so. Most of the plates are signed by well-known Philadelphia engraver Cornelius Tiebout (ca. 1773–1832), but there is no artist's signature. We may suspect that the plates of the orders, like parts of the text, may also have been reworked from Pain or Nicholson. Not so the folding plate of the bridge over the Schuylkill: this was Biddle's own work, signed by him, and engraved by Tiebout.

The style of buildings illustrated by Biddle is rather grander than those in Benjamin's earlier books, and we find an actual building illustrated in these plates (fig. 4). When Benjamin brought out his

[4]Owen Biddle, *The Young Carpenter's Assistant; or, A System of Architecture, Adapted to the Style of Building in the United States* (Philadelphia: Printed by Benjamin Johnson, 1805), p. [3].

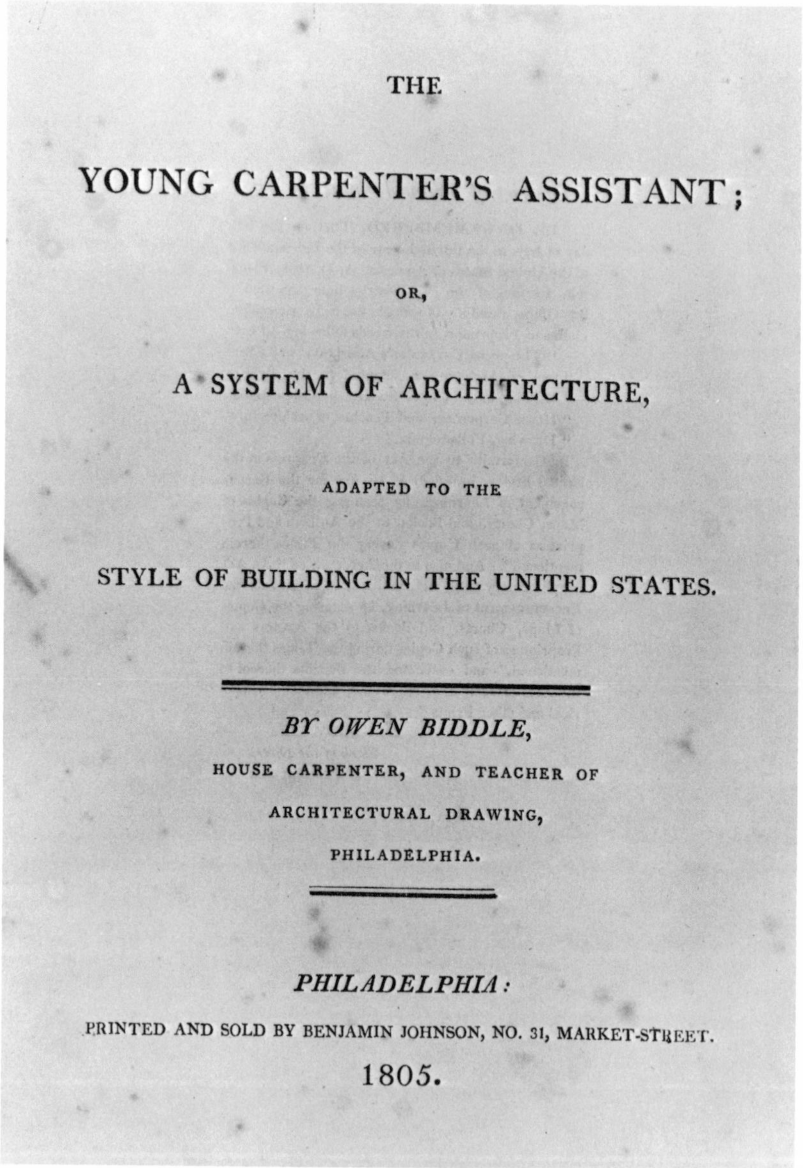

THE

YOUNG CARPENTER'S ASSISTANT;

OR,

A SYSTEM OF ARCHITECTURE,

ADAPTED TO THE

STYLE OF BUILDING IN THE UNITED STATES.

BY OWEN BIDDLE,

HOUSE CARPENTER, AND TEACHER OF

ARCHITECTURAL DRAWING,

PHILADELPHIA.

PHILADELPHIA:

PRINTED AND SOLD BY BENJAMIN JOHNSON, NO. 31, MARKET-STREET.

1805.

Fig. 3. Title page from Owen Biddle, *The Young Carpenter's Assistant* (Philadelphia: Printed by Benjamin Johnson, 1805). H. 9½″, W. 8″. (Winterthur Library.)

Fig. 4. Bank of the United States. From Owen Biddle, *The Young Carpenter's Assistant* (Philadelphia: Benjamin Johnson, 1805), pl. 43. (Winterthur Library.)

American Builder's Companion a year later, he seems to have sensed that Biddle, with his interest in an "American" architecture, had started a trend; his own title describes the contents as a "system of architecture particularly adapted to the present style of building in the United States," and he, too, illustrated a then existing structure—the United States Bank, in Boston, designed by Charles Bulfinch and surmounted by an enormous American eagle.[5] The plates in the book were drawn by Benjamin's collaborator, Daniel Raynerd, described in the first edition of this book as co-author. Raynerd was also a stuccoworker and drew the plates for the orders and other ornament, as well as that of the bank. His training and the copperplate techniques seem well

[5] Asher Benjamin, *The American Builder's Companion; or, A New System of Architecture Particularly Adapted to the Present Style of Building in the United States of America* (Boston: Etheridge and Bliss, 1806), pl. 43.

suited to the Adamesque ceiling ornament and fireplace surrounds shown here; the more pedestrian technical plates were drawn by Benjamin. Several engravers, working with both artists, were responsible for production of these plates.

John Haviland (1792–1852), an English-born Philadelphia architect, may be better known for his pioneering work as a prison architect than as an author, but he should be known also as the first author of an American architectural book to introduce specifically Greek, rather than Roman, orders as prototypes. His 1818 work, *The Builder's Assistant*, with plates engraved by Hugh Bridport, is still a builder's guide in basic content.[6] The amount of text is expanded, however, with much more detailed coverage of carpentry and house painting, and its third volume contains a conservative appendix: "The Philadelphia House Carpenters' Book of Prices and Rules," as of 1819. By this date, individual enterprise and perhaps too great a demand for services had begun to break up the rule of uniform price-setting established by craftsmen's associations such as this. These books resemble nothing so much as an automobile dealer's catalogue. The basic carcass costs so much; throw in this feature or that, a Palladian window or a ceiling rosette, and, as with whitewalls on a car, you pay more. Price books are extremely informative about building economics of their period, but their period did not last. Free enterprise was to break down the system, and with it went some of the understood body of knowledge that had helped to supplement what the builders' guides had furnished.

For a full-blown expression of the Greek revival, we turn to *The Beauties of Modern Architecture* by Minard Lafever (1797–1854), published in 1835 (fig. 5). It contains not only plans and details for town houses in that style (fig. 6) but also illustrations of the "Grecian architecture" that inspired them and an extensive survey of architectural history lifted from British author James Elmes. This invocation of literature and history as a selling tool will reappear over and over

[6]John Haviland, *The Builder's Assistant: Containing the Five Orders of Architecture, Selected from the Best Specimens of the Greek and Roman . . . for the Use of Builders, Carpenters, Masons, Plasterers, Cabinet Makers, and Carvers . . .* , 3 vols. (Philadelphia: John Bioren, 1818–21).

in the literature. In the engraved plates, information has been conveyed with extreme economy in a linear manner both drier and less delicate than that of, for instance, Raynerd, but it accords well with its subject matter. Although the author states that the plates were "drawn expressly" for this work, almost none are signed, so we cannot be sure that Lafever was their creator.

With the advent of the next newly fashionable style, a graphic technique—lithography—seemed to appear almost simultaneously to answer the need for a different type of architectural illustration, and nothing could be more of a violent contrast. The Gothic revival, with its dependence on suggestions of romantic gloom and medieval murk, would have been ill served by the clarity of line that was perfectly adapted to depicting the Greek-revival and earlier federal styles. It was important as well that this new technique be suited to the representation of landscape, for landscape was an essential ingredient of the Gothic-revival style. For almost the first time in American architectural illustration, landscape setting becomes prominent, as in William Bailey Lang's *Views . . . of the Highland Cottages at Roxbury*, a prospectus for a group of cottages to be built near Boston (fig. 7).[7] The technique is perfectly suited for these illustrations of idealized Gothic-revival cottages (fig. 8) in their carefully romanticized settings; one cannot imagine their appearing in the spare unshaded line of Lafever, nor can one easily envision Lafever's pared-down Greek temples in a setting so murkily picturesque.

At about this time the house pattern book appears as a new variation of architectural publication. Unlike the builders' guides, these books are aimed specifically at the client as well as the builder and imply both a greater range of choice of styles and the need for salesmanship in the presentation of house plans as wares from which to be chosen. Attractive plates, as, for instance, in William Ranlett's *Architect*, published in New York in 1849, accompany more complete plans and specifications than we have seen before (fig. 9); with the help of Ranlett, a man and his builder could erect a house that was

[7] I am indebted to Prof. James O'Gorman for clarifying this volume's intended use as a developer's prospectus.

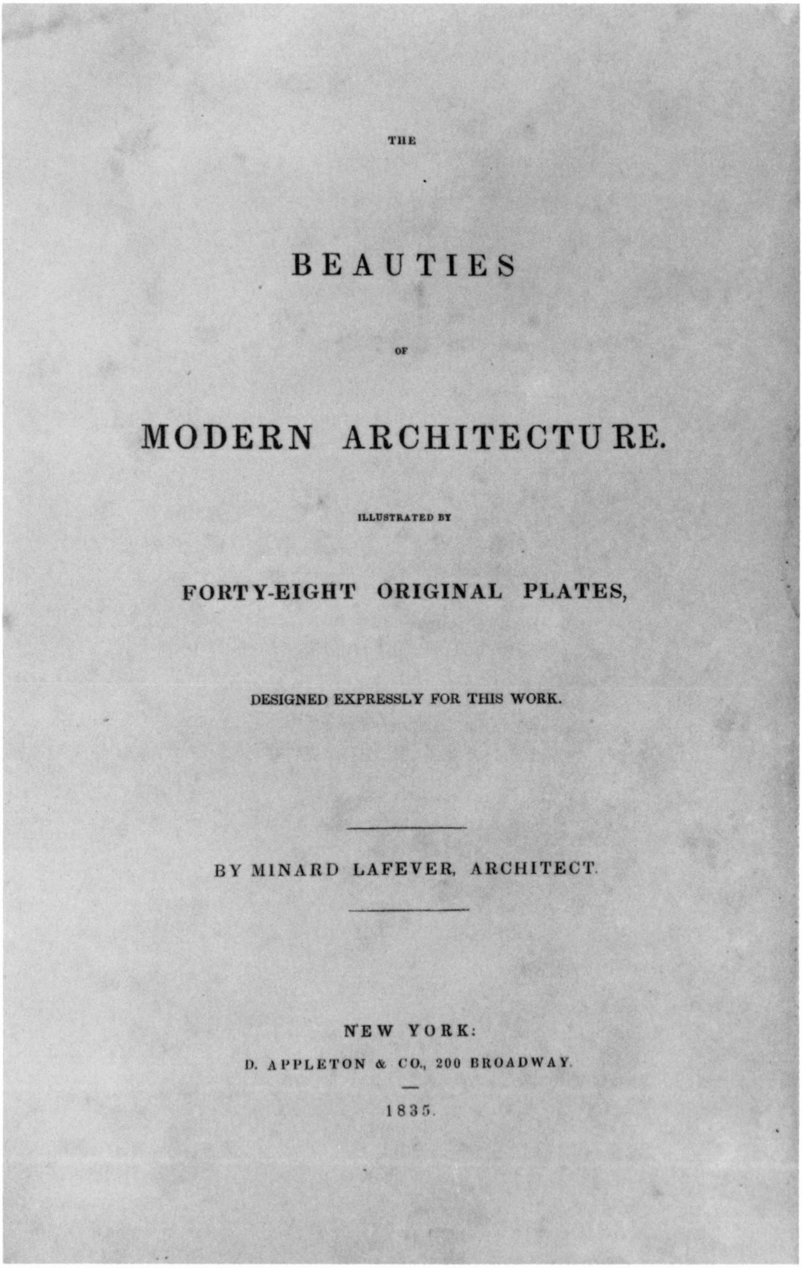

THE

BEAUTIES

OF

MODERN ARCHITECTURE.

ILLUSTRATED BY

FORTY-EIGHT ORIGINAL PLATES,

DESIGNED EXPRESSLY FOR THIS WORK.

BY MINARD LAFEVER, ARCHITECT.

NEW YORK:

D. APPLETON & CO., 200 BROADWAY.

1835.

Fig. 5. Title page from Minard Lafever, *The Beauties of Modern Architecture* (New York: D. Appleton, 1835). H. 10¾", W. 7". (Winterthur Library.)

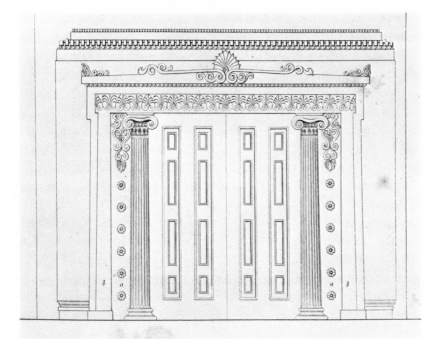

Fig. 6. Detail of double doors and door frame from a town-house design. From Minard Lafever, *The Beauties of Modern Architecture* (New York: D. Appleton, 1835), pl. 25 fig. 1. (Winterthur Library.)

not only fashionable but also as up-to-date technologically as one might wish (fig. 10). Much less has been left to chance or to the assumed knowledge of the builder. A new note is struck in the preface, in which taste is equated with moral beauty and Christian principles to justify the creation of a family's ideal home and its surroundings. The plates are a collaboration between Ranlett himself and the firm of lithographers who printed them. The lithographs are tinted, a technique that suggests the luxury of full-color printing without the expense.

While Ranlett's books seem to have been aimed at a fairly well off middle-class public, the working man was not ignored by architectural writings of the period, as, for instance, in T. Thomas's *Working-Man's Cottage Architecture* (fig. 11). This cheaply produced little book seems deliberately written for the lower income homeowner,

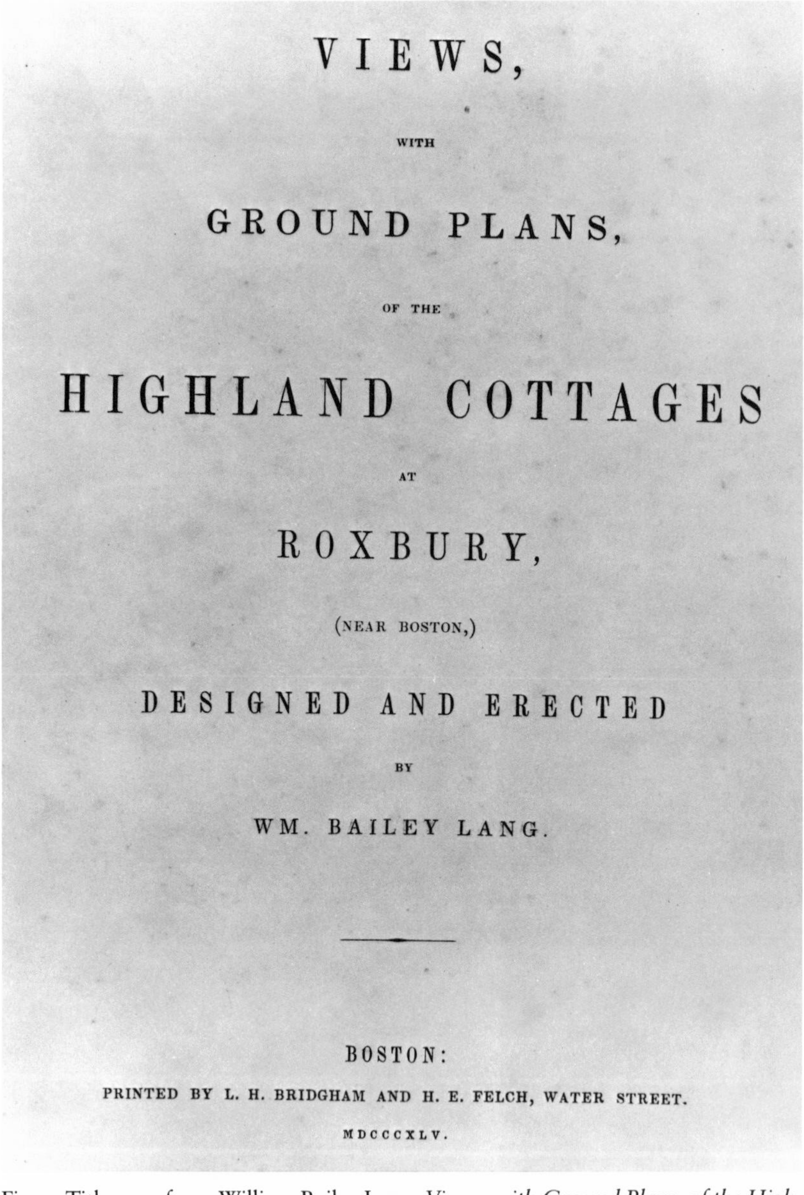

VIEWS,

WITH

GROUND PLANS,

OF THE

HIGHLAND COTTAGES

AT

ROXBURY,

(NEAR BOSTON,)

DESIGNED AND ERECTED

BY

WM. BAILEY LANG.

———

BOSTON:

PRINTED BY L. H. BRIDGHAM AND H. E. FELCH, WATER STREET.

MDCCCXLV.

Fig. 7. Title page from William Bailey Lang, *Views, with Ground Plans, of the High-land Cottages at Roxbury* (Boston: Printed by L. H. Bridgham and H. E. Felch, 1845). H. 11¼", W. 9". (Winterthur Library.)

Fig. 8. *Glen Cottage—Roxbury Highlands.* From William Bailey Lang, *Views, with Ground Plans, of the Highland Cottages at Roxbury* (Boston: Printed by L. H. Bridgham and H. E. Felch, 1845), pl. [6]. (Winterthur Library.)

although the small houses shown are variants of the Gothic-revival style, and the word *cottage* in the title certifies the author as up-to-date. The basic illustrations, unsigned, are a throwback to the style of the builders' guides of the beginning of the century. Little more is provided than a plan and an elevation and a short list of cost estimates (fig. 12). Although it may have been intended for a homeowner with little to spend, it is significant that such a book was written and published at all: in previous centuries, such a client would never have needed or been given explicit instructions of this kind. The author pays tribute to the working classes, who, if "steady and persevering," will ulti-mately enjoy "a home of their own," financed, perhaps, by the Brook-lyn Accumulating Fund Association described in an appendix to the book (and for whom this entire publication may have been a disguised trade catalogue of sorts).

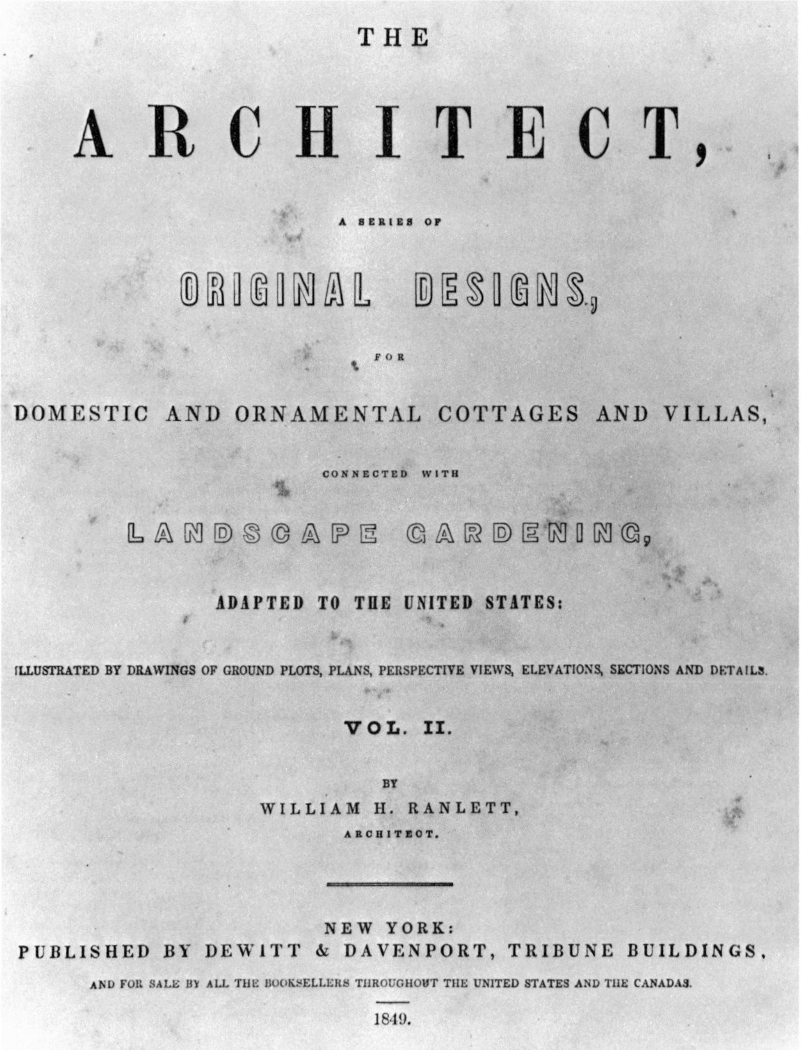

THE

ARCHITECT,

A SERIES OF

ORIGINAL DESIGNS,

FOR

DOMESTIC AND ORNAMENTAL COTTAGES AND VILLAS,

CONNECTED WITH

LANDSCAPE GARDENING,

ADAPTED TO THE UNITED STATES:

ILLUSTRATED BY DRAWINGS OF GROUND PLOTS, PLANS, PERSPECTIVE VIEWS, ELEVATIONS, SECTIONS AND DETAILS.

VOL. II.

BY

WILLIAM H. RANLETT,

ARCHITECT.

———

NEW YORK:

PUBLISHED BY DEWITT & DAVENPORT, TRIBUNE BUILDINGS,

AND FOR SALE BY ALL THE BOOKSELLERS THROUGHOUT THE UNITED STATES AND THE CANADAS.

———

1849.

Fig. 9. Title page from William H. Ranlett, *The Architect*, vol. 2 (New York: Dewitt & Davenport, 1849). H. 14½", W. 11". (Winterthur Library.)

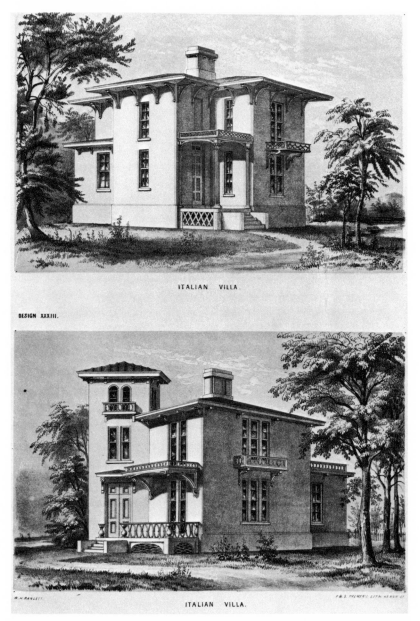

ITALIAN VILLA.

DESIGN XXXIII.

ITALIAN VILLA.

Fig. 10. Designs for Italian villas. From William H. Ranlett, *The Architect*, vol. 2 (New York: Dewitt & Davenport, 1849), pl. 22. (Winterthur Library.)

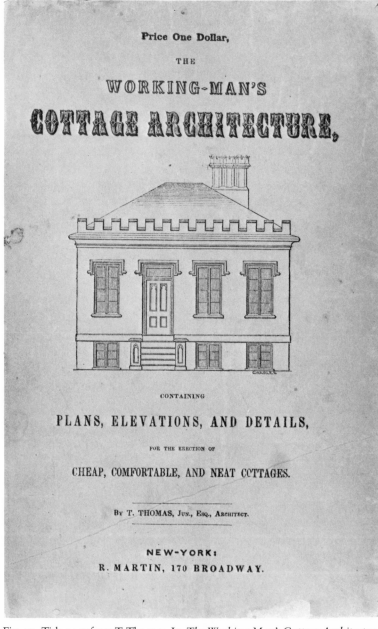

Fig. 11. Title page from T. Thomas, Jr., *The Working-Man's Cottage Architecture* (New York: R. Martin, 1848). H. 8¾", W. 5¾". (Winterthur Library.)

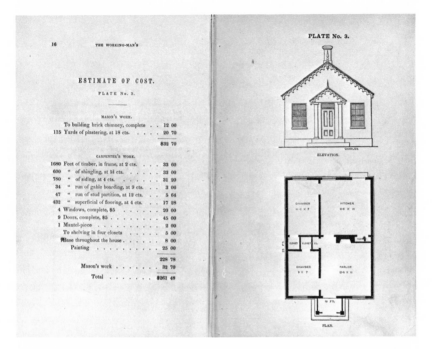

Fig. 12. Estimate of building costs with plan and elevation of a cottage. From T. Thomas, Jr., *The Working-Man's Cottage Architecture* (New York: R. Martin, 1848), p. 16 pl. 3. (Winterthur Library.)

The work of A. J. Downing (1815–52) was, of course, as important to the spread of the Gothic revival as Benjamin's had been for his time and for his mode. Certainly Downing was among the most widely read authors of his period in this field. His *Architecture of Country Houses* and *Cottage Residences* went through numerous editions. His profession of landscape architect seems perfectly fitting for an enthusiast of the picturesque, in which setting and building are interdependent, but he went further still, prescribing styles of furniture and interior appointments. He prefaces *The Architecture of Country Houses* with the remarks that the good house (by which he means, in his own words, "fitting, tasteful, and significant") is a powerful means of civilization—"so long as people live in log huts and follow a hunter's life, we must not be surprised at lynch law and the use of the Bowie knife." Downing goes on to discuss the moral influence of the country home, where the hearth is the focus of the "Beautiful" and the "Good"—and at the same time furnishes quite practical advice on plumbing and warns homeowners to avoid "trashy, colored Show prints of the ordinary kind" as interior ornament.[8] His books, obviously intended to reach the widest possible audience and to sell at a reasonable price, are illustrated by wood engravings—the easily produced, universally used graphic technique of the period, but one that imposed the technique of the engraver between the artist's original concept and the eventual reader. The result was in many cases functional but undistinguished and impersonal.

In contrast to Downing, David Henry Arnot's *Gothic Architecture Applied to Modern Residences*, sumptuously illustrated by chromolithographed plates in several bright colors and gold, must have been meant for a very special audience—the owners and builders of the brownstone row houses then appearing in New York and other eastern cities (fig. 13). In his own text, Arnot derided the "glaring green and white" of the then passé Greek revival and rejoiced that the "fancy for temples" had almost passed, perhaps from the "desire for something more distingué." Arnot's book testifies that there was an audience for advice on building and furnishing the city house at this time, even though Downing had proclaimed the country (or suburban) house an ideal. This volume of Arnot's, however, was surely never intended for mass distribution: it must have been rather expensive to produce (and is scarce today). Arnot's suggestions for interiors (including Gothic-revival furniture) are interesting, and we can speculate that he may have executed these lithographs himself (fig. 14). Certainly the result is unusual and personal. In the work of these two quite different authors, Downing and Arnot, we can pause to think of the changes that had taken place in the half century since architectural publication first began in this country with Benjamin's modest builders' guides: the growth of a diverse audience, the absolute importance of the written word as used in conjunction with illustrations as a

---

[8] The first edition of *Cottage Residences* appeared in 1842, and that of *The Architecture of Country Houses* in 1850. Hitchcock lists these and the many other editions of Downing's books (Hitchcock, *American Architectural Books*, pp. 31–34).

double tool of persuasion, the greater variety of books available, and the changes in their physical appearance.

That the nineteenth century could by this time afford greater opportunity for such variety, in the expression of eccentric personal visions, is testified to by the books written and published by Orson Squire Fowler (1809–77), a believer in phrenology and the water cure, an author who formed his own publishing company, and the popularizer of the octagon house. While geometric fancies had been planned and even occasionally built before, they were generally executed as follies; Fowler, on the other hand, was quite serious about the suitability of the octagon shape to house one and all. "To cheapen and improve human homes, and especially to bring comfortable dwellings within reach of the lower classes" he proclaimed as his aim; however, only a few, quite charming examples remain, whereas the Downingesque cottage can still commonly be seen.[9]

In the post–Civil War era, an economic and building boom brought forth a spate of publications by firms founded to issue inexpensive collections of house plans, with specifications, for the owner-builder. One of these publishers was George E. Woodward (1829–1905). *Woodward's Architecture*, small and cheap, announced as a projected annual publication, included directions for remodeling old houses as well as for the newly fashionable "French or Mansard" roof. Woodward also showed the new balloon frame, which was replacing traditional heavy house framing; it was a technological change of great importance to the housing industry of the period, for it enabled fast, inexpensive erection of buildings with stock dimensional lumber. Woodward elsewhere states quite frankly that he is in the business of selling books containing plans and specifications ("we have carefully avoided all theories, essays, or speculation on the subject of architecture"), but he *did* include an essay by a doctor on the healthful virtues of the fire on the hearth of "old country houses shadowed by some venerable elm"—a foretaste of the nostalgia of the approaching colo-

---

[9] Orson Squire Fowler, *A Home for All; or, The Gravel Wall and Octagon Mode of Building* (New York: Fowler and Wells, 1848), p. [iii]. Fowler acted as his own publisher for this and the many subsequent editions of this book. He also issued his own works on many other topics, including phrenology.

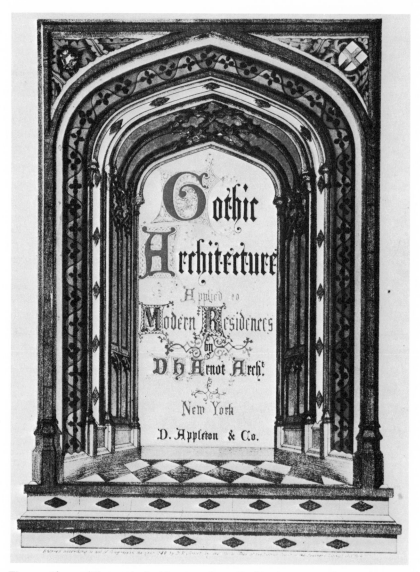

Fig. 13. Chromolithographed title page from D. H. Arnot, *Gothic Architecture Applied to Modern Residences* (New York: D. Appleton, 1851). H. 11½", W. 9". (Winterthur Library.)

Fig. 14. *Perspective of Library*. From D. H. Arnot, *Gothic Architecture Applied to Modern Residences* (New York: D. Appleton, 1851), pl. 36. (Winterthur Library.)

nial-revival style.[10] The wealth of advertising that most of these plan books contain, like the text illustrations executed in serviceable wood engraving, is pictorially fascinating and important for the information it contains on the needs and wants of the average American home builder of the period.

A growing amount of attention was beginning to be paid to the wife, as well as the husband, by authors of architectural literature of the latter years of the century. After the first thirty years or so of the period, interior views appear more often, as do entire volumes on decoration and furnishing, aimed principally at the middle classes. Charles Locke Eastlake's *Hints on Household Taste* was one of the

[10] George E. Woodward and Edward G. Thompson, *Woodward's National Architect* (New York: George W. Woodward, 1869), p. [i]; George Evertson Woodward, *Woodward's Architecture and Rural Art*, 2 vols. (New York: George E. Woodward, 1867–68), 2:78 (issued subsequently as *Woodward's Architecture*, with various subtitles).

most influential of these (fig. 15). His avowed aim was to introduce
relative simplicity into a design scene that seems to have been a battle-
ground of conflicting styles, most of them ornate. Eastlake and his
editor, Charles C. Perkins, deplored the "fatal craving for novelty"
then prevalent and what he perceived as a sterility of invention
"nowhere . . . so marked as in America." He recommended the adop-
tion of no type of furniture "unsuited . . . to modern life," and in
illustrating his own ideas of what he felt to be suitable, he found
himself serving as a design source and his name applied to yet another
style of furniture (fig. 16).[11] The illustrations to his book were the
essential medium for conveying his ideas on design, and from them
"Eastlake" furniture was copied in mass and in detail.

Another author concerned with the interior of the house was
Catharine Beecher (1800–1878), of the accomplished Beecher family.
In her own way she was as much a crusader as her celebrated sister,
Harriet Beecher Stowe. Her concern was the housewife's role in a
changing, industrializing society; she felt that if women were to control
their lives to any extent, they must systematize their daily routine and
their surroundings. One obvious area that demanded such attention
was their own workplace, the home. Beecher then proceeded to rede-
sign the house and its contents, with an emphasis on function. Lest
anyone think that this allowed her ideal housewife to relax for a
minute, some of the chapter headings from one of her many books,
Miss Beecher's Housekeeper and Healthkeeper (fig. 17), might give
pause: "A Healthful and Economical House," "On Home Ventila-
tion," "On the Care of Health," "Domestic Exercise," "Healthful
Food and Drink," "The Preservation of Good Temper in the Housewife," "Habits and Systems of Order." It is no wonder that her last
chapter is called "Comfort for a Discouraged Housekeeper." We must
remember that all these tasks, and more, were the staple of many
women's daily existence; Beecher, at least, suggested bringing some
rationalization to the home and its activities. As might be expected in

---

[11] Charles Locke Eastlake, *Hints on Household Taste in Furniture, Upholstery, and Other Details*, ed. Charles C. Perkins (Boston: James R. Osgood, 1872), pp. vii, xiii, xxv. As Hitchcock notes, the book first appeared in London in 1868.

a work that was intended to reach a wide audience, the wood-engraved illustrations are simple and workmanlike (fig. 18).

A trade catalogue with a difference, Frank L. Smith's *Cosy Home: How It Was Built* (fig. 19), not only shows us the cozy home of the title but also contains actual paint chips, suggesting the correct colors of Atlas paint to use; in this instance, four colors are suggested for this "artistic" dwelling (fig. 20). Yet another trade catalogue, the 1895 brochure *Artistic Homes*, issued by the firm of George Barber of Knoxville, Tennessee, is, like Woodward's works, intended to sell mail-order house plans. Proclaiming that all his plans were actually designed by an architect, Barber issued a vast number of catalogues and brochures and apparently did a thriving business, particularly in the Southeast.[12] One suspects that the proportions of the houses shown in these catalogues may have been enhanced for greater impact. We are just beginning to realize how many of the older neighborhoods in our cities may have had their origins in such catalogues of plans, whose influence far outweighed the expensive monographs issued occasionally to commemorate the mansions of the rich.

By the end of the century, various photographic processes had begun to preponderate in architectural illustration. Ironically, one of the most handsomely produced of all American architectural books, Frank Lloyd Wright's *House Beautiful*, was to be published at this time, but it was a swan song for the graphically illustrated book.[13] This luxury publication, issued by a private press, was not part of the mainstream of architectural illustration that was running elsewhere, as it always had, with the least expensive, most easily produced method. The photograph was to dominate in the future. The shaping of the American home, as seen through the books devoted to its design, had passed from the hands of the traditionally trained house carpenter to the newly professionalized architect and the mass-produced product of builders and mail-order designers, yet the American preoccupation

---

[12] George F. Barber and Company, *Artistic Homes: How to Plan and How to Build Them* (Knoxville, Tenn.: S. B. Newman, 1895).

[13] William Channing Gannett, *The House Beautiful; in a Setting Designed by Frank Lloyd Wright and Printed by Hand by William Herman Winslow and Frank Lloyd Wright* (River Forest, Ill.: Auvergne Press, 1896–97).

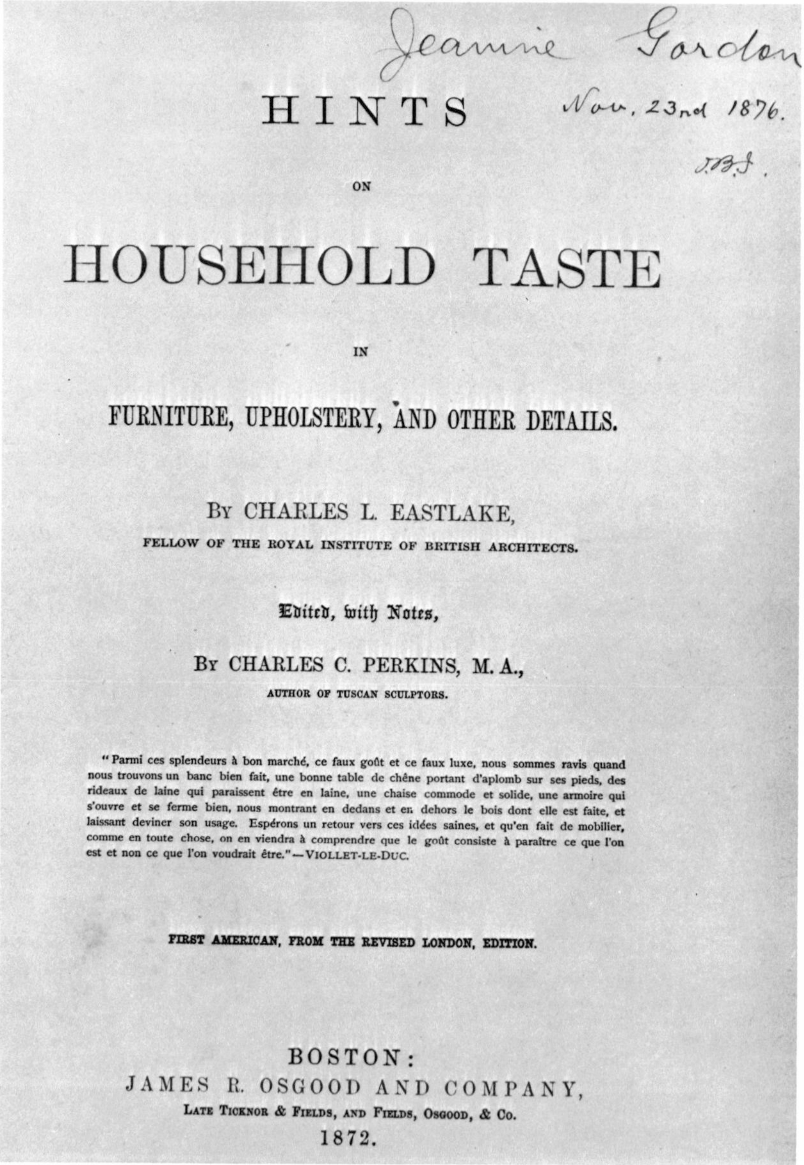

Jeanne Gordon

Nov. 23rd 1876.

HINTS

ON

HOUSEHOLD TASTE

IN

FURNITURE, UPHOLSTERY, AND OTHER DETAILS.

By CHARLES L. EASTLAKE,

FELLOW OF THE ROYAL INSTITUTE OF BRITISH ARCHITECTS.

Edited, with Notes,

By CHARLES C. PERKINS, M. A.,

AUTHOR OF TUSCAN SCULPTORS.

"Parmi ces splendeurs à bon marché, ce faux goût et ce faux luxe, nous sommes ravis quand nous trouvons un banc bien fait, une bonne table de chêne portant d'aplomb sur ses pieds, des rideaux de laine qui paraissent être en laine, une chaise commode et solide, une armoire qui s'ouvre et se ferme bien, nous montrant en dedans et en dehors le bois dont elle est faite, et laissant deviner son usage. Espérons un retour vers ces idées saines, et qu'en fait de mobilier, comme en toute chose, on en viendra à comprendre que le goût consiste à paraître ce que l'on est et non ce que l'on voudrait être."—VIOLLET-LE-DUC.

FIRST AMERICAN, FROM THE REVISED LONDON, EDITION.

BOSTON:

JAMES R. OSGOOD AND COMPANY,

LATE TICKNOR & FIELDS, AND FIELDS, OSGOOD, & CO.

1872.

Fig. 15. Title page from Charles Locke Eastlake, *Hints on Household Taste* (Boston: James R. Osgood, 1872). H. 8¼", W. 5¾". (Winterthur Library.)

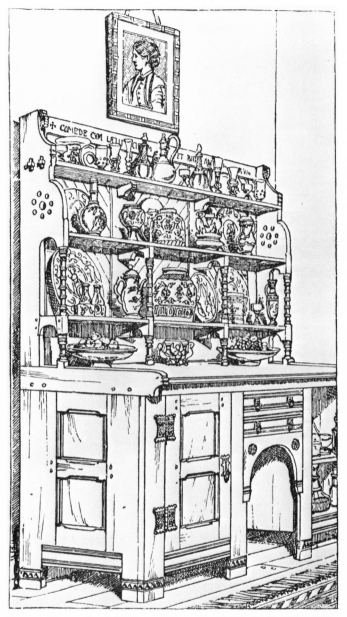

Fig. 16. *Dining-Room Sideboard*. From Charles Locke Eastlake, *Hints on Household Taste* (Boston: James R. Osgood, 1872), pl. 12. (Winterthur Library.)

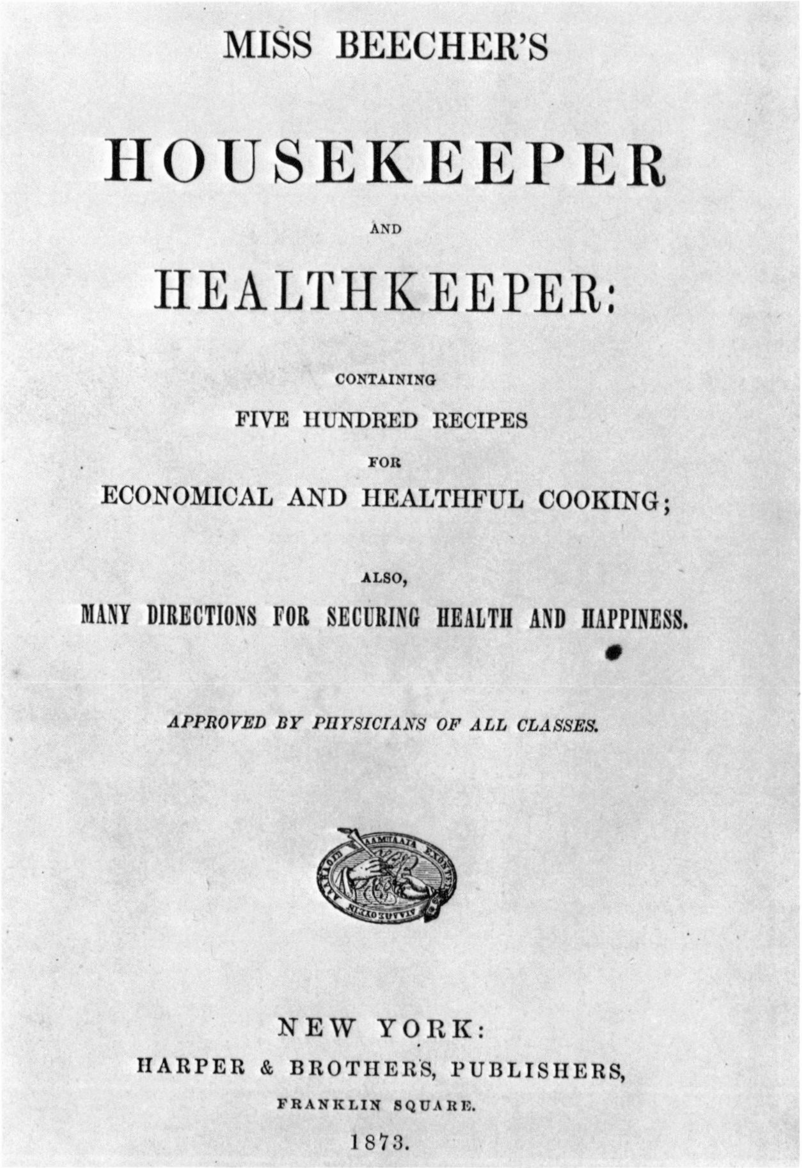

MISS BEECHER'S

HOUSEKEEPER

AND

HEALTHKEEPER:

CONTAINING

FIVE HUNDRED RECIPES

FOR

ECONOMICAL AND HEALTHFUL COOKING;

ALSO,

MANY DIRECTIONS FOR SECURING HEALTH AND HAPPINESS.

APPROVED BY PHYSICIANS OF ALL CLASSES.

NEW YORK:

HARPER & BROTHERS, PUBLISHERS,

FRANKLIN SQUARE.

1873.

Fig. 17. Title page from [Catharine E. Beecher], *Miss Beecher's Housekeeper and Healthkeeper* (New York: Harper & Brothers, 1873). H. 7¼″, W. 4¾″. (Winterthur Library.)

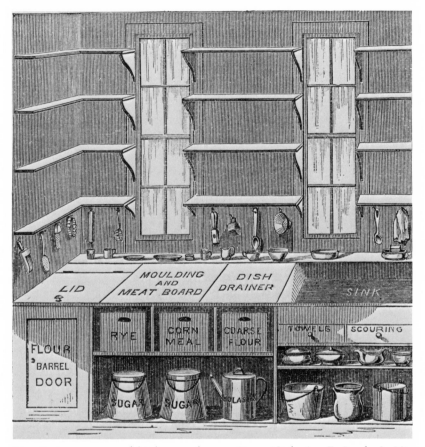

Fig. 18. Arrangement of kitchen work area. From [Catharine E. Beecher], *Miss Beecher's Housekeeper and Healthkeeper* (New York: Harper & Brothers, 1873), p. 142 fig. 19. (Winterthur Library.)

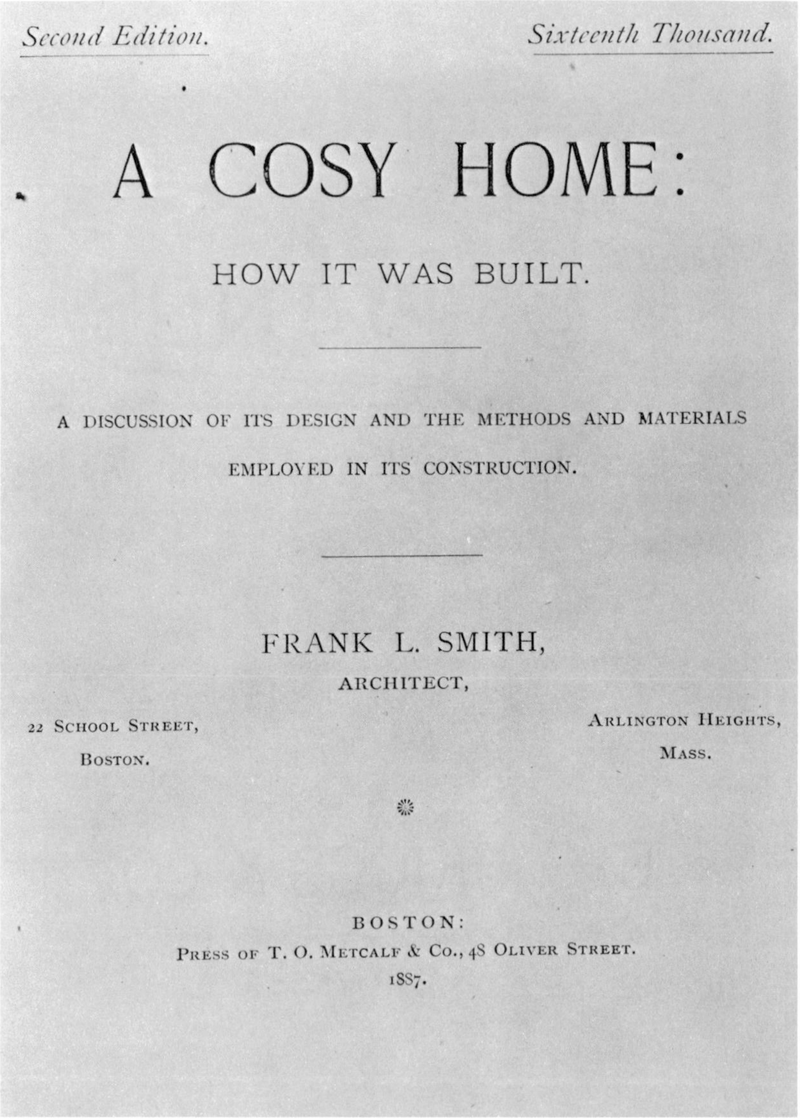

Second Edition.   *Sixteenth Thousand.*

A COSY HOME:

HOW IT WAS BUILT.

A DISCUSSION OF ITS DESIGN AND THE METHODS AND MATERIALS

EMPLOYED IN ITS CONSTRUCTION.

FRANK L. SMITH,

ARCHITECT,

22 SCHOOL STREET,   ARLINGTON HEIGHTS,

BOSTON.   MASS.

BOSTON:

PRESS OF T. O. METCALF & CO., 48 OLIVER STREET.

1887.

Fig. 19. Title page from Frank L. Smith, *A Cosy Home: How It Was Built* (2d ed.; Boston: T. O. Metcalf, 1887). H. 6¾″, W. 5½″. (Winterthur Library.)

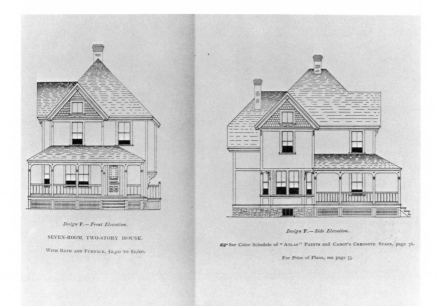

Fig. 20. Designs for elevations of a seven-room, two-story house. From Frank L. Smith, *A Cosy Home: How It Was Built* (2d ed.; Boston: T. O. Metcalf, 1887), pp. 30–31. (Winterthur Library.)

with a home of one's own had not changed that much, nor did its visual presentation change quickly. The literature remained conservative, and it plagiarized itself repeatedly. It tended to present few surprises to its largely middle class audience and to clothe itself in reassuringly ordinary illustrative style—I feel, with intent. Although these illustrations embodied a succession of dream houses, to present them in a manner that did not suggest, threateningly, great sums of money to acquire seems to have been a soothing sales tool. The camera, too, can lie in the service of salesmanship, and today's descendants of these earlier volumes can be found, not on the coffee table, but on the newsstand—still professing ideals, conveying technical information, and selling a good thing.

The Arts and Crafts Book in America

Susan Otis Thompson

AMERICAN PRINTING IN THE 1890s and the early years of this century derived its most visible and distinctive style from the arts and crafts movement. The arts and crafts style was more quickly and dramatically adopted than almost any other style in the history of printing. This period at the turn of the century was outstanding not only in American printing history but also internationally. Within that context, American printers as a group achieved for the first time a position of world renown and leadership. Carl Purington Rollins noted, "from 1890 to 1914 the spirit of adventure seized the printers, [and] . . . in no similar length of time was so much interesting and stimulating work issued from the American press."[1] We see the beginnings in these years of the careers of what may be termed the heroic generation of American artist-craftsmen: Rollins, Daniel Berkeley Updike, Bruce Rogers, Frederic W. Goudy, W. A. Dwiggins, Will Ransom, Dard Hunter, Will H. Bradley, and Thomas Maitland Cleland. They all started out in the arts and crafts style, although they moved on later, for the most part, to more re-strained and classical traditions.

This arts and crafts style is associated with the influence of William Morris's Kelmscott Press and is thus part of what is called the

---

[1] For a lengthier discussion of American book printing, see Susan Otis Thompson, *American Book Design and William Morris* (New York: R. R. Bowker, 1977). Carl Purington Rollins, "The Golden Age of American Printing," *New Colophon* 2, pt. 7 (September 1949): 299–300.

Kelmscott revival of fine printing.[2] Much has been written favorably about this return of printing to artistic principles, but the style itself has often been maligned. Perhaps the time has come for reevaluation.

Most people are familiar with the arts and crafts movement of England that developed in reaction to the decorative excesses and dehumanizing conditions of the industrial revolution in the Victorian period. Morris, as a young man at Oxford in the 1850s, was deeply influenced by the medieval elements of romanticism that we call the Gothic revival, especially as formulated in the writings of John Ruskin, and to some extent exemplified by Dante Gabriel Rossetti and his followers, the Pre-Raphaelites. Morris flirted with a career in the church, then in architecture, then in painting. But when he married Jane Burden in 1859 and had Red House built for him by Philip Webb, it seemed a natural development for him to form a company with some of his friends. This company would provide items of interior decoration for clients with tastes that favored what he and his friends had furnished for Red House.[3]

Morris, Marshall, Faulkner, and Company, with its medievalistic merchandise, had almost immediate success. The emphasis was on handicrafts, the philosophical basis for which was derived from Carlyle, Pugin, and Ruskin. The machine was a dehumanizing agent that debased both the workman and the product; only by the methods of the Middle Ages, when workmen designed and single-handedly crafted their work, were the results worthy of approbation, aesthetically and morally. The company's goods and services were expensive but became very popular among the English upper classes, and gradually during the ensuing decades of the nineteenth century a whole movement grew out of the initial impetus of Red House. This movement stood for unity of design and manufacture, integrity of materials, and respect for the historical Gothic, although a more modern idiom actually replaced the Gothicism.

[2] For more information on Kelmscott Press, see Henry Halliday Sparling, *The Kelmscott Press and William Morris: Master-Craftsman* (London: Macmillan Publishing Co., 1924).

[3] For more information on Morris's life, see J. W. Mackail, *The Life of William Morris*, 2 vols. (London: Longmans, Green, 1899); and Philip Henderson, *William Morris: His Life, Work and Friends* (New York: McGraw-Hill, 1967).

There were followers in other nations, especially in America. The catalogue of the 1972 Princeton exhibition on the American arts and crafts movement takes 1876 as the beginning of a movement, properly speaking, in the United States because of the International Centennial Exhibition in Philadelphia and because H. H. Richardson adopted the Queen Anne style of architecture in the mid 1870s. Robert Judson Clark, the organizer of the exhibition, divided the American arts and crafts movement into three periods: 1876–93, a time of British and Oriental influences; 1893–1901, a time of national self-confidence stemming from the World's Columbian Exposition in Chicago and the heyday of the movement with arts and crafts societies being established throughout the country; and 1901–16, the years between the Pan-American Exposition and the American entrance into World War I, often referred to as the "Craftsman" movement since *Craftsman* magazine was the chief spokesman for that generation of designers. It ceased publication in December 1916.[4]

The timetable for printing corresponds roughly to this outline. Predecessors of the arts and crafts style can be recognized in the 1880s; the early 1890s were years of the style's formation by the printing avant-garde, mainly in Boston; after 1895, when American Type Founders Company (ATF) released the Jenson typeface for sale, there was a wave of arts and crafts printing from commercial presses and trade publishers; just at the turn of the century the private-press wave began. Arts and crafts as a printing style largely died out in the years before the First World War.

Morris, from early in his career, was interested in fine books as well as buildings. But it was the Kelmscott Press itself that provided the catalyst for a full-fledged style of book design that can be designated arts and crafts. The story of the founding of the press is well known. On a famous night in 1888 at the Arts and Crafts Exhibition Society, Emery Walker showed lantern slides of enlarged fifteenth-century typefaces and inspired Morris to take up neoincunabular bookmaking on a serious scale. Morris designed a roman typeface, had it

[4] Robert Judson Clark, ed., *The Arts and Crafts Movement in America, 1876–1916* (Princeton, N.J.: Princeton Art Museum, 1972).

cut and cast, bought an Albion press, installed it in Hammersmith near Kelmscott House, hired workmen, had special paper made, ordered ink from abroad, and in 1891 issued his own *Story of the Glittering Plain* in a limited edition.[5]

There were other influences leading up to the developed arts and crafts style of the nineties. The most obvious of these is the Gothic-revival book itself. During the middle decades of the century, there were many books published that actually copied in chromolithography the illuminations of manuscripts and incorporated Gothic details into other areas of book design. This neo-Gothic style continued to a diminished extent throughout the century.[6]

Less important, there was also a style called "antique," which reflected the general love of historicism, of anything from the past, and used "antique" details from early printing up to the neoclassical style of the eighteenth century. Antique printing was largely a jobbing style but was not unheard of in books.[7]

Related to this was the pseudocrude "chapbook" style of Joseph Crawhall and Andrew Tuer at Leadenhall Press, especially in Crawhall's books. These imitated in a self-consciously sophisticated fashion the old-time woodcut-illustrated tracts hawked by wandering salesmen.

There was also in the eighties a strong movement toward typographical design by prominent artists, such as Herbert Horne, A. H. Mackmurdo, Walter Crane, and the Americans Howard Pyle and Elihu Vedder.

Finally, two major trends were significant background influences. One has already been mentioned: the revolt against machines, which had taken over all aspects of bookmaking. The nineteenth century gave us power presses, mechanized binding with cloth, papermaking, typecasting and typesetting, and photography. In the realm of bookmaking this was particularly evident in the reaction to the books of

[5] See Joseph R. Dunlap, "The Road to Kelmscott" (D.L.S. diss., School of Library Service, Columbia University, 1972).

[6] For the best coverage of this style, see Ruari McLean, *Victorian Book Design and Colour Printing* (2d ed.; Berkeley: University of California Press, 1972).

[7] Vivian Ridler, "Artistic Printing: A Search for Principles," *Alphabet and Image*, no. 6 (January 1948): 4–17.

the so-called cheap publishers.[8] Before the International Copyright Act of 1891 was passed, many American publishers took advantage of the lack of control to turn out books of popular English authors without paying royalties. They also made the formats as inexpensive as possible so that prices could be kept down in answer to the new mass market of industrial civilization. The result, of course, was hideous books deplored by those interested in physical appearance. The ability to provide cheap decoration by mechanical means was also overused in the Victorian period and deplored by many.

The other large, nineteenth-century trend, bibliophily, relates to this interest in format. There were perhaps more conscious book lovers in the sense of caring about formats a century ago than there are today. The combination of printing and art was much discussed among professional printers as well as among collectors and was more than a historical interest. Arthur W. Turnure's periodical, the *Art Age*, published in New York in the 1880s, was almost entirely devoted to the theory of artistic printing. The professional printers' journals also stressed it.

Thus it was that the printing world seemed to be waiting for the catalyst that triggered the arts and crafts period. Morris was already well known to American graphic artists, and when *The Story of the Glittering Plain* came out in 1891 the reaction was enormous. It was made available in photographic reproduction from Roberts Brothers in Boston, Morris's American publishers, as well as being imported from Kelmscott Press. The many press comments were only the tip of the iceberg—printers soon began to copy Morris's style, thus setting off this dramatic episode in the history of book design. Later Kelmscott books continued the style and were circulated in America. One was even jointly published by Way and Williams of Chicago: Rossetti's *Hand and Soul* in Golden type (fig. 1).

The arts and crafts style, as it evolved in the hands of American printers, can be precisely defined. This is the style not of the Kelmscott books themselves, but of the books influenced by them. Materials are the first consideration. The binding could be paper boards with a cloth

[8] See Raymond H. Shove, *Cheap Book Production in the United States, 1870 to 1891* (Urbana: University of Illinois Library, 1937).

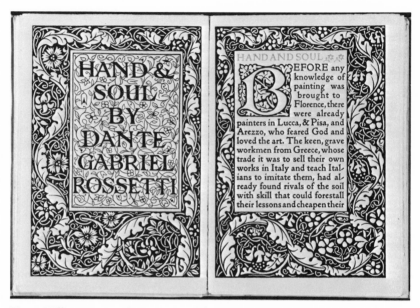

Fig. 1. William Morris, designer, spread from Dante Gabriel Rossetti, *Hand and Soul* (Hammersmith: Kelmscott Press, 1895). H. 5⅝″, W. 8″. (Rare Book and Manuscript Library, Columbia University.)

backstrip, limp or stiff vellum, often with silk ties, or blind-stamped leather with raised bands and sometimes with clasps. The paper tended to be white, thickish, handmade, and laid, with watermarks and deckle edges. Usually the endpapers were plain. Black ink was used in contrast to the white paper, and red was frequently used as a second color, especially for title pages, large initials, and shoulder notes. Sometimes another color, such as blue or green, would be used.

Second, there is the question of design. The typeface was often one modeled after Nicolas Jenson's fifteenth-century type by way of Morris's Golden type, or some other old-style typeface such as Caslon might be used. Gothic was often employed for display and sometimes for texts. But there was an avoidance of italic or modern-style type. The title page was often a spread, with woodcut borders, initials and ornaments, and Gothic lettering, sometimes on a background of arabesque or foliate tracery. If type was used, there was often a block arrangement of words, all caps, flush left and right, with fleuron line fillers. Sometimes the title page would be relegated to frontispiece treatment opposite the incipit page or abbreviated to a "label title" telling only the subject of the book. The half title tended to be in caps, flush left, in the upper left-hand corner of the page; the table of contents and other preliminaries in caps, arranged in block form.

In the text layout, lines would be closely spaced without leading. Fleurons were often used as line fillers and for new paragraphs, instead of indentations. Both pages of an opening would be regarded as one unit, with the margins in this order of increasing width: gutter, head, fore, tail. Running titles were set not as headlines, but as shoulder notes. Decorated initials were used at the beginning of sections, with the adjacent text lines in caps. Illustrations would be black-and-white woodcuts, usually within borders. Woodcut borders were sometimes used for all text pages.

The colophons in these books were especially important, often giving more information than on the title page as to the facts of production, including the names of the artists and craftsmen involved, and sometimes couched in archaic language. The text would usually be all in caps, block set with fleurons and a woodcut printer's device.

Other aspects of arts and crafts books included heavy inking and impressions for the presswork; a full range of sizes and shapes for the format; a small, limited edition with numbered, signed copies, produced by hand methods; and for subject matter, medievalistic texts, literary classics such as *Sonnets from the Portuguese*, works of bibliophily, and hitherto unpublished belles lettres.

This description shows how medieval the arts and crafts books appeared. Their makers, in copying Morris, were also copying German incunabula, the printed books of the fifteenth century from northern Europe, where printing was born, which in turn had copied the Gothic manuscripts of the late Middle Ages. The earliest printed books of the West were based on the latest examples of the preceding technology. At the beginning of the twentieth century, just as mechanization was completing its takeover of all the processes of bookmaking, there arose a style harking back to the earlier period in protest against the dehumanizing of the book by machines.

There was another prominent book style at the turn of the century which has been dubbed the "aesthetic," after the artistic movement—

that of Pater, Wilde, and Whistler—that used it. The style is opposed to the arts and crafts in that it takes the Renaissance books of the sixteenth century as its basic model: small format, small type, italic and old style, wide leading and margins, little decoration except for a few Renaissance headpieces and initials. The flavor of this style is classical restraint, in contrast to the romantic exuberance of arts and crafts. It was used by Chiswick Press in England and by John Lane at Bodley Head and has come over into twentieth-century printing as a longer-lasting influence than arts and crafts.[9] Incidentally, both arts and crafts and aesthetic were, in a sense, part of the larger picture of art nouveau and had art-nouveau ornament applied to them at times.

The first important figure among the avant-garde leaders of printing in the American arts and crafts movement was Daniel Berkeley Updike, in the days before he became America's most famous printer. The first book he was responsible for designing is *On the Dedications of American Churches*, printed at Riverside Press in Cambridge, Massachusetts, in 1891. It was paid for by his wealthy friend from Providence, Harold Brown, who later also financed the famous *Altar Book* of 1896. The woodcut that accompanies the inverted-triangle title is repeated as a tailpiece with a medievalistic Latin colophon (fig. 2). The text is in Franklin old-style type with running titles in Gothic. The edition was 500, of which 150 were printed on large paper, the whole for private distribution. It was given a favorable notice in the first issue of the *Knight Errant*, a Boston periodical issued by other leaders of the avant-garde.[10]

Riverside Press was owned by Houghton Mifflin and Company, for whom Updike worked. In fact, 1891 was the year he moved to the press itself. The complete list of books that he designed for Houghton Mifflin is not known; however, he referred to one in a prospectus—*A Day at Laguerre's* by F. Hopkinson Smith (fig. 3). This is the first American book found so far that clearly indicates that the designer had seen *The Story of the Glittering Plain*. The artwork is

[9] For more information, see Elizabeth Aslin, *The Aesthetic Movement: Prelude to Art Nouveau* (New York: Praeger Publishers, 1969).

[10] For an account of Updike's career, see *Updike: American Printer and His Merrymount Press* (New York: American Institute of Graphic Arts, 1947).

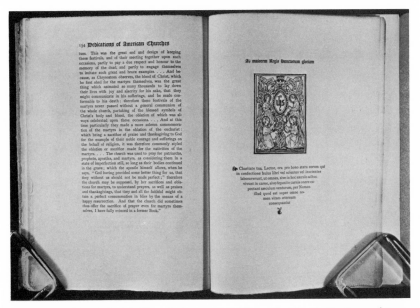

Fig. 2. Daniel Berkeley Updike, designer, spread from *On the Dedications of American Churches* (Cambridge: Riverside Press, 1891). H. 9⅞", W. 14½". (Rare Book and Manuscript Library, Columbia University.)

probably by J. E. Hill, who worked for Updike on other projects. There are floriated initials at the beginnings of the stories and shoulder-note running titles.

Updike issued a series of prospectuses when he left Houghton Mifflin to set up his own office in Boston. These, too, are in the arts and crafts style. The first one, a four-page folder dated 1893, *To the Trade*, has a border and an initial also probably by Hill. The text states: "Limited editions of attractive little books of poems or essays printed on hand-made paper, with initials and bordered title-pages, in the modern aesthetic English style, he makes a specialty."[11]

The next circular, dated October 15, 1894, *A Few Words about Printing, Book Making, and Their Allied Arts*, has decorated initials and shoulder notes and is composed in the new American Type Founders' Jenson, the first commercial type modeled on Morris's Golden

[11][D. B. Updike], *To the Trade* (Boston: Merrymount Press, 1893), p. [2], Rare Book and Manuscript Library, Columbia University.

Fig. 3. Daniel Berkeley Updike, designer, title page from F. Hopkinson Smith, *A Day at Laguerre's and Other Days Being Nine Sketches* (Boston and New York: Houghton Mifflin, Riverside Press, 1892). H. 7″, W. 4½″. (Susan Otis Thompson.)

type. This folder may be the first published use of Golden type, which was not released to the trade for sale until early 1895. Updike had intended to use the type in the *Altar Book*, but Joseph Phinney of Dickinson Type Foundry in Boston, who was responsible for its manufacture, had released it for use to the University Press at Cambridge. Updike turned to Bertram Grosvenor Goodhue to design another face based on Golden, called Merrymount.

The text of this 1894 circular is also ground-breaking, for it is perhaps the first announcement of the new profession of book designer: "there are arising on every side, workers whose place is not that of the man by whom a printer's work is used, nor of the printer himself, but of one, who, by a knowledge of the requirements of clients on the one hand, and the abilities of the printer on the other, is able to produce a better result than either could do alone."[12]

The final circular is the announcement of Merrymount Press itself, dated November 25, 1895, with a woodcut by Mary J. Newill.[13] Updike would no longer be dependent on using presses in other printing offices.

The first publisher to make a specialty of arts and crafts books was the new Copeland and Day of Boston. This was one of the so-called literary publishers of the 1890s, a group that also included the famous Stone and Kimball of Cambridge and Chicago. These were small houses run by idealistic young men to publish contemporary literature in pleasing formats at moderate prices. Copeland and Day's first book was the 1893, privately distributed *Decadent*, put out anonymously but known to be by architect Ralph Adams Cram. The artwork was by his friend and architect Goodhue, who had done the cover for the *Knight Errant* and was to do other fine works of graphic art in the arts and crafts style.

The first book of Copeland and Day for actual publication was Rossetti's *House of Life*, printed in a limited edition by the University

[12] [D. B. Updike], *A Few Words about Printing, Bookmaking, and Their Allied Arts* (Boston: Merrymount Press, 1894), p. [1], Rare Book and Manuscript Library, Columbia University.

[13] [D. B. Updike], *Merrymount* (Boston: Merrymount Press, 1895). Another arts and crafts circular was [D. B. Updike], *To the Clergy and Laity of the Episcopal Church and to All Others Who Are Interested in Ecclesiastical Printing: Greeting* (Boston: Merrymount Press, 1894/95). Both in the Rare Book and Manuscript Library, Columbia University.

Press with decorations by Goodhue (fig. 4). It is the first of four in the English Love Sonnet Series, which also included Wilfred Scawen Blunt, Elizabeth Barrett Browning, and Shakespeare (fig. 5). They all were decorated by Goodhue in a manner directly based on Kelmscott but showing Goodhue's originality. The type is Bookman, or Antique Old Style, a roman face that goes back to the mid nineteenth century but was much used at the turn of the century because its heavy, almost equally weighted lines seemed to go well with the heavy lines of arts and crafts woodcuts.

Still another Goodhue–Copeland and Day item is Louise Imogen Guiney's *Nine Sonnets Written at Oxford*, for distribution to friends at Christmas 1895 (fig. 6). It is a tiny pamphlet in Bookman with an astonishing amount of Gothic decoration. The use of leaves as line fillers, typical of the period, is particularly spotty in these pages; nonetheless, Goodhue's artwork makes it an attractive little book.

Bruce Rogers was another important member of the arts and crafts avant-garde. He started out in Indianapolis, where in 1890 he met Joseph M. Bowles. In 1893 Bowles began publishing *Modern Art*, a magazine that was a major carrier for the gospel of arts and crafts as applied to printing. While still in Indianapolis, they worked together on R. B. Gruelle's *Notes: Critical and Biographical*, in which they deliberately adapted Morris's style and used Bookman type. When Bowles moved to Boston in 1895 because lithographers Louis Prang and Company had agreed to underwrite the publication of *Modern Art*, he began to put the magazine out in arts and crafts dress based on the style he and Rogers had evolved.[14]

Rogers followed Bowles to Boston and did some free-lance work for the literary publishers, including another arts and crafts book for Way and Williams. *The Banquet of Plato* was printed at Lakeside Press in Clarendon type, with outline vine initials and tailpieces in Rogers's *Modern Art* manner (fig. 7). In 1896 Rogers went to work for Riverside Press, where he supervised book design and in 1900

[14] For Rogers's ideas on printing, see Bruce Rogers, *Pi: A Hodge-Podge of the Letters, Papers, and Addresses Written during the Last Sixty Years* (Cleveland: World Publishing Co., 1953).

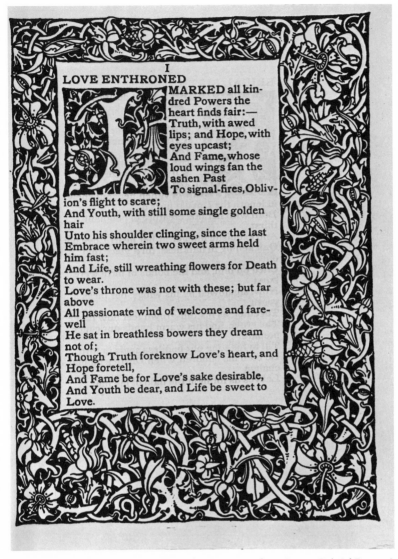

Fig. 4. Bertram Grosvenor Goodhue, designer, page from Dante Gabriel Rossetti, *The House of Life* (Boston: Copeland and Day, 1894). H. 8¼", W. 6¼". (Rare Book and Manuscript Library, Columbia University.)

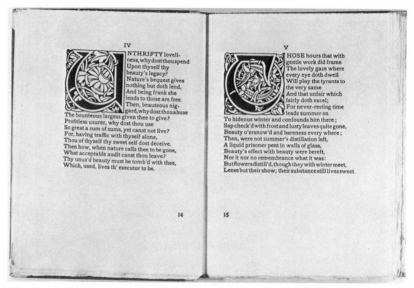

Fig. 5. Bertram Grosvenor Goodhue, designer, spread from *Shakespeare's Sonnets* (Boston: Copeland and Day, 1897). H. 7⅛", W. 11¼". (Susan Otis Thompson.)

Fig. 6. Bertram Grosvenor Goodhue, designer, spread from Louise Imogen Guiney, *Nine Sonnets Written at Oxford* (Boston: Copeland and Day, 1895). H. 6", W. 9". (Rare Book and Manuscript Library, Columbia University.)

Fig. 7. Bruce Rogers, designer, title page from Percy Bysshe Shelley, trans., *The Banquet of Plato* (Chicago: Way and Williams, 1895). H. 6½", W. 4⅜". (Joseph R. Dunlap.)

began the series of limited editions that brought him world fame. He also designed two typefaces based on Jenson: Montaigne and Centaur.

Will H. Bradley is the next great figure in the arts and crafts avant-garde. He got his start in Chicago as a conventional artist, but his style was dramatically changed when Aubrey Beardsley's version of Malory's *Morte d'Arthur* was published by Dent in London in 1893. This first book of Beardsley's was in pseudo-Kelmscott style and profoundly influenced the second phase of Bradley's artistic life, as evidenced by his 1895 edition of R. D. Blackmore's *Fringilla* (fig. 8).[15]

Stephen Crane's *War Is Kind* (1899) is one of Bradley's best-known books. Here the Kelmscott influence has largely been left behind, or perhaps replaced by the influence of Charles Ricketts's version of Oscar Wilde's *Sphinx* (1894). This first edition of *War Is Kind* was designed and printed by Bradley at the University Press in 1899 for publisher Frederick A. Stokes of New York (fig. 9). The cover is gray boards printed in black. The whiplash line of *War Is Kind* is less evident than the perpendicular line of a later stage of art nouveau. It is a tall, thin, octavo divided into elongated panels by rules, and the elongated line is repeated in the cover picture by the woman's figure, flowing hair, sword, trees, and vases. The title page resembles the cover with its elongated candles. There are illustrations in the text, but some pages are plain, even without running titles. Most of the decorations are black, which suits the thick gray wove, deckle-edge paper but does not go with the Caslon text type, which is also too thin for the heavy, dark paper. It is a strong, harsh book, not for all tastes, but it suits Crane's poetry.

In 1895 Bradley had left the Chicago area for Springfield, Massachusetts, where he set up his own Wayside Press and published seven numbers of the periodical called *Bradley His Book* (1896–97), inspired by Stone and Kimball's famous *Chap-Book* for which Bradley had done several posters. The July 1896 cover is typical of his colorful art (fig. 10). ATF Jenson is used for the text. The last, unpublished issue was February 1897, with a frontispiece by W. W. Nicholson (fig. 11).

[15] For an autobiographical account, see *Will Bradley: His Chap-Book* (Mount Vernon, N.Y.: Peter Pauper Press, 1955).

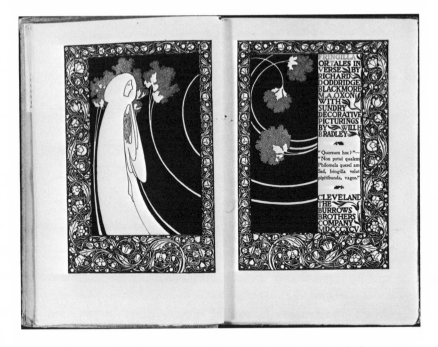

Fig. 8. Will H. Bradley, designer, spread from Richard Doddridge Blackmore, *Fringilla; or, Tales in Verse* (Cleveland: Burrows Brothers Co., 1895). H. 8¾″, W. 12″. (Rare Book and Manuscript Library, Columbia University.)

The *American Chap Book*, done by Bradley for ATF between September 1904 and August 1905, was a series of instruction booklets that influenced a whole generation of American printers. The artwork goes back to arts and crafts in the heavy, blunt, rounded lines and in the close spacing. Decorative and typographic elements are set close when not actually superimposed, leaving little unfilled space. There is an emphasis on color, often muted tones. Tinted paper is often used. Another characteristic is repeated motifs disposed uniformly, especially floral and other plant forms. The headings are often in large type, letter spaced.

With Bradley, we have moved from the avant-garde period to the one when arts and crafts penetrated commercial printing, including general trade-book publishing. This was seen primarily in two ways: the use of Jenson type and the addition of an extra title page on coated paper with a fancy border, not at all related to the text.

Fig. 9. Will H. Bradley, designer, spread from Stephen Crane, *War Is Kind* (New York: Frederick A. Stokes, 1899). H. 8¼″, W. 10¼″. (Rare Book and Manuscript Library, Columbia University.)

There were more sophisticated examples, however. Henry Van Dyke's *Poetry of the Psalms* (1900) shows the arts and crafts style Updike developed for trade publishers Thomas Y. Crowell and Company and used on a series of books traceable from 1897 to at least 1908. The type is Clarendon, which strongly resembles Bookman. There are touches of red ink, decorated initials, woodcut title-page ornaments, and Gothic type for display. In San Francisco, booksellers Paul Elder and Morgan Shepard published modishly artistic books after the turn of the century (fig. 12), occasionally using artists like Goudy.

The late 1890s began the wave of private presses inspired by the example of Kelmscott. One of the most famous graphic designers in America, Thomas Maitland Cleland, began in this way. He saw Kelmscott books in the window of a New York bookstore and began

Fig. 10. Will H. Bradley, designer, cover from *Bradley His Book* 1, no. 3 (July 1896). H. 9⅞″, W. 5″. (Rare Book and Manuscript Library, Columbia University.)

Fig. 11. Will H. Bradley, designer, spread from *Bradley His Book* 2, no. 4 (February

BRADLEY
HIS BOOK
FEBRUARY, 1897. VOL. II. NO. 4

Narcissus. Jean Wright.

THE HAPPY POET PAGANS SUNG AND SAID *
ONCE LIVED A BOY WHOSE GRACIOUS BEAU-
TY MADE ** THIS DARK WORLD RADIANT
FOR A LITTLE SPACE; **** AND ALL WHO
LOOKED UPON HIS PERFECT FACE ** THEY
NEEDS MUST LOVE HIM FOR ITS LOVELINESS.

THUS MANY A NYMPH, WHOSE PASSIONATE
WARM HEART * KNOWING NOT HOW TO CURB
ITS TENDERNESS * BROKE WITH THE WEIGHT
OF UNREQUITED LOVE, ** SIGHED OUT A
PRAYER FOR PITY TO GREAT JOVE, ** THAT
HIS COLD YOUTH BE PIERCED BY EROS' DART.

** VAIN HOPE. FOR AS IT CHANCED UPON A
TIME, * DEEP IN A FOREST POOL, AS CRYSTAL
CLEAR, ** HIMSELF HE SAW, AND HELD NO
OTHER DEAR * THEREAFTER. STERN JUSTICE
WAVERING, * METED A TENDER JUDGEMENT
FOR HIS CRIME; **** EARTH COULD ILL
SPARE SO BEAUTIFUL A THING. * A DELICATE
PURE FLOWER, HE FOR ALL TIME ** WILL
STAR THE WOODLAND IN THE EARLY SPRING.

1897). H. 11″, W. 16″. (Susan Otis Thompson.)

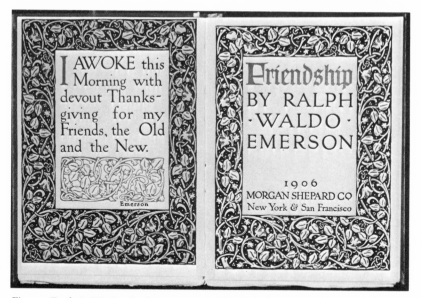

Fig. 12. Frederic W. Goudy, designer, spread from Ralph Waldo Emerson, *Friendship* (New York and San Francisco: Morgan Shepard Co., 1906). H. 6⅛", W. 8¼". (Susan Otis Thompson.)

printing in his father's basement in 1898. A little book, Josephine Preston Peabody's *In the Silence*, was even completed in 100 copies in June 1900. The next one, Tennyson's *Lady of Shalott*, was begun in New York and finished in Boston in September 1900 in 240 copies. The third book, Lady Dilke's *Shrine of Death and the Shrine of Love* (January 1901; 290 copies), has the most arts and crafts characteristics and names Cleland's Cornhill Press in the imprint. The fourth and last book from his Cornhill Press was Florence Housman's *Blind Love* (March 1901; 500 copies).[16]

There were many other small private presses. One of the best known is Clarke Conwell's Elston Press, begun in New York City but soon moved to New Rochelle. His wife, Helen Marguerite O'Kane, was a graphic artist who worked for trade publishers as well as for Elston. Rossetti's *House of Life* is noteworthy for the power of the bold designs successfully enclosed in a relatively small surface (fig. 13).

[16] For an overview of his work, see T. M. Cleland, *The Decorative Work of T. M. Cleland: A Record and Review* (New York: Pynson Printers, 1929).

PART I. YOUTH AND CHANGE. SONNET I. LOVE ENTHRONED.

I MARKED all kindred Powers
the heart finds fair: —
Truth, with awed lips; and
Hope, with eyes up-cast;
And Fame, whose loud wings
fan the ashen Past
To signal-fires, Oblivion's
flight to scare;
And Youth, with still some
single golden hair
Unto his shoulder clinging, since the last
Embrace wherein two sweet arms held him fast;
And Life, still wreathing flowers for Death to wear.
Love's throne was not with these; but far above
All passionate wind of welcome and farewell
He sat in breathless bowers they dream not of;
Though Truth foreknow Love's heart, and Hope foretell,
And Fame be for Love's sake desirable,
And Youth be dear, and Life be sweet to Love.

Fig. 13. Helen Marguerite O'Kane, designer, page from Dante Gabriel Rossetti, *The House of Life* (New Rochelle: Elston Press, 1901). H. 10¼″, W. 7¾″. (Rare Book and Manuscript Library, Columbia University.)

The Elston books are on sumptuous handmade paper, and the inking and presswork are impeccable.

The man who was able to combine the arts and crafts world of the private press and commercial success was Frederic W. Goudy. After working as a bookkeeper, running Booklet and Camelot presses in Chicago, and beginning his prolific career of type designing, Goudy started Village Press in 1903 in Park Ridge, Illinois, with Will Ransom, who had earlier had his own Handcraft Press in Snohomish, Washington. The type used had been designed for a clothing company by Goudy after Golden; when the company did not accept it, he renamed it Village type and used it in all his books before the 1905 *Lyf of Seynt Kenelme*. These books are on handmade paper with wide margins and in limited editions with board bindings and excellent presswork.[17]

Goudy and his wife moved their press in 1904 to Hingham, Massachusetts, where W. A. Dwiggins soon joined them and decorated two books. J. M. Neal's *Good King Wenceslas* (1904) has illustrations by Arthur J. Gaskin and outline vine borders by Dwiggins. Browning's *Rabbi Ben Ezra* (1904) also has a frontispiece illustration by Dwiggins.

There were two publishers at the turn of the century who were not private or trade, but who did more than any others to awaken Americans to the art of the book by mail-order selling of fine editions at low prices to thousands. Thomas Bird Mosher, literary pirate of Portland, Maine, is an anomaly in an arts and crafts chronicle, for his major book style was aesthetic, not arts and crafts. Morris was one of his idols, however, and he published some Kelmscott pastiches. One, Rossetti's *Hand and Soul*, was the seventh in his Miscellaneous Series (fig. 14). He used ATF type and ornaments and ordered Kelmscott paper from England. The binding was blue boards with labels; the editions were 450 at $1.50 and 100 copies on Japan vellum at $2.50. Where he differed from Morris was in printing the initials in red (once done for Blunt's *Love Lyrics* at Kelmscott and abandoned) and in pressing his sheets to take out the type impression.[18]

---

[17] For a review of Goudy's work, see F. W. Goudy, *A Half-Century of Type Design and Typography, 1895–1945* (New York: Typophiles, 1946).

[18] For more information on Mosher, see Norman H. Strouse, *The Passionate Pirate* (North Hills, Pa.: Bird and Bull Press, 1964).

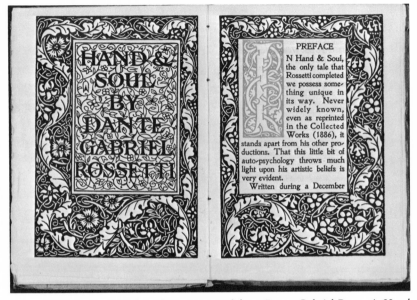

Fig. 14. Thomas Bird Mosher, designer, spread from Dante Gabriel Rossetti, *Hand and Soul* (Portland, Maine: Mosher, 1899). H. 5¾″, W. 8¼″. (Susan Otis Thompson.)

The other popular mail-order publisher was in East Aurora, New York. Elbert Hubbard, a former soap salesman, succeeded in turning his Roycrofters colony into handicrafters of books, furniture, copperware, and modeled leather goods that provided a vastly prosperous business. He became one of the most colorful and controversial lecturers and writers on the American scene before going down with the *Lusitania* in 1915.[19]

Books were the first, and always the most important, of the Roycroft products. Hubbard shipped them out by carloads all over the country where they reposed on innumerable parlor tables. For years these volumes have been derided because of their low prices, Hubbard's own texts which they often reproduced, and their chamois bindings, known as limp ooze, window cleaners, or mouse skin. Many of the books, however, turn out to be not only representative but also

---

[19] The best biography of Hubbard is Freeman Champney, *Art and Glory: The Story of Elbert Hubbard* (New York: Crown Publishers, 1968).

charming examples of the art of the time. They are all on good, hand-made paper imported from Europe. The type for the most part is either Bookman or Caslon. The hand illuminations are amateurish but often pleasing. Fine bindings were available at higher prices. Moreover, the printed designs are by some fine artists. The first of these is the least known today: Samuel Warner, an Englishman who obviously knew the work of Beardsley. In Tennyson's *Maud*, his inspiration is definitely Kelmscott (fig. 15). The type is ATF Satanick, based on Morris's Troy. The paper is beautifully crisp and white, the binding a pleasing shade of burgundy chamois with matching silk doublures and marker. The presswork is superb, and the taste used in putting the book together extends to the fine touch of printing the title in a darker red than usual, to match the binding. W. W. Denslow, who became famous and rich as the illustrator of the *Wizard of Oz* (1900), designed books for Hubbard and did many well-known cartoons for the *Philistine*, Hubbard's controversial magazine (fig. 16).

The third major designer arrived at East Aurora in 1903 at the age of nineteen from Chillicothe, Ohio. Dard Hunter came as an admirer of Hubbard but later disavowed his own work for the Roycrofters because he felt it was meretricious. Today his books seem a genuine expression of American art nouveau, especially as influenced by Vienna. The style is visible in *Respectability: Its Rise and Remedy*, possibly an example of his work (fig. 17), while his signed *Justinian and Theodora* has been called the Roycroft masterpiece (fig. 18).[20]

The end of the arts and crafts movement in bookmaking came in the early twentieth century when printers changed their allegiance from the German incunabular style of Kelmscott to the Italian incunabular style of Thomas James Cobden-Sanderson's Doves Press. In the 1906 Boston Society of Printers' exhibition catalogue called *The Development of Printing as an Art*, Updike and Rogers put this into words: "during the last few years the somewhat Gothic feeling of the Kelmscott Press books has been slowly abandoned for the lighter and more classical styles of type founded on Italian models of the

---

[20]For more information on Hunter's stay in East Aurora, see Dard Hunter, *My Life with Paper* (New York: Alfred A. Knopf, 1958).

HATE the dread-
ful hollow behind
the little wood,
Its lips in the field
above are dabbled
with blood-red
heath,
The red-ribb'd
ledges drip with a
silent horror of
blood,
And Echo there, whatever is ask'd her,
answers "Death."

For there in the ghastly pit long since a
body was found,
His who had given me life—O father!
O God! was it well?—
Mangled, and flatten'd, and crush'd, and
dinted into the ground:
There yet lies the rock that fell with
him when he fell.

Did he fling himself down? who knows?
for a vast speculation had fail'd,
And ever he mutter'd and madden'd, and
ever wann'd with despair,
And out he walk'd when the wind like a
broken worldling wail'd
And the flying gold of the ruin'd wood-
lands drove thro' the air.

Fig. 15. Samuel Warner, designer, page from Alfred Tennyson, *Maud* (East Aurora: Roycrofters, 1900). H. 7¾", W. 5". (Susan Otis Thompson.)

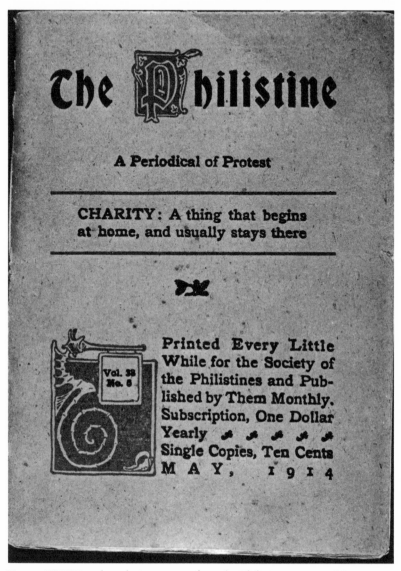

Fig. 16. W. W. Denslow, designer, cover from the *Philistine* 38, no. 5 (May 1914).
H. 6″, W. 4½″. (Susan Otis Thompson.)

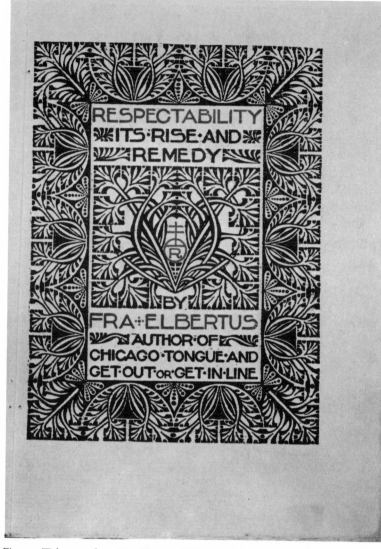

Fig. 17. Title page from Fra Elbertus [Elbert Hubbard], *Respectability: Its Rise and Remedy* (East Aurora: Roycrofters, 1905). H. 7¾″, W. 5½″. (Susan Otis Thompson.)

Fig. 18. Dard Hunter, designer, spread from Elbert and Alice Hubbard, *Justinian and Theodora: A Drama Being a Chapter of History and the One Gleam of Light during the Dark Ages* (East Aurora: Roycrofters, 1906). H. 7¾″, W. 11½″. (Winterthur Library.)

fifteenth century — a movement in which The Doves Press, London, has been chiefly instrumental."[21] John Henry Nash, famous printer of San Francisco, for many years did indeed closely follow the Doves style. The general influence of arts and crafts in the sense of regarding printing as an art is still with us, however, even in an age when computers seem to be taking over.

[21] *The Development of Printing as an Art* (Boston: Boston Society of Printers, 1906), p. 20.

Drawn in Ink

Book Illustrations by Howard Pyle

Elizabeth H. Hawkes

URING HIS THIRTY-YEAR CAREER, Howard Pyle (1853–1911) became one of America's most popular illustrators as well as a successful writer, teacher, and mural painter (fig. 1). More than three thousand of his illustrations were published in a host of magazines and in over a hundred books ranging from school primers to histories of the United States by such eminent writers as Henry Cabot Lodge and Woodrow Wilson. His drawings embellished the novels and poetry of such diverse writers as Alfred Tennyson, William Makepeace Thackeray, Robert Louis Stevenson, William Dean Howells, and Arthur Conan Doyle.

Pyle himself wrote twenty-one books dealing with a variety of subjects, including folklore, the Middle Ages, colonial America, and pirates and the sea. His specialty was children's fiction. Many of his books were compiled from stories that first appeared in popular magazines. At the turn of the century, novels were frequently serialized in magazines and then published as books. Also, collections of short stories and poems, which first appeared in magazines, were sometimes issued later in book form.

Working in several media—ink, oil, gouache, and watercolor— Pyle experimented with different techniques that might provide for better-quality reproductions on the printed page. Nearly all the books he wrote were decorated either partially or entirely with ink drawings.

Fig. 1. Photographic portrait of Howard Pyle (1853–1911), ca. 1897. (Howard Pyle Collection, Delaware Art Museum.)

Most of the books he illustrated for other authors were in ink or black and white oil until about 1900, when publishers began to commission colored oils to satisfy the public's appetite for color printing made possible by technological innovations.

By reviewing the books he illustrated in ink, it is possible not only to trace the stylistic development of his work but also to examine some of the artistic influences that helped to shape his style. Although he approached both magazine and book illustration in a similar way, for the purposes of this essay the discussion will be limited to his ink drawings published in books.

Born in Wilmington, Delaware, in 1853, Howard Pyle began his art training at the age of sixteen at a small art school in Philadelphia under Belgian-trained Adolph van der Wielen.[1] After three years of study, he returned to Wilmington to work for the family leather business and at the same time began to submit poems and illustrated stories to *Scribner's Magazine*. In 1876, shortly after his first work was published in *Scribner's*, Pyle decided to move to New York to be closer to the publishers and to study there. He was in New York for three years, returning in 1879 to Wilmington where he continued his career as an illustrator.

Pyle's first book illustrations were gouache drawings printed in a children's textbook, *McGuffey's Fifth Eclectic Reader*, published by Van Antwerp, Bragg of Cincinnati in 1879. These drawings, still youthful and not very distinguished, accompanied stories by Nathaniel Hawthorne and Charles Dickens. The textbooks, unlike those of today, emphasized reading aloud and had drills on articulation, inflection, and poetic pauses.

The first opportunity to illustrate a complete book came in 1881 when Pyle was commissioned by Dodd, Mead, and Company to provide colored drawings for two children's books: *Yankee Doodle: An Old Friend in a New Dress* (the nursery-rhyme song) and Tennyson's *Lady of Shalott*. For these books Pyle made line drawings in ink and colored them with watercolor. These drawings were reminiscent of the nursery-book illustrations by English artists Walter Crane, Kate Greenaway, and Randolph Caldecott. Since the English books were so popular in America, Dodd, Mead tried to emulate the style and hoped to capture the American market.

Pyle's first serious and successful effort at book illustration was *The Merry Adventures of Robin Hood* published by Scribner's in

---

[1] There has been confusion as to the identification and proper spelling of the name of Howard Pyle's teacher. Charles David Abbott, *Howard Pyle, a Chronicle* (New York: Harper and Brothers, 1925), p. 11, identified Pyle's teacher as "Mr. Van der Weilen," and this name continues to appear in recent publications about Pyle. According to the 1872 Philadelphia City Directory, however, artist F. A. van der Wielen resided at 1334 Chestnut St. Van der Wielen (1843–76) is listed in both Bénézit and Thieme-Becker as a Belgian painter who studied in Antwerp and worked in Philadelphia. For a description of Van der Wielen's school, see Cecilia Beaux's autobiography, *Background with Figures* (Boston: Houghton Mifflin Co., 1930), and *Cecilia Beaux: Portrait of an Artist* (Philadelphia: Pennsylvania Academy of the Fine Arts, 1974). The name is misspelled as Van der Whelen in these publications; however, in *Beaux*, a drawing is inscribed "after F. A. van der Wielen, Feb. 26th 1873" (cat. 2). This further confirms the correct spelling.

1883. Pyle wrote the text by retelling the old English folk tale in a quaint but very readable style. He had first conceived of using the Robin Hood theme for a book while studying in New York and had written to his mother asking to borrow her copy of Thomas Percy's *Reliques of Ancient English Poetry* which she had read to him during his childhood. Percy recounted some of the adventures of Robin Hood, as did Joseph Ritson in his eighteenth-century anthology of old English ballads, which also served as a source for Pyle's modern version.[2]

Pyle's *Robin Hood* features twenty-three full-page drawings, and many of the chapters are decorated with headpieces and tailpieces. Many of the illustrations have decorative floral borders reminiscent of the work of designer and book illustrator Walter Crane, in particular his *Grimms' Household Stories*, a collection of fairy tales published in England in 1882, coincidentally one year before Pyle's *Robin Hood*. It is very likely that Pyle knew of this work by Crane, who was a leading figure in the English arts and crafts movement in the last half of the nineteenth century and whose work was highly regarded by Pyle.

The illustrations for *Robin Hood* are packed with details of the English countryside as Pyle imagined it: stone castles, half-timbered inns, and dense forests. The final chapter of the book tells of the death of Robin Hood. After coming down with a fever, he seeks aid at a nunnery and then, bedridden, shoots his last arrow and dies with his steadfast friend, Little John, at his side (fig. 2).

The book became a landmark in American publishing and reflects the impact of the English arts and crafts movement. Following arts and crafts ideas, Pyle conceived the book as an aesthetic whole, in which the illustrations, text, typeface, and binding were unified in style and concept. Instead of being cut by hand on woodblocks by engravers as was common during the early 1880s and as was done in Crane's books, however, Pyle's line drawings were photographed onto metal plates and mechanically engraved. In this way he took full advantage of recent technological developments in printing. This new process eliminated the need for a middle step, in which engravers redrew and possibly changed the artist's designs. *Robin Hood* was published in

[2]Abbott, *Pyle*, p. 114.

Fig. 2. Howard Pyle, *Robin Shooteth His Last Shaft*, 1883. Ink on paper; H. 9½",
W. 6¾". For Howard Pyle, *The Merry Adventures of Robin Hood* (New York: Charles
Scribner's Sons, 1883). (Central Children's Room, Donnell Library Center, New York
Public Library.) The curved bracket at the left side of the enclosed wall shelf is based
on a similar one in Dürer's *St. Jerome in His Cell* (fig. 5).

England as well as America, and, according to Joseph Pennell, even William Morris was greatly impressed and surprised that something artistically good had finally come out of America.[3]

Robin Hood was followed by another tale inspired by medieval times, *Otto of the Silver Hand* (1888), also published by Scribner's. This tender story tells of a gentle, motherless boy raised in a peaceful monastery by monks and then returned to his father's castle in a Germany divided by warring factions. There, Otto learns firsthand about the evil ways of greedy, vengeful men.

In his drawings for the medieval stories *Robin Hood*, *Otto of the Silver Hand*, and his later King Arthur books, Pyle tried to create historically accurate settings, costumes, and architecture. To achieve this accuracy, he referred to prints by fifteenth- and sixteenth-century artists such as Albrecht Dürer, Hans Burgkmair, Lucas Cranach, and Hans Holbein. Pyle owned Georg Hirth's *Bilderbuch*, a six-volume collection of reproductions of old master prints selected to illustrate the history and customs in Europe from the sixteenth to the eighteenth century.[4] Also in Pyle's library were books on knighthood, armor, alphabets, ornament, costumes, furniture, and architecture, all of which served as valuable source material for his illustrations.

Some of the objects and designs that appear in Pyle's drawings for *Otto of the Silver Hand*, as well as for other book illustrations of the 1880s, can be traced directly to the *Bilderbuch*. For example, the composition of his illustration of Abbot Otto is very similar to Dürer's *Erasmus of Rotterdam*, although reversed. A number of the objects in the Otto drawing were based on Dürer's engraving of *St. Jerome in His Cell*, such as the decorative edge of the table leg, hourglass, crucifix, stuffed pillows, and even the glass in the casement window (figs. 3, 4, 5).

Then, when Pyle wanted to include some domestic items in the scene showing the old nurse Ursela holding baby Otto after his mother had died, he turned to Dürer's woodcut *Birth of the Virgin* (*Bilderbuch*, pl. 7) for such details as the two-handled bucket, the weave (although

---

[3] Joseph Pennell, *Graphic Arts* (Chicago: University of Chicago Press, 1920), p. 92.
[4] *Kulturgeschichtliches Bilderbuch aus Drei Jahrhunderten*, ed. Georg Hirth, 6 vols. (Leipzig, 1881–90).

not the shape) of the sewing basket, and the pitcher. The women in the Dürer print are also holding children, although none is in the same pose as Ursela.

During the mid 1880s Pyle wrote and illustrated many short fables, fairy tales, and poems based on old folk legends which were first published in the children's magazine *Harper's Young People* and featured princesses, kings, animals that talk, and even trolls. Most of these stories were collected in book form and marketed for the Christmas trade. Pyle's first collection of fairy tales was *Pepper and Salt* (1886). The cover of the book is embellished with an adaptation of a medieval illuminated letter, and the frontispiece shows a jester (who looks remarkably like Pyle as a young man) playing a pipe and reading to a group of children seated nearby. The preface shows the same jester standing by a castle inviting children to have a "little pinch of seasoning [pepper and salt, obviously] in this dull, heavy life of ours." The stories are interspersed with poems which are hand lettered and decorated with drawings.

The stories usually end with a moral such as in the poem "Pride in Distress" (fig. 6), in which Mistress Polly Poppenjay who "held her head aloft with pride" failed to see a large puddle of water in her pathway and plunged into it. Pyle closed with a warning to curb one's pride.

The *Pepper and Salt* drawings vary in subject from the Middle Ages to the eighteenth century and are indebted to Pyle's close study of the Crane and Greenaway toy books. Like Crane, he successfully incorporated the hand-lettered texts of the poem and the captions with the drawings.

Following *Pepper and Salt* came another collection of stories from *Harper's Young People* called *The Wonder Clock*, in which twenty-four tales (one for each hour of the day) are told by old Father Time and his still-older grandmother. The drawings are full of Pyle's stock fairy tale characters: handsome princes, old bearded kings, long-haired princesses dressed in richly ornamented costumes, the evil and ugly stepmother, the fumbling soldier, and a host of magical, otherworldly figures such as the half-bird–half-man creatures, giants, dwarfs, ogres, and a host of talking animals.

Fig. 3. Howard Pyle, *Abbot Otto, of St. Michaelsburg, Was a Gentle, Patient, Pale-Faced Old Man.* From Howard Pyle, *Otto of the Silver Hand* (New York: Charles Scribner's Sons, 1888). (Delaware Art Museum Library.)

Fig. 4. Albrecht Dürer, *Erasmus of Rotterdam*. From *Kulturgeschichtliches Bilderbuch aus Drei Jahrhunderten*, ed. Georg Hirth, vol. 1 (Leipzig, 1881), pl. 505. (Delaware Art Museum Library.)

Fig. 5. Albrecht Dürer, *St. Jerome in His Cell*. From *Kulturgeschichtliches Bilderbuch aus Drei Jahrhunderten*, ed. Georg Hirth, vol. 1 (Leipzig, 1881), pl. 461. (Delaware Art Museum Library.)

Fig. 6. Howard Pyle, *Pride in Distress*, 1884. Ink on paper; H. 13″, W. 9¼″. For Howard Pyle, *Pepper and Salt* (New York: Harper and Brothers, 1886). (Howard Pyle Collection, Delaware Art Museum.)

These *Wonder Clock* drawings, like those for *Robin Hood* and *Otto*, give the impression of being woodcuts done in a Düreresque style. The figures are clearly outlined, and the folds of the drapery are richly modeled with series of short parallel lines. It is obvious that Pyle relied on Dürer's woodcuts and engravings reproduced in the *Bilderbuch* as a source for details. In the *Wonder Clock* frontispiece the osier fence is very similar to the one shown in Dürer's *Virgin Crowned by Two Angels* (*Bilderbuch*, pl. 459), and the treatment of the figure Time is suggestive of Dürer.

The captions for many of the *Wonder Clock* drawings are embellished with intricate initial letters done in various styles. For example, the initial letter for *The Great Red Fox Goeth* is clearly derived from sixteenth-century German letters shown in the *Book of Initial Letters and Ancient Alphabets for Ornamental Purposes* in Pyle's own library (figs. 7, 8).

By relying on the *Bilderbuch* and other books in his collection for information about ornament, clothing styles, and even a type of medieval fence construction, Pyle strove to achieve historical accuracy in his work. Furthermore, he wanted to use a style that would reflect the period of his subjects. Therefore, in the case of *Otto of the Silver Hand*, a story set in sixteenth-century Germany, he found it natural to work in a Düreresque manner. In addition, this "woodcut style" could be easily translated into ink drawings and adapted to the new photomechanical printing processes used by the American magazine and book publishing firms.

If one had any doubt about Pyle's reliance on Dürer, there is a rare and, in fact, puzzling drawing, *The King Being Lost in ye Forest*, where Pyle borrowed an entire figure on horseback from Dürer's *Knight and Halberdier* (figs. 9, 10). In the story, the king, who is lost, promises his beautiful daughter in marriage to the raven in exchange for being led out of the forest. This example of Pyle's rather extravagant borrowing seems to be, however, an exception in his work.

In 1889 when he wrote to Pennell, who was preparing the landmark *Pen Drawing and Pen Draughtsmen*, Pyle admitted: "I never did feel free and easy with that medium [pen and ink], and only use it to suggest the stiff style of medieval work. My best drawings of this kind are those, I think, in my last winter's work published by Chas. Scribner's Sons—Otto of the Silver Hand." In his book Pennell points out Pyle's close affinity with the work of Dürer and adds with some slight hint of sarcasm: "I admit, with certain American critics whom I respect, that in some qualities it is very hard to tell where Dürer ends and Howard Pyle begins"; however, he goes on to praise Pyle's ability "to saturate himself with the spirit of the age in which the scenes are laid, and to give his work the color and character of the biggest man [Dürer] of that age." Pennell admired not only Pyle's adaptation of earlier styles but also his understanding and use of modern technical developments in printing.[5]

Other contemporary writers and critics admired Pyle's medieval style. In 1896 Crane noted Pyle's considerable study of the method of Dürer. In an essay about American pen drawings, Ernest Knaufft described the *Robin Hood* illustrations as drawn in the manner of sixteenth-century woodcuts and called it "a pleasant revival of the antique" and a novelty in America. Also, Sadakichi Hartmann referred to Pyle as "one of the few great masters of linear composition of the day" and was enthusiastic about the designs "powerfully conceived in the true spirit of the early woodcut, and approaching Dürer in their purity of line."[6]

In summary, Pyle's ink drawings of the 1880s reveal his personal adaptation of the graphic style of Dürer and other artists of the fifteenth and sixteenth centuries, as well as a keen awareness of the work of nineteenth-century English artists, especially Crane, who were similarly inspired by artists of an earlier time. On the whole, Pyle did not simply copy, but rather imaginatively adapted earlier styles and motifs in his work in the same spirit of other nineteenth-century artists who were dedicated to the revival of earlier styles.

[5] Howard Pyle to Joseph Pennell, April 13, 1889, Joseph Pennell Papers, Library of Congress, Washington, D.C. I am grateful to Anne C. Palumbo for bringing this letter to my attention. Joseph Pennell, *Pen Drawing and Pen Draughtsmen* (New York: Macmillan, 1889), p. 209.

[6] Walter Crane, *Of the Decorative Illustration of Books Old and New* (London: George Bell and Sons, 1896), p. 273; Ernest Knaufft, "American Pen Drawings," in *Modern Pen Drawings: European and American*, ed. Charles Holmes (London: Studio, 1901), p. 94; Sadakichi Hartmann, *A History of American Art* (Boston: L. C. Page, 1901), p. 102.

The Great Red Fox goeth to the store-house and helps himself to the good things.

Fig. 7. Howard Pyle, *The Great Red Fox Goeth*, 1886. From Howard Pyle, *The Wonder Clock* (New York: Harper and Brothers, 1888), p. 283. (Delaware Art Museum Library.)

Fig. 8. Initial letters from German woodcuts, 1536. From *Polygraphic Curiosa: The Book of Initial Letters and Ancient Alphabets for Ornamental Purposes* (London: D. Bogue, n.d.), pl. 26. (Delaware Art Museum Library.)

he king being lost in ẏ ffozest meets with the Great Black Raven.

Fig. 9. Howard Pyle, *The King Being Lost in ye Forest*, 1885. From Howard Pyle, *The Wonder Clock* (New York: Harper and Brothers, 1888), p. 67. (Delaware Art Museum Library.)

Fig. 10. Albrecht Dürer, *Knight and Halberdier*. From *Kulturgeschichtliches Bilderbuch aus Drei Jahrhunderten*, ed. Georg Hirth, vol. 1 (Leipzig, 1881), pl. 2. (Delaware Art Museum Library.)

By 1889 and 1890, a dramatic change occurred in Pyle's drawings. His linework became progressively thinner and more delicate; Pyle called it a "scratchy" line.[7] Some of his drawings show a serious concern for capturing transitory effects of light and motion. Others reveal his use of symbolic, allegorical imagery. Also, during the nineties he became a master at using ink wash which could be reproduced by the recently developed halftone process. His drawings done during these years are characterized by a variety of styles, each chosen to fit a particular type of story and suited to the technical aspects of their reproduction.

Pyle's new drawing style is apparent in his fifth children's book, *Twilight Land* (1895). Like *Pepper and Salt* and *The Wonder Clock*, this book is a collection of stories written, beginning in 1889, for *Harper's Young People*. In 1892 Pyle wrote to Harper's about plans to compile the stories in a book to be published by Christmas. It was not until 1894, however, that he completed the last two stories, wrote the introductory section, and drew the additional headpieces and decorated title. The book, dedicated to his daughter Phoebe, is a collection of bedtime stories of exotic, magical tales set in faraway places which have quasi-Mediterranean and Middle East settings, rather than the northern European locale of most of his earlier stories.

In the preface Pyle describes *Twilight Land* as a "wonderful, wonderful place . . . where all is sweet and quiet and ready to go to bed."[8] He then describes the Inn of the Sign of Mother Goose where all the storybook characters (Aladdin, Cinderella, the tailor who killed seven flies at a blow, and Sinbad, among others) assemble and tell stories, one for each chapter.

Some of the drawings in the book show scrawny, elongated creatures, often from unusual points of view such as the genie flying in front of the sun with the scheming prime minister in tow (fig. 11) or the "spirit of the stone" with batlike wings who transports a soldier to a faraway place.

[7]Pyle to Henry Harper, November 1, 1891, Howard Pyle Collection, Delaware Art Museum, Wilmington.
[8]Howard Pyle, *Twilight Land* (New York: Harper and Bros., 1895), p. 1.

Fig. 11. Howard Pyle, *The Genius Snatched the Minister up and Flew away with Him*, ca. 1894. Ink on board; H. 12″, W. 8¾″. For Howard Pyle, *Twilight Land* (New York: Harper and Brothers, 1895). (Howard Pyle Collection, Delaware Art Museum.)

Other drawings show exotic palaces such as in *There Was Feasting and Merrymaking* (fig. 12) where Selim the Baker, transported to an enchanted island, is seated on a splendid throne and watches the beautiful dancing girls clinking their cymbals and tapping tambourines. Pyle conveys the motion of their flowing hair, filmy skirts, and graceful arms, and he captures the impression of shimmering light on their costumes. Unlike his Düreresque drawings, there is not a clear outline; instead, the linework is fine and broken. Sometimes, small black areas contrast with complex patterns of thin, delicate lines, and large portions of the white paper are left purposely blank.

A number of these *Twilight Land* drawings are reminiscent of the drawings of Pyle's contemporary Daniel Vierge, a Spanish artist who enjoyed wide popularity in France and America. In his book on pen drawing, Pennell discussed and illustrated work by several European illustrators who were trying to capture effects of light and shadow: for example, Vierge in his Spanish subjects; Mariano Fortuny, who tried to translate the lighting effects he observed on a visit to Africa; and Martin Rico, who frequently placed his subjects directly in front of the sun. One can only speculate what impact Pennell's book might have had on Pyle. In any case, the work of these European artists was becoming more widely known in America in the late 1880s when Pyle was beginning to pursue a new direction in his drawings.[9]

In the early 1890s Pyle illustrated two small volumes of poetry by Oliver Wendell Holmes in which he adapted his new pen-and-ink style to the subject of the American historical scene. Holmes's *One Hoss Shay*, a slim, leather-bound volume, was published in 1892 by Houghton Mifflin and printed by Riverside Press in Cambridge, Massachusetts. The book included three humorous poems. The first, "The Deacon's Masterpiece," tells of a one-horse shay built so well that it did not have a single weak spot and therefore never broke down until a hundred years later when it collapsed all at once into a heap, leaving the driver sitting on a rock. Another poem, "How the Old Horse Won the Bet," describes the parson's old horse who to everyone's surprise

[9] Henry Pitz, *Howard Pyle* (New York: Clarkson N. Potter, 1975), p. 124; Pitz points out the similarity of Pyle's and Vierge's work. Pennell, *Pen Drawing and Draughtsmen*, pp. 28, 41, 52.

Fig. 12. Howard Pyle, *There Was Feasting and Merrymaking*, ca. 1891. Ink on board; H. 12″, W. 10″. For Howard Pyle, *Twilight Land* (New York: Harper and Brothers, 1895). (Howard Pyle Collection, Delaware Art Museum.)

wins a race, while "The Broomstick Train" whimsically reports about witches on broomsticks operating the trolleys.

Pyle's lighthearted drawings reflect the mood of the poems. Again we can look to Vierge as a source for this style. Knaufft claimed that Pyle's style for *One Hoss Shay* was based on drawings by French illustrator Maurice Leloir in which outline played a minor role and parallel lines, instead of cross-hatching, formed the shading. Pyle himself described the *One Hoss Shay* drawings as his "scratchy pen and ink illustrations" in a letter to his friend and long-time publisher Henry Harper. For Pyle the book had been a labor of love, and he was pleased that Holmes also liked the drawings.[10]

A second volume of poetry, *Dorothy Q*, by Holmes was published in 1893, also illustrated by Pyle. These drawings were done in a similar manner with the "scratchy" and expressive linework. Pyle managed to capture in the drawings for "Grandmother's Story of Bunker Hill Battle" a sense of the atmosphere and drama of the battle scenes of the American Revolution. One example is *The Frightened Braves of Howe*, a scene of the British fleeing to their barges with the sky full of battle smoke (fig. 13).

The next year, 1894, Pyle illustrated still another book of Holmes's writings, *The Autocrat of the Breakfast-Table*. The book is a collection of witty, entertaining essays and poems recording imaginary conversations at the breakfast table in a Boston boardinghouse. These "written conversations" were first published in *Atlantic Monthly* and then in book form in 1858. When Houghton Mifflin decided to publish a new illustrated edition, art editor Winthrop Scudder persuaded Pyle to make the drawings, even though Pyle was at that time very busy and almost turned down the job. Scudder wrote in a cajoling manner: "I have felt from the beginning that your work on this book would give you a great deal of pleasure, delight the good doctor, and satisfy the general public, who are so well acquainted with the *Autocrat*."[11]

Most of the illustrations for the *Autocrat* were done in ink wash, a medium that could be reproduced by halftone process or by wood

---

[10] Knaufft, "American Pen Drawings," p. 94; Pyle to Harper, November 1, 1891, Howard Pyle Collection.

[11] Abbott, *Pyle*, p. 156.

Fig. 13. Howard Pyle, *The Frightened Braves of Howe*, ca. 1893.
Ink on board; H. 9″, W. 6½″. For Oliver Wendell Holmes, *Dorothy Q, together with a Ballad of the Boston Tea Party and Grand-mother's Story of Bunker Hill Battle* (Boston: Houghton Mifflin Co., 1893). (Howard Pyle Collection, Delaware Art Museum.)

Fig. 14. Howard Pyle, headpiece, 1893. Ink on paper; H. 11″, W. 8⅝″. For Oliver Wendell Holmes, *The Autocrat of the Breakfast-Table* (Boston: Houghton Mifflin Co., 1894). (Howard Pyle Collection, Delaware Art Museum.)

engraving. Pyle had first used this technique for magazine illustration about 1890. For the *Autocrat* he used both allegorical and realistic subjects for his drawings. There were several full-page black and white oil illustrations, but most of the works were in ink wash and handled very freely and imaginatively echoing the content of the chapter. For example, the heading for a chapter dealing with growing old shows a hooded figure in black with a sickle, while a figure in white holds the cup of life (fig. 14).

Pyle had begun to use allegorical figures in his work several years earlier in illustrations for a series of poems by William Dean Howells for *Harper's Monthly Magazine*. For the poems published in the March 1893 issue, Pyle designed a full-page oil and several ink head-pieces, tailpieces, and initial letters. There is an interesting exchange of correspondence between Pyle and *Harper's* art editor F. B. Schell revealing Pyle's attitude toward the symbolic nature of the poems and drawings as well as offering insight into the relationship of author, illustrator, and publisher.

In a letter written in August 1891 to Schell, Pyle describes his deep involvement with the assignment: "I have worked upon it more conscientiously and with as much enjoyment as I have perhaps, upon anything that I have ever done. Though it may sound hysterical, I have really put heart and soul into it." Then Pyle went on to say that the poem "Question" made a great impression on him but that he felt rather sheepish about sending them the oil (fig. 15). He imagined that they would say: "What's the matter with Pyle, has he gone crazy?" The painting, different from anything he had ever done, shows a kneeling figure asking Death when and where the questioner would die.[12]

In the same vein Pyle explained some of the symbolism to *Harper's* editor Henry Alden: "I began to let the Poem 'soak in' and tried to project myself into the author's feeling when he wrote it. I think I myself have felt just such experiences as the Poem describes and I have tried to embody in the painting pictorially what I felt psychologically . . . in the figure holding to the skirts of Death . . . in the thorny fields and the rocks."[13]

Apparently Schell had objected to the content of some of the grotesque headpieces, but Pyle reassured him that there would be no more skeletal heads in the series and offered to make some other changes. Pyle pointed out that these drawings were "novel and quite out of [his] usual style."[14] Explaining that the designs for the head- and tailpieces had been made with brush instead of pen, he hoped that

[12] Pyle to F. B. Schell, August 15, 1891, Harper's Collection, Pierpont Morgan Library, New York.
[13] Pyle to Henry Alden, August 28, 1891, Harper's Collection.
[14] Pyle to Schell, August 15, 1891, Harper's Collection.

Fig. 15. Howard Pyle, *Question*, 1891. From William Dean Howells, "Mono-
chromes," *Harper's Monthly* 86, no. 514 (March 1893): 547. (Delaware Art
Museum Library.)

Fig. 16. Howard Pyle, *November*, ca. 1891. From William Dean Howells, *Stops of Various Quills* (New York: Harper and Brothers, 1895). (Delaware Art Museum Library.)

they would be engraved on wood to keep the richness and softness he intended. If the drawings were reproduced by halftone process, he feared they would become harsh and hard.

Pyle sent Harper's an estimate of $375 for the set of sixteen ink drawings and one oil or $350 if the oil painting was returned to him. When Harper's asked him to lower the price, Pyle, clearly angered, responded: "I am always slow in falling into any new line of work and that rule has been borne out in the present case. The full page I painted twice and the headband I began and completed at least 4 times."[15]

The Howells poems with the Pyle drawings were finally published in *Stops of Various Quills* (1895). From the correspondence it appears that Pyle designed the book's cover as well as the layout. He sent along a dummy with notes describing the overall arrangement of the text and asked that it be set according to his specifications.

Pyle's allegorical drawings show ethereal angels with large, graceful wings (fig. 16), the Grim Reaper in black hood, a brooding man with an hourglass and empty goblet symbolizing approaching death,

[15] Pyle to Schell, September 2, 1891, Harper's Collection.

as well as the image of death in the form of a gruesome skeleton playing the fiddle. This symbolist, mystical content was new for Pyle, and he repeated this type of work again in Edwin Markham's *Man with the Hoe* (1900). Other American artists commonly used symbolic figures in their work in the 1890s. Painters such as Elihu Vedder and Kenyon Cox and sculptors Augustus Saint-Gaudens and Daniel Chester French incorporated winged angels and hooded figures in their work, as did other adherents of the renaissance revival in America.

During the final years of the 1890s and again in 1901, Pyle was commissioned to illustrate several books on American historical subjects by Woodrow Wilson and Henry Cabot Lodge to be published by Harper's and Scribner's. Pyle painted these illustrations, considered to be among his most important works, in oil, using ink only for the head- and tailpieces.

He did not abandon his use of ink, however, or, for that matter, his interest in medieval subjects. In 1902 he proposed to Scribner's the idea of publishing a book of the legends of King Arthur and the knights done in the general manner of his Robin Hood book twenty years earlier. This project expanded into a series of four volumes: *The Story of King Arthur and His Knights* (1903), *Champions of the Round Table* (1905), *Sir Launcelot and His Companions* (1907), and the *Grail and the Passing of Arthur* (1910).

The books were largely based on Sir Thomas Malory's version of the Arthurian tales, originally compiled in the fifteenth century. Malory's tales were filled with scenes of murder, betrayal, and wickedness, and Pyle had to modify them for children who were his main audience. He wanted to inspire his readers with the chivalric deeds of his characters and therefore deleted many of the gruesome parts of the story.

The King Arthur books are richly embellished with full-page illustrations, hand-lettered titles, illuminated initials, and many decorative head- and tailbands. These works differ greatly from his Robin Hood drawings which look more like woodcuts with sharp black outlines. The most brilliant King Arthur designs are built of rich, complex textures and various patterns of delicate linework. In *The Lady of ye Lake* the cross-hatching on the dress conveys a sense of the silkiness and deep folds of her garb (fig. 17). These fine, precise lines contrast

Fig. 17. Howard Pyle, *The Lady of ye Lake*, 1903. Ink on board; H. 14½″, W. 11¼″. For Howard Pyle, *Story of King Arthur and His Knights* (New York: Charles Scribner's Sons, 1903). (Howard Pyle Collection, Delaware Art Museum.)

Two Knights do battles before Cameliard

Fig. 18. Howard Pyle, *Two Knights Do Battle before Cameliard*, 1902. Ink on board; H. 14½", W. 11¼". For Howard Pyle, *Story of King Arthur and His Knights* (New York: Charles Scribner's Sons, 1903). (Howard Pyle Collection, Delaware Art Museum.)

with the broader, fluid patterns done with brush on the trees and grass in the background.

The figures in the King Arthur drawings are usually cut off just below the waist and are starkly placed against a flat background. There is an incredible richness in the contrasting play of textures and in the variety of tones Pyle used. Although the portrait of King Arthur (which served as the book's frontispiece) is in black and white, there is an impression of color in the gold neck chain and the dazzling jewels on his costume. The rich textures of enchanter Merlin's fur collar and heavy cloak seem tactile.

In *Two Knights Do Battle before Cameliard*, the landscape and castle provide a background of enchantment and wonder for the battle taking place between King Arthur and an unworthy suitor for the hand of Lady Guinevere (fig. 18). The drawing shows Pyle's adeptness at combining stippling and fluid brushstrokes in contrast with the dense, dark foliage and the gleaming whiteness of the paper. The King Arthur drawings suggest Pyle's affinity with the work of Aubrey Beardsley, who was a master at creating rich patterns and textures in pen and ink.

The remaining three volumes followed at two- or three-year intervals, but the drawings for the last book lack the brilliance of the first King Arthur volume. Pyle was by then very busy illustrating other stories, writing, and painting murals, and one senses that the last volume was almost a burden completed in a hurry shortly before he went abroad in 1910. The next year, while in Italy, Pyle met his untimely death at the age of fifty-eight.

The King Arthur series marks the climax of Pyle's work in ink. Throughout his career Pyle had experimented with the ink medium and used it imaginatively for book illustrations ranging from his woodcut style in the Robin Hood drawings, to works in which he tried to capture the effect of light and motion, to his densely patterned King Arthur designs. He was versatile in adapting styles from the past and from his contemporaries but coming up with a work that was uniquely his own. Although Pyle painted many illustrations in oil, his ink drawings formed an important part of his career and represented some of his most satisfying artistic achievements.

The Development of Photomechanical Book Illustration

Lois Olcott Price

T HE HISTORY OF BOOK ILLUSTRATION throughout the nineteenth century is, in some respects, the history of the search for the perfect reproductive process. To the technologically minded Victorians, this meant a photomechanical process that would allow an artist's drawing or a photograph to be reproduced at minimal cost and with total fidelity to the original. To the artist or photographer, it meant a photomechanical process that would eliminate the subjective and highly variable intrusion of the engraver between the original and the published illustration. To the publisher, this meant a typographically compatible process that could be reproduced reliably and inexpensively and printed on any paper.

This search for the ideal process by printers, photographers, chemists, and inventors continued throughout the century. Competition was keen, spurred on by prize competitions, international exhibitions, and hopes for substantial financial rewards that frequently erupted into patent disputes and court battles. The emergence of each new process was greeted eagerly by printers, artists, and the general public. In half a century, new processes and technical improvements shortened the time necessary to make a printing plate from months to hours, making possible the inclusion of illustrations in inexpensive publications. Photomechanical reproduction gave the general public images of art and the world never before available and provided illustrators and photographers with a vastly larger audience for their work.

It is therefore necessary in reviewing the development of photomechanical book illustration to suspend the late twentieth-century aversion to reproductions and feel the excitement of the chase as inventors pursue the elusive perfect process.

More patents were filed and processes developed than can possibly be discussed in this brief essay, so this discussion is confined to black-and-white processes that either received some significant commercial use or were important to the development of a major commercial process. For purposes of this discussion, these processes are divided according to primary printing technique: intaglio, planographic, and relief. This makes identification of the processes easier and has some chronological justification since the earliest processes were intaglio and the latest were relief, with the development of the planographic processes falling in between.

Technical Considerations

Any discussion of photomechanical processes requires some understanding of a few basic photomechanical principles. The most fundamental of these is the production and use of photographic negatives and positives. A negative is produced when a transparent support coated with a light-sensitive substance, usually a silver halide in a gelatin or a collodion emulsion, is exposed to light. The light converts the silver halide to metallic silver in quantities directly proportional to the amount of light received. After developing the plate to intensify the image and fixing it to remove the unexposed silver halide, a finished negative is visible. The highlight areas of the original are represented by opaque areas of metallic silver. The middle tones are represented by thinner translucent areas of silver, and the dark tones are represented by transparent areas with little or no silver. In other words, the tonal relationships are the exact reverse of the original subject. All photomechanical processes begin with a negative. Frequently, however, a positive transparency is necessary to the process. To produce a positive image, a transparent support coated with a light-sensitive substance is placed behind and in contact with the negative and exposed to light through the negative. This produces an image whose tonal relationships are the same as those of the original subject.

The second fundamental photomechanical principle is based on the effect of light on gelatin or similar substances such as albumen when they are combined with potassium bichromate. The chemical reaction caused by light imparts three properties to bichromated gelatin. First, when gelatin is mixed with potassium bichromate and then exposed to light, it becomes hard and insoluble in water in direct proportion to the amount of light it receives. If a support of metal, glass, or paper is coated with gelatin and potassium bichromate and exposed to light through a negative or a positive transparency, an image of hardened gelatin will be formed. The unexposed areas can be washed away and the partially exposed areas washed away somewhat in a warm-water bath. Second, since the bichromated gelatin also becomes impervious to water in direct proportion to the amount of light it receives, a cold-water bath which does not dissolve the gelatin will cause the unexposed and partially exposed areas to swell and create an image in relief. The amount of swelling is inversely proportional to the amount of light received. Finally, the light-exposed, water-impervious areas of the wet plate are also receptive to grease-base ink in direct proportion to the amount of exposure. The grease-base ink is rejected by moist, unexposed areas. (This behavior is similar to that of a lithographic stone.) These three properties of bichromated gelatin form the basis of most photomechanical processes.

Intaglio Processes

The search for a photomechanical process began before the first successful photograph was announced by Louis Daguerre (1789–1851) in 1839. The first print produced by photomechanical means was the work of Joseph-Nicéphore Niepce (1765–1833), a Frenchman later associated with Daguerre. In 1822 he produced a reproduction of a print of Pope Pius VI which he called a heliograph. Niepce's process involved the use of bitumen of Judea which has properties similar to those of bichromated gelatin. He dissolved the bitumen in oil of lavender, which is similar to turpentine, and spread the solution on a pewter plate. Niepce then exposed the plate to light through an engraving oiled to render it translucent and allow it to be used as a positive transparency. A long exposure to light was necessary to penetrate the oiled paper and to harden the bitumen immediately below the non-image areas. In areas of the plate protected from light penetration by the printed image, the bitumen remained soft and was readily washed away. The insoluble bitumen remained to act as a resist when the plate was placed in an etching bath. After etching, the image could be printed as an intaglio plate. Only a few plates were ever successfully etched, and the results of Niepce's experiments were not published until much later; few heliographs were ever printed. They were, however, the first photomechanical reproductions, and Niepce's experiments contributed to the development of heliogravures and photolithographs.

The excitement aroused by the introduction of the daguerreotype in 1839 overshadowed Niepce's experiments. Daguerreotypes are small, minutely detailed, unique photographic images produced without a negative by inserting a sensitized silver plate in a camera and exposing, developing, and fixing it. Enchanted with the results, the public demanded a method of reproducing these images. The first reproductions of daguerreotypes were made using the traditional hand processes like the aquatints published in *Excursions Daguerriene* (1841). These prints were beautifully executed, and the printmaker retained the photographic character of the original; however, the production of the plate was time-consuming, and the intervening hand of man was evident in the treatment of texture, distance, and detail.

A few plates in this extraordinary book were, however, printed directly from the original daguerreotypes. The silver-face daguerreotypes were etched in a bath of nitric acid using the silver-mercury amalgam that formed the highlights as the resist. The etching achieved was too shallow to produce a clear print, and wear on the soft silver plate was an immediate problem. These shortcomings could be alleviated only by extensive and frequent reworking of the plate by hand.

In 1842, Armand-Hippolyte-Louis Fizeau (1819–96) developed and patented an improved process for daguerrian printing plates. By applying a gold resist to the highlights, he was able to achieve a deeper etch which he sometimes supplemented with an aquatint ground. By electroplating the etched plate with copper to slow wear, he was able to pull a reasonable number of prints from the plate; the quality of reproduction still left much to be desired, however, and the process destroyed the original daguerreotype.

Although the daguerreotype dominated photography for the next decade, the development of photography and photomechanical techniques lay along an entirely different path. At the same time Daguerre was perfecting his process, Englishman William Henry Fox Talbot (1800–1877) had discovered that when he exposed a piece of paper sensitized with a silver halide in a camera or under a waxed print or a collage of leaves, a negative image was formed. He announced his discovery of photogenic drawing in 1839. He soon found that he could wax one of his negative images to make the paper translucent and then use it to print an unlimited number of positive images on sensitized paper. These images are known as callotypes, talbotypes, or salt prints. In 1844, he published the first book illustrated with original photographs, *The Pencil of Nature*. Aside from the time and labor involved in individually exposing, developing, and tipping-in every photograph in every copy of the book, salt prints had a further disadvantage: they tended to fade.

Talbot then began the search for a permanent printing process for his photographs. In 1852, he patented a process he called photoglyphy. After coating a steel plate with gelatin containing potassium bichromate, he covered the plate with a piece of black gauze folded so that the threads crossed at a 45-degree angle. He then exposed the whole assemblage to light under a composition of leaves and lace or under a waxed salt print acting as a positive transparency. After the exposure was complete, Talbot washed away the soluble unexposed gelatin, leaving a negative image on the plate crisscrossed by a fine network of lines left by the gauze. Talbot then etched the plate using the hardened gelatin image as the resist. The etchant bit most deeply where the gelatin was thin or nonexistent and bit to a lesser depth or not at all where the gelatin was thick. The etched image of the gauze left a network of intaglio lines that varied in depth with the design and provided a grain of tiny reservoirs to hold the ink when the plate was printed. Talbot continued to improve his process, substituting an aquatint ground for the gauze, but his images still lacked clear detail, especially in the darker halftones. Talbot's process received no commercial use because of his restrictive patents, but his discoveries led to the development of photogravure later in the century.

In the meantime, others continued to investigate new approaches to photomechanical reproduction. Photogalvanography was introduced by Paul Pretsch (1808–73), manager of the Imperial Printing Establishment in Vienna, in 1854. In this process, a glass plate thickly coated with bichromated gelatin was exposed under a positive transparency. The exposed plate was then placed in a cold-water bath. In those areas not hardened by exposure to light, the gelatin absorbed water and swelled, producing a relief image. As the plate dried, the swollen gelatin developed a reticulated surface that acted as a grain. A mold of gutta-percha was made of this relief image and then electrotyped in copper to produce an intaglio printing plate.

Although the finished plate still required costly reworking by hand, it was the most successful process available in 1856 when Pretsch published *Photographic Art Treasures; or, Nature and Art Illustrated by Art and Nature*. The book produced an immediate sensation, and, in the words of one contemporary, people were "perfectly crazy with astonishment and delight."

Meanwhile, in France, Claude-Félix-Abel Niepce de Saint Victor (1805–70) was trying to perfect the heliographic process discovered by his uncle Joseph-Nicéphore Niepce. Working with engraver Augustin François Lemâitre, he made several changes in the process including the substitution of steel for the original pewter plates. These changes resulted in a commercially viable printing process, although the plates still required reworking by hand. As examples of his process, Saint Victor published his portrait as the frontispiece of two books, *Récherches Photographique* (1855) and *Traité Practique de Gravure Heliographique* (1856). Charles Nègre (1820–79), a French artist and photographer, further improved on Saint Victor's process. He exposed a steel plate coated with bitumen or bichromated gelatin under a negative, then he electrotyped a layer of gold over the developed plate and covered it with a layer of aquatint rosin before he etched it. The gold, which served as an acid resist, was deposited most continuously in the highlight areas, intermittently in the halftones, and scarcely at all in the shadows. The rosin provided an aquatint grain. Nègre patented his process, called heliogravure, in 1856. Although the process was tricky, the successful plates produced moderately detailed images and a good range of halftones. Until the introduction of photogravure, the process received limited commercial use, especially in France and elsewhere on the Continent.

Photogravure became, soon after the process was published, the ultimate intaglio photomechanical process. It could reproduce details accurately and gave a full, rich range of tones. And most important, it required little or no reworking by hand. The process was introduced in 1879 by a Viennese painter, Karl Klič (1841–1926), who based his discoveries on the earlier work of Talbot. Klič kept the details of the process secret, revealing it only to those who paid him a license fee, but the secrecy lasted only until 1886 when the full details were published by Hans Lenhard of Vienna, in *Der photographische mitarbeiter*, the periodical he edited.

Photogravure used a nonsilver photographic process, the carbon print, as its basis. Carbon prints were produced by first coating a heavy sheet of paper with a thick layer of bichromated gelatin containing pigment, usually carbon black. The coated paper was produced commercially and known as carbon tissue. After exposure under a negative, the carbon print was developed in a bath of warm water that dissolved the unexposed, unhardened gelatin. The hardened gelatin was then transferred to a final paper support. The image was composed of varying thicknesses of pigmented gelatin, with the shadows composed of the thickest and therefore the most heavily pigmented areas and the highlights formed by the paper seen through the thin, almost unpigmented areas of gelatin. The tone was continuous, and the detail was excellent.

To make a photogravure, a sensitized sheet of carbon tissue was exposed under a positive transparency, and then the paper was developed in a warm-water bath to remove the unexposed gelatin. While in the bath, a copperplate coated with an aquatint rosin became the final support of the gelatin image. This plate, covered with varying depths of pigmented gelatin, was then etched in successive baths of ferric chloride. The acid etched the thin areas of gelatin, representing the shadows, most deeply. The etched plate was then cleaned and faced with steel in an electrolytic bath, after which it would yield 1,000 to 1,500 impressions.

For commercial uses, a screen was soon substituted for the aquatint ground. Before development, the pigmented gelatin image was transferred to an ungrained copperplate and exposed again under a grid of clear lines and opaque holes. This superimposed a resist grid over the image. After etching, the grid formed a regular texture to hold the ink. In the high-speed process of rotogravure, the etched plate was placed on a rotary cylinder that could be automatically inked and wiped.

Photogravures at their best are characterized by rich, full, vigorous tones, the three-dimensional ink deposits found in other intaglio prints, and good halftone detail. The aquatint grain is readily visible under magnification, but, unlike traditional aquatint, the transitions between tones are gradual rather than sharply defined (figs. 1, 2). Screen photogravure shows the same gradual tonal transitions, but the screen pattern replaces the aquatint grain (figs. 3, 4). Although handwork was not necessary on most photogravures, many prints show evidence of the burnisher and roulette under magnification.

Woodburytype

All the tonal photomechanical intaglio reproductive processes involve the use of a grain to break up the image and hold the ink. All the tonal planographic and relief halftone processes also use a grain or a screen to break up the image. There is only one continuous-tone photomechanical process—the Woodburytype. This process does not fit comfortably into any of the categories used to classify prints. Its closest relative is the carbon print described in the discussion of photogravure.

The Woodburytype, and slight variations known as photomezzotint, Woodburygravure, Stannotype, and photoglyptie, was developed by Walter Bentley Woodbury (1834–85), who patented the process

Fig. 1. *Oxen plowing.* Photogravure; H. 7¾″, W. 11⅛″. (Collection of Debbie Hess Norris: Photo, Winterthur.)

Fig. 2. Photomicrograph (400x) of photogravure shown in figure 1. (Photo, Winterthur.)

in 1864. Sir Joseph Wilson Swan (1828–1914) developed a similar process at the same time called the photomezzotint. Both processes were acquired by Woodbury Permanent Photographic Printing Company in England. In 1867, Goupil and Company of Paris acquired Woodbury's patent rights and called its version of the process photoglyptie. The American rights were acquired by John Carbutt of Phila-

Fig. 3. *Jules Lecomte-du-Nouy.* Screen photogravure; H. 6¼″, W. 5″. (Collection of
Debbie Hess Norris: Photo, Winterthur.)

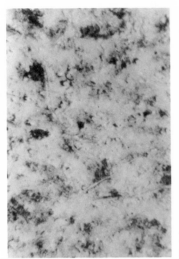

Fig. 4. Photomicrograph (400x) of screen photogravure shown in figure 3. (Photo, Winterthur.)

delphia in 1870. Woodburytypes were commonly used for book and periodical illustration between 1875 and 1900. An important book that used the process was *London Street Life* (1877) by John Thompson, an early documentary photographer.

Production of a Woodburytype began with a plate covered with a thick layer of bichromated gelatin that was exposed to light under a negative and developed in warm water to produce a positive image in relief. This relief image of exposed hardened gelatin was further hardened with alum. The gelatin was then harder than lead, so an embossed mold was formed when the gelatin was pressed against a lead blank in a hydraulic press. To produce the finished image, warm gelatin containing a pigment was poured into this lead mold and a sheet of paper pressed over the back. When the gelatin set, it adhered firmly to the paper and could be removed from the mold and passed through an alum bath to harden it. Like the carbon print, the thick areas of gelatin contained more pigment and therefore appeared darker, while the thin areas contained almost no pigment and therefore assumed the color of the paper to which the gelatin was adhered.

Fig. 5. *Representations de Mme. Adelina Patti.* Woodburytype; H. 10⅜″, W. 8″. (Collection of Debbie Hess Norris: Photo, Winterthur.)

Fig. 6. Photomicrograph (400x) of Woodbury-type shown in figure 5. (Photo, Winterthur.)

Because of their grainless continuous tone, Woodburytypes exhibit excellent detail, and they are relatively inexpensive to produce (figs. 5, 6). Their biggest drawback in book production was the necessity of mounting each finished image on a page. This difficulty was partially overcome by a process modification in 1891, but the Woodburytype still could not compete with the typographically compatible halftone process.

Planographic Processes

The early photomechanical techniques were all intaglio processes. As the nineteenth century progressed, however, lithography became an increasingly popular illustrative method. It was inevitable, therefore, that those searching for a photomechanical process would begin to experiment with planographic reproductive methods.

The first successful photolithographs were the product of a cooperative effort. Two chemists, Barreswil and Alphonse Davanne, worked in collaboration with optician N. P. Lerebours and printer R. J. Lemercier. In 1852, they revived Joseph-Nicéphore Niepce's helio-graph process and applied it to stone rather than metal. They coated a stone with bitumen of Judea, exposed it under a negative, and then dissolved away the unhardened, unexposed areas. The stone was then etched with acid using the remaining bitumen as a resist. The parts of the stone protected from the acid by the bitumen would then accept the greasy lithographic ink rejected by the water-saturated etched areas. The absence of the traditional greasy lithographic design mate-rials in producing the image resulted in a less effective etch, so a single stone yielded only a limited number of impressions, although the prints exhibited good halftones. In 1854, Lemercier published *Litho-photographie; ou, Impressions obtenus sur pierre a l'aide de la photo-graphie*, a series of prints of details of Strasbourg and Chartres.

Lemercier's process, however, was soon supplanted by a technique developed by Alphonse Louis Poitevin (1819–82). In 1855, Poitevin discovered that light renders bichromated gelatin not only insoluble but also water resistant. He coated a grained stone with bichromated gelatin and exposed it to light under a negative. He then moistened the image whose unexposed highlights absorbed the water while the exposed shadows rejected it. When the stone was rolled with a greasy lithographic ink, it adhered only to the water-repellant shadows. Poite-vin then etched the stone using the gelatin and the ink as the resist which resulted in a more effective etch allowing him to pull 300 prints from each stone. He started a small lithographic shop and produced a number of plates for various publications, but in 1857 he sold his patent rights to Lemercier. Because he was an experienced printer, Lemercier could pull 700 prints from a stone. He continued to use this process for the rest of the nineteenth century.

Meanwhile, in England, E. and J. Bullock of Lemington began printing excellent photolithographs by a process patented in 1865. The Bullocks used a transfer paper coated with bichromated gelatin whose surface they impressed with an aquatint grain before exposing it under a negative. The exposed paper was then moistened, rolled with a greasy ink, and pressed against the lithograph stone. The direct contact of the ink with the stone allowed the stone to be etched in the same manner as a traditional lithograph with the same degree of effectiveness, yielding about 2,600 prints from each stone.

In 1859, J. W. Osborne of the Government Survey Office in Melbourne developed a similar method that, without the use of aquatint grains, was used to produce linear subjects such as maps, prints, and rare books. A few months later, Col. Sir Henry James (1803–77) of the Government Survey Office at Southhampton used the same process but transferred the image to zinc rather than stone, resulting in a further savings of time and money. In 1862, James and Capt. A. DeCourey Scott published a book entitled *Photozincography* that contained examples of their work. The process was used throughout England and Europe. Zinc was soon substituted for stone in other line photolithographic processes and for some halftone work. It was also adapted for high-speed printing on a rotopress.

Photolithographs, unless they are clearly reproductions from some other medium such as etchings or photographs, are difficult if not impossible to differentiate from traditional lithographic processes. It is often impossible to determine whether drawings were done on the stone or transferred to the stone by either a traditional or a photographic process. And then there is the confusing use of aquatint grain overlying the lithograph's characteristic grain. The general character of a print will reveal it as a lithograph, but the role photography played in its production often cannot be determined. Also, once an image was transferred to the stone by any method, reworking using any of the traditional lithographic materials could be and frequently was undertaken.

The other major planographic photomechanical process was the collotype, also called the Albertype, heliotype, gelatin print, Lichtdruck, collograph, autograph, phototype, indotint, photophane, artotype, and glyptograph. The process was first used by F. Joubert, a French engraver who published examples of his work in the *Photographic Journal* of 1860 but who never published the details of his procedure.

Joseph Albert (1825–66), a Bavarian court photographer, developed the process to the point where he could achieve fine halftone prints, and the technique gained wide acceptance after 1870. Albert

Fig. 7. *Interior of Marian Church*. Collotype; H. 11¼", W. 9⅛". (Collection of Debbie
Hess Norris: Photo, Winterthur.)

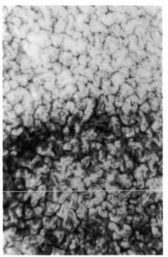

Fig. 8. Photomicrograph (400x) of collotype shown in figure 7. (Photo, Winterthur.)

applied bichromated gelatin to a ground glass surface and allowed it to dry. As it dried, often in an oven, it contracted to form a reticulated surface. After exposure under a negative and moistening, the light-hardened areas could be rolled with a greasy lithographic ink that was held in the grain of the reticulated surface. Each plate required two printings, one with thick ink for the shadows and one with a thinner ink for the halftones.

In 1869, Ernest Edwards (1837–1903), a London portrait photographer, introduced an improved version of the process which he called the heliotype. Edwards's process differed only slightly from Albert's, but the changes he made resulted in more vigorous prints. The process was used by Edwards and his Heliotype Company to illustrate Charles Darwin's *Expression of the Emotions in Man and Animals* (1872). An American branch in Brooklyn, Photogravure Company, printed the plates for Eadweard Muybridge's *Animal Locomotion*, published in Philadelphia in 1887. Collotypes were used for fine illustrations where clarity of tone in defining the image rather than vigor was important (figs. 7, 8). Collotypes were also popular for hand coloring because of their soft tones and were also sometimes glazed to resemble albumen photographs.

Relief Processes

The development of photomechanical reproductive techniques had now produced three commercially and technically viable processes capable of producing excellent reproductions—the intaglio photogravure and the planographic lithograph and collotype. All three processes produced excellent book illustrations from almost any medium, but there was still one major drawback—no process was typographically compatible with letterpress, so each illustration had to be printed separately and then bound into the book as a single sheet. Text and illustrations could be integrated on the same page only by the use of complicated maneuvers that compromised either the type or the illustration. The search for a typographically compatible and durable process was therefore of particular interest to publishers and those who, during the nineteenth century, provided the greatest proportion of book and magazine illustrations—the wood engravers.

Efforts to use photographic means to transfer the image to be engraved to the woodblock began the year Daguerre announced the success of his experiments. The first crude example was published in 1839 in the *Magazine of Science and School of Arts*, but the technique was not perfected or widely used until the mid 1860s.

Before the use of photography, the artist's original drawing (if he did not execute it directly on the block) was adhered to the woodblock and destroyed during the engraving process or reduced or redrawn or both by an intermediate hand for transfer to the woodblock. Many engravers considered the original drawing no more than a basic guide to their creative work. The use of photography to transfer the original image to the block had two immediate consequences. Photography could either reduce or enlarge the original image and still provide an exact reproduction on the block. It also allowed the original image to be preserved and to be compared with the engraver's finished work. These consequences produced a major change in the style of wood engraving dictated by the desire to reproduce design, tone, and texture with total fidelity. This change had mixed results aesthetically and could not, ultimately, overcome the competition from the typographically compatible photomechanical processes.

In 1850, Firmin Gillot, a Parisian lithographer, developed a process for producing a relief printing plate that was suitable for line work, although it could not print halftones. Gillot called his prints paniconographs, but the process soon became known as gillotage. In 1872, Gillot's son Charles improved the process. It was widely used in the United States after 1880 to reproduce drawings in newspapers and periodicals.

Gillot coated a zinc plate with bichromated albumen (which behaved in a manner similar to bichromated gelatin) and exposed it to light under a negative. The plate was then lightly inked, and the soluble unexposed areas of albumen were washed away in a water bath. The plate was then heavily inked to provide a resist and etched. The resulting relief could then be used on either a flat bed or a rotary press.

Firmin Gillot also collaborated with Charles Nègre to produce a relief process suitable for halftone work. The first example of their work was published in *La Lumiere* on May 5, 1856. The Gillots published a book entitled *Album de gravure paniconographique et photogravure* in the early 1870s that contains examples of both line and halftone work.

The halftone process, which Nègre christened "gravure paniconographique en relief," consisted of inking the surface of a finished collotype plate with a greasy ink and then pressing it against a clean zinc plate. The ink transferred to the zinc acted as an acid resist when the plate was etched sufficiently deeply to produce a relief image. The tones produced by this process were coarse, but the printing plates were typographically compatible.

John Culven Moss, a leading figure in the history of American printing, used his version of Gillot's line process when he founded Photoengraving Company in 1872. He produced process line engravings from pen-and-ink drawings or any other image of a uniform intensity. To reproduce halftones, Moss gave a photograph of the image to his trained artists who used pen and ink to produce a design of uniform intensity on top of the photograph, using the traditional techniques of line and stipple to simulate tone. The photographic image was then bleached away, leaving only the pen-and-ink drawing to be photographed and reproduced. The result was known as Moss process halftone. Although this process produced typographically compatible halftones, it still used the expensive and subjective hand of a skilled craftsman.

Working during the same period, Louis E. Levy introduced another line relief process called the swelled gelatin or Levytype. After exposing a plate coated with bichromated gelatin to light under a negative, he developed it in cold water, causing the unexposed areas to swell. A plaster mold was made from the gelatin relief, and a wax relief was made from the plaster. Any necessary handwork such as building up the whites was done at this stage. Then the wax was electrotyped to produce a relief printing plate. This process was especially well suited to reproducing line work with uneven contours such as prints or drawings executed on textured paper in charcoal or graphite. It was used for illustrations in cheap editions of expensive books like encyclopedias and was still a major technique for newspaper illustrations in the 1890s.

Frederic Eugene Ives (1856–1937) of Philadelphia and Charles Petit of Paris independently arrived at a similar halftone process in 1878. The first newspaper halftone was published in the New York *Daily Graphic* in 1880. Ives formally introduced his process in 1881, but it was supplanted a year later by the halftone process introduced by Georg Meisenbach, a Munich engraver. This process, with improvements made by Ives patented in 1886, became the modern halftone process. A fine screen with transparent holes and opaque lines was placed between the camera and the image to be reproduced. Then a plate coated with bichromated gelatin was exposed under this negative and etched to produce a relief printing plate. The print pulled from this plate was composed of a grid of lines and dots of the same intensity but varied size.

Although this halftone process was typographically compatible, it did not entirely solve the publishers' problems. The use of fine screens with up to 400 lines per inch produced superior images that could only be printed on smooth, highly calendered, often coated paper. Coarse screens with 60 to 160 lines per inch produced plates that would print on textured paper, but the images were relatively coarse and lacked detail. To cope with this problem, publishers either printed entire books on smooth coated paper or printed the text on uncoated paper and inserted plates printed on coated stock. This created the same production problems they had faced with the processes that were not typographically compatible. Process halftone is among the easiest techniques to identify because of the characteristic pattern of dots created by the screen (figs. 9, 10). Particularly fine examples, however, can be misleading until examined under magnification.

The choice of a photomechanical process to reproduce a particular drawing, painting, or photograph was dictated primarily by the publisher and by his considerations of time and expense rather than by the characteristics of the drawing. As any comparison of original material with the published illustrations will show, the choice of reproductive techniques had a profound effect on the final illustration. In *Practical Notes on the Preparation of Drawings for Photographic Reproduction* (London, 1880), Col. J. Waterhouse advised artists to consider the probable means of reproduction in designing their illustrations. He considered photogravure the best process for pen-and-ink drawings. Process line he considered clumsy, with a distinct loss of detail and coarsening of design. According to Waterhouse, photolithography on zinc also tended to be coarse, and lines drawn too close together tended to merge. Photogravure and collotype, he concluded, produced the best halftones as well as excellent detail, but both were costly and time-consuming to print. Photolithography and process halftone were cheap and fast but frequently blurred detail and tonal distinctions. As Waterhouse advised artists to proceed with these considerations in mind, so should we in identifying processes and evaluating illustrators on the basis of their published works. Some artists struggled to understand and master the strengths and limitations of a particular process, while others ignored or misunderstood the problem and left publishers to cope with inappropriate materials as they saw fit.

Photomechanical processes did not eliminate the intervening hand of man—printers continued to change and manipulate the printing plate. Under magnification, photogravures and collotypes frequently show signs of extensive reworking. An illustration originally designed for and printed by a particular process was sometimes retrieved from

Fig. 9. H. Regnault, *Portrait of General Prim*. Madrid, 1869. Process halftone taken from the painting; H. 16½", W. 12¾". (Collection of Lois Olcott Price: Photo, Winterthur.)

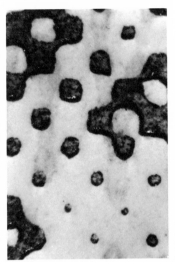

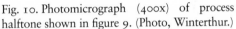
Fig. 10. Photomicrograph (400x) of process halftone shown in figure 9. (Photo, Winterthur.)

the printer's file and republished by a different process years later. Halftone plates were reworked to resemble wood engravings in many illustrations for popular magazines published around 1900.

As the study and understanding of nineteenth-century illustrators and their work grows, scholars will need to become increasingly familiar with photomechanical techniques in evaluating the artist's work and in differentiating the work of the artist from the work of the printer.

Bibliography

Gernsheim, Helmut, with Alison Gernsheim. *The History of Photography from the Camera Obscura to the Beginning of the Modern Era.* 2d ed. New York: McGraw-Hill, 1969. The best single source on photomechanical techniques. It contains an extensive bibliography.

Baley, Roger Child. *The Complete Photographer.* London: Methuen, 1906.

Crawford, William. *The Keepers of Light: A History and Working Guide to Early Photographic Processes.* Dobbs Ferry, N.Y.: Morgan & Morgan, 1979.

Denison, Herbert. *A Treatise on Photogravure and Its Practice.* London: Iliffe, n.d. Reprint. Visual Studies Workshop, 1974.

Eder, Josef M. *History of Photography.* 4th ed. Translated by Edward Epstean. New York: Columbia University Press, 1945.

Edwards, Ernest. *The Heliotype Process.* Boston: Osgood, 1876.

Hackleman, Charles. *Commercial Engraving and Printing.* Indianapolis: Commercial Engraving Publishing Co., 1921.

Jussim, Estelle. *Visual Communication and the Graphic Arts: Photographic Technologies in the Nineteenth Century.* New York: R. R. Bowker Co., 1974.

Lemercier, Alfred. *La lithographie Français de 1796 à 1896.* Paris: C. Lorilleux, 1899.

Lemercier, Lerebours, Barreswil, and Davanne. *Photo lithographie; ou, Impressions obtenues sur pierre à l'aide de la photographie.* Paris: Goupil, Gide & Baudry, 185-.

Lilien, Otto M. *History of Industrial Gravure Printing up to 1900.* London: Lund Humphries, 1957.

McCabe, L. R. *The Beginnings of Halftone: From the Notebooks of Stephen H. Horgan.* Chicago: Inland Printer, 1924.

Nègre, Charles. *De la gravure heliographique, son utilité, son origine, son application.* Nice: Gauthier, 1867.

Schnauss, Julius. *Collotype and Photo-lithography Practically Elaborated.* London: Iliffe, 1889.

Taft, Robert. *Photography and the American Scene: A Social History, 1839–1889.* New York: Macmillan Co., 1938.

Wakeman, Geoffrey. *Victorian Book Illustration: The Technical Revolution.* Detroit: Gale Research Co., 1973.

Waterhouse, Col. J. *Practical Notes on the Preparation of Drawings for Photographic Reproduction.* London: K. Paul, 1890.

Wood, Sir Henry Trueman Wright. *Modern Methods of Illustrating Books.* London: Stock, 1887.

Appendix

North American Print Conferences

A series of locally organized conferences held in the United States and Canada on subjects relating to the history of prints in North America.

1 *Prints in and of America to 1850.* March 19–21, 1970, Winterthur Museum, Winterthur, Del. Proceedings, edited by John D. Morse, published by University Press of Virginia, 1970.

2 *Boston Prints and Printmakers, 1670–1775.* April 1–2, 1971, Colonial Society of Massachusetts, Boston. Proceedings, edited by Walter Muir Whitehill and Sinclair Hitchings, published by University Press of Virginia, 1973.

3 *American Printmaking before 1876: Fact, Fiction, and Fantasy.* June 12–13, 1972, Library of Congress, Washington, D.C. Proceedings published by Library of Congress, 1975.

4 *Philadelphia Printmaking: American Prints before 1860.* April 5–7, 1973, Free Library of Philadelphia; Historical Society of Pennsylvania; Library Company of Philadelphia; and Philadelphia Museum of Art. Proceedings, edited by Robert F. Looney, published by Tinicum Press, 1976.

5 *Eighteenth-Century Prints in Colonial America.* March 28–30, 1974, Colonial Williamsburg, Va. Proceedings, edited by Joan Dolmetsch, published by University Press of Virginia, 1979.

6   *Art and Commerce: American Prints of the Nineteenth Century.* May 8–10, 1975, Museum of Fine Arts, Boston, Mass., in association with other Boston institutions. Proceedings published by Museum of Fine Arts, Boston, 1978; distributed by University Press of Virginia.

7   *Prints of New England.* May 14–15, 1976, American Antiquarian Society and Worcester Art Museum, Worcester, Mass. Proceedings, published by American Antiquarian Society, edited by Georgia B. Barnhill, forthcoming.

8   *American Maritime Prints.* May 6–7, 1977, New Bedford Whaling Museum, New Bedford, Mass. Proceedings, edited by Elton W. Hall, published at the Whaling Museum by Old Dartmouth Historical Society, 1985.

9   *Prints of the American West.* May 4–6, 1978, Amon Carter Museum, Fort Worth, Tex. Proceedings, edited by Ron Tyler, published by Amon Carter Museum, 1983.

10   *American Portrait Prints.* May 15–17, 1979, National Portrait Gallery, Smithsonian Institution, Washington, D.C. Proceedings, edited by Wendy Wick Reeves, published by University Press of Virginia, 1984.

11   *Canada Viewed by the Printmakers.* May 6–8, 1980, Royal Ontario Museum, Toronto. Proceedings, edited by Mary Allodi, forthcoming.

12   *New York State Prints and Printmakers, 1825–1940.* May 14–16, 1981, Syracuse University; Everson Museum of Art; and Erie Canal Museum. Proceedings, edited by David Tatham, published by Syracuse University Press, 1986.

13   *Mapping the Americas.* October 15–17, 1981. Historical Society of Pennsylvania, Philadelphia. Proceedings, edited by Peter Parker, forthcoming.

14   *The American Illustrated Book in the Nineteenth Century.* April 8–9, 1982, Winterthur Museum, Winterthur, Del. Proceedings, edited by Gerald W. R. Ward, published by Winterthur Museum; distributed by University Press of Virginia, 1987.

15   *Images by and for Marylanders, 1680–1940.* April 27–30, 1983, Maryland Historical Society, Baltimore, in association with other Baltimore institutions. Proceedings, edited by Laurie A. Baty, forthcoming.

16   *The Graphic Arts in Canada after 1850.* May 9–12, 1984, Public Archives of Canada and National Gallery of Canada in cooperation with National Library of Canada and Remington Art Museum, Ogdensburg, N.Y. Proceedings, edited by Jim Burant, forthcoming.

17   *Aspects of American Printmaking, Nineteenth and Twentieth Centuries.* April 25–27, 1985, Grace Slack McNeil Program in American Art, Wellesley College, and Museum of Our National Heritage, Lexington, in cooperation with Boston Athenaeum, Museum of Fine Arts, and Boston Public Library. Proceedings, edited by James O'Gorman, forthcoming.

18   *Prints and Printmakers of New York City.* April 10–12, 1986, New-York Historical Society, New York, N.Y. Proceedings, edited by Wendy Shadwell, forthcoming.

19   *Prints and Printmakers of New Orleans and the South.* April 29–May 1, 1987, Historic New Orleans Collection, New Orleans, in cooperation with Louisiana State Museum and New Orleans Museum of Art. Proceedings, edited by John A. Mahe II, forthcoming.

Index

The American Illustrated Book in the Nineteenth Century
was typeset, printed, and bound by Meriden-Stinehour Press.
The type is Linotronic Sabon; the halftone photography is in
300-line screen. The text paper is Mohawk Superfine Text,
Softwhite, Eggshell Finish; the endleaves are Curtis Tweed-
weave Text; the book is bound in Roxite Buckram.
Paul Hoffmann saw the book through the press.
The indexer was Ruth G. Low.
The designer was Patricia R. Lisk.